SING TO ME

SING TO ME

MY STORY OF MAKING MUSIC,
FINDING MAGIC, AND SEARCHING
FOR WHO'S NEXT

LA REID

WITH JOEL SELVIN

TO

ME

HARPER

An Imprint of HarperCollins*Publishers*

The names and identifying characteristics of some of the individuals featured throughout this book have been changed to protect their privacy.

Interior: page 2: Courtesy of Ditte Isager/Edge Reps; page 32: Steven Tucker; page 37: courtesy of Cheryl Brooks; page 50, 53, and 59: courtesy of Michael Mitchell/Perspective Image; page 58: www.cincinnativiews.net; ; page 61: courtesy of Sheri Roberson Drye; page 68: Richard E. Aaron/Getty Images; page 83: Ron Galella/Getty Images; page 87: Dave Hogan/Getty Images; page 105: Randall Dunn; page 111: ©1991, Kevin C. Rose; page 121 and 123: Al Pereira/Getty Images; page 127: ©ImageCollect.com/Andrea Renault/Glob Photos, Inc.; page 131, 187, 254, and 306: KMazur/Getty Images; page 154: Randall Dunnpage; page 159, 205, 227, and 234: L. Busacca/Getty Images; page 134: Raymond Boyd/Getty Images; page 148: NBC/Getty Images; page 154: Randall Dunn; page 155: Quinn Hood; page 161: Jeff Kravitz/Getty Images; page 171: ©ImageCollect.com/Paul Skipper/Globe Photos, Inc. 2001; page 193, 210, and 261: S. Granitz/Getty Images; page 212: Stefanie Keenan/Getty Images; page 219: Ida Mae Astute/Getty Image; page 221: L. Cohen/Getty Images; page 223 and 238: R. Diamond/Getty Images; page 228: courtesy of Ciara Harris; page 240: ©ImageCollect.com/Bymillan Ryba/Globe Photos, Inc. 2004; page 249: Jamie McCarthy/Getty Images; page 265: Mat Szwajkos/Getty Images; page 296: Kevin Winter/Getty Images; page 298, 303, 305: Theo Wargo/Getty Images; page 326: Gabe Ginsberg/Getty Images; page 348: ©ImageCollect.com/Globe Photos; page 364: Christopher Pol/KCA2015/Getty Images; page 372: Anthony Saleh.

Photo Insert: page 2 (top): courtesy of Rhonda White; page 2 (bottom), page 4 (top left): courtesy of Sherry Roberson Drye; page 3:courtesy of Michael Mitchell/Perspective Image; page 4 (bottom): Berliner Studio/REX Shutterstock; page 5 (bottom): Quinn Hood; page 6 (top): courtesy of Eddie "F" Ferrell; page 6 (bottom): Courtney Walters; page 7 (top left and right): photos by former LaFace Records creative director DL Warfield @dlwarfield; page 7 (bottom): Dimitrios Kambouris/Getty Images; page 8 (top left), page 11 (top), page 12 (top left and bottom): K. Mazur/Getty Images; page 8 (top right): Larry Busacca/Getty Images; page 8 (bottom): Larry Busacca; page 9: Terence Carter; page 10 (top left): J. Countess/Getty Images; page 10 (top right, bottom): Johnny Nunez/Getty Images; page 11 (bottom right): Zoe Young; page 13: Kevin Winter/AMA 2010/Getty Images; page 14: X Factor/Getty Images; page 15 (top right): ©Image Collect/Andrea Renault/Globe Photos, Inc. 2004; page 15 (bottom): Courtney Lowery; page 16 (top right): FilmMagic/Getty Images; page 16 (bottom): C. Flanigan/Getty Images.

HarperCollins books may be purchased for educational, business, or sales promotional use. For information please write: Special Markets Department, HarperCollins Publishers, 195 Broadway, New York, NY 10007.

FIRST EDITION

Designed by William Ruoto

Library of Congress Cataloging-in-Publication Data has been applied for.

ISBN: 978-0-06-227475-5

16 17 18 19 20   OV/RRD   10 9 8 7 6 5 4 3 2 1

THIS BOOK IS DEDICATED TO THE
LOVING MEMORY OF MY DEAR MOTHER,
EMMA B. REID.

CONTENTS

SING TO ME

THE
AUDITION

'd never auditioned a child before. My partner Kenny "Baby-face" Edmonds and I had written and produced records with a couple of boy groups, but working with kids wasn't something I'd envisioned doing when we started our own record company. I vaguely figured I would listen to a song or two and tell the kid to come back in a few years, but the minute this fourteen-year-old boy walked into my office that afternoon in 1993, I could tell that there was nothing that felt remotely child-like about Usher Raymond IV.

These were high times at LaFace Records, the label I had started with Babyface in Atlanta four years earlier. The company was beginning to make a name for itself. We had an album about to be released by an unknown singer named Toni Braxton that would become a multiplatinum smash. The label had its first multimillion-seller, the soundtrack to the Eddie Murphy movie *Boomerang*, and we had sold millions of records with another previously unknown group called TLC. Babyface had become a star in his own right after releasing two stellar solo albums and writing dozens of big hit songs with me as his regular producing partner.

On the heels of all this, we had recently relocated the LaFace office from Norcross to a bright, beautiful space we'd built out on the fifteenth floor of the Capital City Plaza building in Buckhead. We built the conference room in the ten-thousand-square-foot office to be shaped like a piano, which made a curved wall in the lobby. Nobody ever mentioned that particular design feature, so we probably spent a lot of money for something that went largely unnoticed. The staff was growing, as our operation expanded behind our two multimillion-sellers. The sleek, modern office lent the label an air of prosperity that I hoped would define us in the years to come.

But with all the success had come some serious adversity. Our top-selling group, TLC, was unhappy about money, and that was causing problems between me and my wife, Pebbles, who also happened to be the manager of the group. And, after scaling the heights of the music business together, from late nights at chitlin' circuit dives in the Midwest to the top of the charts, my partner Babyface and I were inexplicably drifting apart.

What made the growing distance between me and Kenny even more difficult was that when LaFace started, it was a small operation, just a handful of close friends who moved out from Los Angeles together. In the early days, LaFace was a family affair—me, Kenny, our office manager, Sharliss, my wife, Pebbles, Kenny's brother-in-law Derek Ladd, Kenny's childhood friend Daryl Simmons, my childhood friend Kayo. My younger brother, Bryant, moved from Cincinnati, where we grew up, to Atlanta and came to work for us. Bryant and I always had similar tastes in clothes and style—we shared music a lot when we were growing up. His world revolved around music, fashion, and sports. He was funny and charming and knew what he was about. Once we signed Toni Braxton, we assigned her to him, and he became the keeper of all things Toni.

Bryant also scouted talent, and it was through him that I first heard the name Usher. My brother brought several writers and producers to the label. He caught Usher at a local talent show—he'd gone to check out another act on the program—and called me from the show to tell me about him. I wasn't especially enthusiastic, but Bryant insisted that the kid was something I needed to see.

Though I hadn't been running a label for long, finding talent had become a specialty of mine. Our hit records so far had come from artists who had never made a record before I auditioned them. You never know what to look for at an audition; everyone is different, special in their own ways. You have to remain receptive, open, but without losing your critical and analytical side. It is a tricky combination of balancing intelligence and intuition and being able to tell the difference between having a vision and a hallucination.

I auditioned talent in my office three or four times a week, part of my regular workday. There was a corridor that led to the side-by-side twin offices occupied by Kenny and me. My office was a big, fluffy, all-white space with furniture from Kreiss and huge speakers powered by my McIntosh amplifier. Posters of our artists hung on the walls. People would come in and out to ask questions, to show me artwork, to get a moment of my attention. I always had an open-door policy and people knew they could walk in anytime.

It was around two in the afternoon, and I had been listening to some new songs by Toni Braxton, when this fourteen-year-old kid dressed in blue came to my office with his mother, Jonetta, and my brother, Bryant. His appearance looked a little small-town, but his surprising swagger was all big-city. Usher had grown up in Chattanooga and learned he could sing at an early age. Thinking a bigger city would be a better place for him to be discovered, his mother had moved the family to Atlanta, where she worked as a medical technician. She acted as his manager. He had never auditioned for a record label before.

My routine at auditions rarely varied and was much the same that day. After a quick introduction and handshake with Usher and his mother, I sat back down and asked, "What are you going to sing for us?"

I always know in a few seconds. There are very few people who can pass an audition. I usually know when they walk in the room before they open their mouth—even if they open their mouth only to speak and not sing. I've already made up my mind. The last few minutes is just me being kind to them. I've been told I'm rude in auditions, but I'm not. I might not look up from my computer, but I pay attention. I never tell anybody what I think, unless I'm blown away. I like the theater of leaving it hanging, so that when you do deliver the news, you create a life-changing moment.

He handed me a tape of an instrumental track. I put it in the cassette player and pressed Play. He stood in front of my desk and started to sing a song Kenny and I wrote that had been a record-breaking number one hit for Boyz II Men on the *Boomerang* soundtrack called "End of the Road." He was killing it. He didn't get through sixteen bars before I interrupted him.

"Stop, whoa," I said. "I need to get some girls. I want everybody to hear you."

Our bustling office was filled with employees and interns from local colleges. We rounded up all the pretty girls. They filled the chairs in my office, perched on desks, leaned in the doorway. About fifteen people crowded in. Usher took it from the top.

He zeroed in on Phyllis Parker, who worked for us, probably the most beautiful woman in the room, and dropped to his knee in front of her, singing, placing his hand on her thigh and looking dead in her eyes. He was seducing her with the confidence of someone who had done it before.

This kid wasn't afraid, he wasn't intimidated, he wasn't overwhelmed by the surroundings or the fact that he was singing for a record company president. He didn't have any apprehension at all. He jumped in like a pro. It turned out he had some stage experience in a group he sang with and had done a *Star Search* audition, but he was still raw and green. He came by his self-confidence naturally.

When he opened his mouth to sing, he didn't sing it like Boyz II Men, he sang it like it was his own song. His tone was perfect for the way he sang the song; he gave it his own, original sound, which is what I always look for with people—that special voice stamp that is only yours, that will not be mistaken for anyone else. The voice there was all his own. He was his own person. He was already Usher.

He was confident and poised way beyond his years. His eyes

told the story. He had eyes of steel. He knew he would be a star. I could see that commitment in his eyes. He was charming. He could dance his ass off. He had an unbelievable vocal tone and he was a sponge. He sensed exactly what I was looking for. I knew all this in an instant.

When he finished, the room exploded in applause and I stood up.

"Welcome to LaFace Records," I said.

1

GIVE THE DRUMMER SOME

incinnati was a factory town, automotive factories and steel plants, an industrial city. We called it the Up South—if Birmingham was the Down South, we were the Up South. Cincinnati could feel like a Southern city, but in a crazy way, it had a sort of cosmopolitan flair. It didn't feel like Kentucky—which was only across the river—and it didn't feel like Cleveland. It was its own place, not necessarily a spot where anything seemed possible, but a blue-collar city where people worked for a living.

My mother, Emma Reid, had a factory job as a seamstress making vinyl tops for cars at Parkway Manufacturing. She was always working, and when she wasn't busy at the factory, she was making beautiful clothes, draperies, tablecloths, and bedspreads for us at home. She also occasionally freelanced for an interior design firm, so our house was like a little sewing shop with sewing machines and bolts of exotic fabric lying around—antique satin, linen, gabardine, Sea Island cotton. "That's cashmere," she would say. "It's very expensive—don't touch that."

From the time I was little, Mom made all my clothes, which got me paying attention to fashion early on. She could make anything, often re-creating styles so that we could afford them. There was a really popular expensive shirt that all the kids used to wear called a Nik Nik, made of satin with cool designs on it. Some of the better-off kids would have them, but they were too expensive for us. My mother went to the fabric store and bought the same fabric and made Nik Nik shirts for me and my brother. We were in the club. Nobody knew we didn't buy them.

My mom did just about everything on her own—I never knew my father and never even saw a photograph of him until I was a teenager. I met him a couple of times after I was grown-up, but we didn't connect. Instead, my mom raised us as a single mother, and she was wonderful. I have two older sisters, Ivy and Rosaland, and a younger brother, Bryant, who is four years younger. Mom grew up with ten siblings, and her sister

Katrina, or Kate, lived across the street with her two daughters, Luana and Heidi. My mom watched her girls while Katrina went to college classes, so they were always around, which meant I basically was raised around four girls, my two sisters and my two cousins.

Growing up, I never felt poor, even though we lived in Mount Auburn, which could be a rough part of town. I didn't know it was the ghetto, though; it was simply a neighborhood to me. Our home was always a happy place where we always had anything we needed. We had to do our chores and make sure the place was clean before Mom came home, but she took good care of us. I learned everything from her. Her read on people was incredible. She used to give me these little insights, saying things like, "You know something, guilty people don't trust anybody."

Like most things in my young life, music came to me through my mother. My earliest memory of music is from when I was about five years old and was in her kitchen. Mom and Aunt Kate were talking and cooking, as the transistor radio blared out "Please Mr. Postman" by the Marvelettes. I watched them chat and pop their fingers to the beat, but the music was what captivated me. The feeling I experienced when I heard that song is as familiar as yesterday. It made me feel *something*. And I loved the feeling.

After that, I noticed that there was always music playing. My mother loved rhythm and blues and vocal jazz artists like Dinah Washington, Billie Holiday, and Ella Fitzgerald. James Brown was a big star in my house. *Live at the Apollo* was my favorite album as a kid, and I learned to mimic Brown's riffs, even though I can't sing to this day.

Every weekend the music mingled with the tinkle of ice cubes, happy chatter, and the clink of chips at my mother's weekly poker games. Our home was always festive, and as far back as I can remember, every weekend the house filled with friends and relatives.

Spinning 45s in my mom's house

All the adults would be there, gambling, drinking, having a good time, and that was my chance to be independent and discover music. I ran the stereo, the music guy, playing whatever records I wanted because Mom didn't care about anything else when she was concentrating on her poker games.

I have always been fascinated by how things in life—whether they are ideas or interests—get started. I always felt I could do anything I put my mind to; I don't know where that came from, but it has been with me since I can remember. When I was about eight years old at my mother's house on Highland Avenue in Cincinnati, where we moved, there was a washing machine with one of those old-fashioned wringers in the basement, where we'd go to wash our clothes. One day, I was down there with my sister Ivy, and as she was wringing out the laundry, I looked up and said, "Ivy, one day I'm going to be rich."

"That's really cute," she said.

But I never forgot it. It was as if my life spoke to me early and told me what I was going to do. I've always thought you can actually program your mind—your brain sets the coordinates even before you know what you're saying—and that's what I did, only I never focused strictly on money in my life. That was never the chase. I never made decisions in my career based on money. (I don't advocate doing so unless you're a businessperson, and then you should be focused on nothing *but* money.)

My first job was working with my uncle Rueben at his barbershop on Saturdays when I was nine years old. The shop was downtown in the busiest section of the black business district. Occasionally white guys came in for a shave or haircut, but mostly the barbershop was something of a black community center. My job was to brush the hair off customers after a cut for tips. I also cleaned up, ran errands, and did whatever I was asked. I brought the money I earned home to my mother. Sometimes she would keep it. Sometimes she would give half back to me, sometimes all of it.

Rueben was clean and suave—a debonair kind of guy whom I could look up to. He owned his own business, so he was an independent man. I took note that he was the boss, that what he said went, that everybody followed his instructions, and that he never had problems. The other barber in the shop, Leroy, was slicker, slightly shady, but Rueben had a large presence, a lot of personality, and it was his shop. In his line of work, being a barber was as much about having personality as it was about cutting hair, because it was really a hang. It was something black people did on weekends, go get a haircut and a shave or go to the beauty salon (like white people don't get haircuts on the weekend).

Everything I didn't learn from my mom, I learned in the barbershop. I discovered everything there. I learned about sports from people coming in to watch *Wide World of Sports* and started to follow the Cincinnati Reds, as well as Muhammad Ali, who had only recently changed his name from Cassius Clay. Above all, though, I learned about music.

All the hustlers would drop by to sell whatever—coke, clothes, that sort of thing—but I always paid attention when they had records. My uncle would flip through the records and pull out Jimmy Smith, Miles Davis, any obscure tenor player that he liked, and buy the albums for a dollar each. Music was a big thing to him, even if he didn't play it that often at the shop. He would keep the television on when he was working, but when he went home to relax and be himself, he listened to music. As a successful man, Uncle Rueben owned his own home, got a new car regularly, dressed nice, and had the latest gadgets. For a sound system, he owned a Technics turntable and floor-standing speakers, and he took special care of his records, always cleaning them, handling them by the edge.

After one day at the barbershop, I'd walked uptown to the record shops to buy the latest 45s. The music shops had speakers outside the storefronts, and the day I heard Aretha blasting "Respect," I thought it was the best record I had ever heard (still might be). I went in and bought it right then and there. I always bought James Brown—he was my favorite artist. James was Soul Brother Number One and the hardest working man in show business. King Records, the label that recorded James Brown, was headquartered in Cincinnati in a neighborhood called Evanston. I used to take karate lessons—everybody took karate in those days—and my karate school was right around the corner from King Records. Every time I went to class, I walked past the building. I never saw anything or anyone, but I always looked.

Rhythm intoxicated me, and eventually it occurred to me that I wanted to play along. I started visiting musical instrument shops after work to listen to people fumbling around with the instruments. One day I broke down and bought a pair of drumsticks, but I had nothing to play them on, so I banged on any hard surface that had a bounce—windowsills, tabletops—teaching myself to play along with the hits.

That was only the start, though. The day the drums really entered my life was when my uncle Albert showed up at my grandmother's house. My mother, her sister, and my grandmother were excited to see him, as it was the first time they'd seen him in many years. They had never spoken of him, so I knew nothing about this tall, smart, and handsome man who walked into my grandmother's home bringing all his bags, but I quickly learned he was the hero of the family because he was extremely intelligent and well read. A know-it-all who was never wrong, he could talk about anything to anybody.

As he said his hellos, I couldn't keep my eyes off the strange, round cases in his luggage. I wondered what could be in them. He unpacked the mystery cases and pulled out his drums. He lived in Pittsburgh and played drums in a jazz band. He set up the drums and he played a bit for me. I was instantly smitten. From that day forward, I became fixated on drums.

Though my uncle Raymond, who was also a drummer, might have been a little better than Albert, I got my drumming chops from my uncle Albert. He started to teach me how to play, the rudiments. He showed me stick exercises that teach you how to achieve independence, coordination, and all the different things you can do on drums. He gave me a pair of drumsticks and a practice pad, basically a piece of wood with a rubber coating on it.

"Take this and learn," he said. "Practice your paradiddles, practice your flamadiddle, practice your flamcue, practice your ratamacue."

I could never play the things he played. He played jazz. He took me to jam sessions, and I got to meet other musicians. I sat there for hours and watched as they jammed, entranced at what I was hearing. They played improvisational jazz—no set song, just a jazz jam. Despite the talent in the room, being there felt natural to me. I felt like I belonged, and even though I was young, the guys treated me as though I belonged there, too. That meant a lot because validation is very important among musicians. You could tell it was a world you needed to be invited to join. When a civilian came in, the musicians would stop and speak more properly, and everything would change. But when the outsider left, they would get back to talking that talk.

At the same time that was happening, I was still listening to James Brown records, which is enough to make anyone want to play drums. I learned how to play "Cold Sweat" by James Brown. He also had a song in which he said "Give the drummer some! Give the drummer some!" that I learned to play. Uncle Albert thought that was trash, but I always liked funk drumming and stayed with it despite my uncle's misgivings. And though he didn't like my taste in music, he kept supporting me and teaching me things.

When I was ten, I woke up Christmas morning to find my mother had bought me a set of toy drums. I went crazy. After that, I drove everyone else in the house nuts, playing them day and night. I didn't know what I was doing, and the toy drum set never made a big enough report to get beyond a muffled clatter, but I was obsessed. I played by myself along to records and learned every song I heard, from James Brown to Motown.

School proved to be the place where my fascination with

music turned serious. When I was twelve years old and started seventh grade at Merry Junior High School, I began taking music classes, starting with the violin. Since I already knew how to play drums, I quickly became a favorite of the teacher. He loaned me a snare drum that I took home and played with my toy drum set, actually getting a pretty good sound.

In class, I could hear when people were out of tune and it would drive me crazy, so my teacher put me in charge of tuning the class instruments. I couldn't play violin worth a damn, but I could hear any little harmony that was out. By the time I went from violin class to band class alongside the rest of the orchestra—the horns, the woodwinds, the brass, and the percussion instruments—I knew how to play violin a little bit. I started to grow in my confidence. In ninth grade, I joined the marching band, where I played the bass drum, the heartbeat of the band.

As I became more comfortable with my drumming, my musical tastes began to broaden. After working for several years at the barbershop, I took a job cleaning up on Johnson's Party Boat, which was an event charter on the Ohio River. My new best friend from junior high, Dee Dee, landed us the job through his brother, who also worked there. It was a sixty-foot boat with a large ballroom, a jukebox in the corner, and a bandstand, a few tables, and chairs. A man named Cap ran the operation. We worked for him there on weekends from after school on Friday until Sunday night, making sometimes sixty or eighty dollars in a weekend—big money for a junior high school kid. I was twelve years old spending weekends on a boat—times have changed. I wouldn't let my twelve-year-old do that.

We were supposed to stay bunked in our cabin during the parties and come out afterward to clean, but hearing live music and seeing people partying made it impossible to follow those rules. We would go out and watch anyway, and that's where I started to hear pop music.

Is that me? Yup, at age twelve.

Growing up as I did in a black household, soul music was a fact of life. The Beatles and the Beach Boys came from a different world than mine, and my eyes were opening. Where the R&B records I knew always featured a prominent beat for dancing and funky playing, the white rock records concentrated more on songs and harmonized vocals, set against a clean, crisp sound. It was an amazing experience for a little kid. We grew up fast.

We worked on the boat until Dee Dee's brother punched Cap in the face—that was the end of our boat run. We'd earned enough money, though, to buy some slick clothes, and, more important, for me to purchase my first drum set, a black Pearl kit.

I moved my drums into the garage and practiced only when nobody was home. I wasn't trying to keep anything secret, but I guess that was what happened. My stepdad, JB, who lived with us for a time, didn't even know I played until he heard me one day.

JB had moved in with us when I was about six years old, but we were never close. He was closer to my sisters and never bothered to get to know me. He acknowledged me and I acknowledged him, and that was about the end of it. He had another family with nine kids, but he divorced his wife and moved in with us. His family hated us because they would visit and it was like going to the rich people's houses for them. We were not rich, but we owned our home in Mount Auburn, a better neighborhood than where they lived, and we had two brand-new expensive cars outside, a Mercury Cougar and a Cadillac. JB had two jobs. He worked at National Distillers during the day. At night, he was a pimp. My mother used to say he was a "popcorn"—he was lightweight, not the real thing. He had a couple of girls and that was about it. I never understood the mentality of that, or why my mom allowed it. We never discussed it.

Because he never bothered to get to know me, he didn't even know I was a musician until one day when he came home while I was playing. Afterward, when I came into the house, this guy who never said anything to me looked at me and said, "Hey, Antonio, you sound pretty good." That was the only endearing thing he ever said to me. When I was about sixteen he got into an argument with my mother. He held his hand up like he was going to hit her and I beat the shit out of him. He moved out shortly after that.

When I entered Hughes High School in 1969, my music class there became the greatest thing in the world, but even better was how the music teacher became one of the most inspirational figures of my life. Not long before, we'd moved to the suburbs—a nicer home in Madisonville, a mixed neighborhood where I don't think there were more than three or four black families living on our block. Everybody had lawns in their front yard. My mother drove me to school all the way across town on her way to work.

My high school was like the TV show *Fame*. It wasn't a performing arts school, but it felt like it. At the end of the year, the school always held a talent show called the Merry Go Round. I did it every year, and mom went to every talent show I played. If she loved the music, she'd praise me, and if she didn't, she'd tell me that, too. I liked my band class, chorus, jazz ensemble, marching band, drama, and art classes in school. They all shaped me. There were some seriously gifted musicians in my high school, musical prodigies, actually. I asked this one incredible piano player in my class if he had ever heard of a song called "Benny and the Jets."

"How does it go?" he asked.

I tried to hum it a little bit and the guy began picking it out. I was amazed that he could start playing the tune right off the bat.

Our vocal class had the craziest, most talented bunch of people. Terry Brown, a tall, cool young guy who sang in a group of his own called the Mystics, was our music teacher. He was an inspirational figure to all his students, but especially to me. Mr. Brown took a special interest in me, encouraged me greatly, and started me down the path. First of all, he was cool. Handsome and well dressed, Mr. Brown kept his Afro exactly the right length. He had all the best singers in school in his class, and they were all into male vocal groups like the Temptations, the Four Tops, the Stylistics, and the Delfonics. The class was divided into different groups, and the best was the Backstabbers, who had great harmonies and killer dance steps, and were like a high school version of the Temptations. I didn't sing, but Mr. Brown let me stay there all day and soak it in. We'd go to the music class in the morning and stay until school was out.

Because he was borderline successful with his own group, everyone looked up to Mr. Brown. He stressed good work habits, always telling us practice, practice, practice. Practice before every show. Practice after the show, if you can. Always try to get better. Don't ever go onstage unrehearsed. He taught us everything about music; performing, singing, reading, and writing music. He wasn't only a teacher, but also a friend.

Technically it was a traditional choir class, but we used to do all kinds of music in there, and jam all day long. I would play drums, bongos, piano, whatever was around. That class was the seed from which I first grew some practical knowledge about music beyond simply loving it.

Eye-opening as it was, Mr. Brown's class was just a start; moving to that school really changed things for me, both

with drums and with everything else. Girls started to seriously matter when I was about fourteen. My friends and I
constantly thought about them, but we didn't know how
to seduce them; we were afraid of them. My cousin said we
should drink to calm down before we talked to the girls. We
had a few drinks and I *hated* it, didn't like the feeling of it at
all. I lost my composure and it gave me a headache. Next we
found out about diet pills, black beauties. Uppers like that
could actually make me feel smarter, although neither booze
nor drugs turned out to be my thing.

Instead, the drums were my thing—everybody knew I
played drums. I walked around school with drumsticks in
my hand. All the time. Teachers would take them from me in
class because I was making noise and give them back at the
end of the class. If they ever refused to give them back, my
mother would come to school and demand them back. She
didn't take any shit.

Mr. Brown's class was not the first time I laid eyes on
Kayo—since his name was Kevin Roberson, we were in the
same homeroom, which was determined alphabetically—but
I had no idea he was such a funky bass player until I saw him
there. We teamed up and became best friends. We backed up
the school talent shows and the choir. We played behind the
Backstabbers.

One day while I was strolling the halls, Mr. Brown stopped
me and asked if I had a set of drums and if I would be interested in auditioning for his group. When I went to the
audition, there were a few other drummers. One guy, Bobby
Harris, intimidated me. He had a killer drum kit and a bad
Afro. But as he started to play, I was like, *I can take this
guy*. He was older than me, more handsome and more charismatic, but he didn't have that pocket, that solid feel for the
center of the groove.

When it was my turn to play, they asked me if I knew Stevie Wonder's "Living for the City." I did and I jumped on it. I got the gig. We traveled to Chicago the next weekend to play a club called the Skyway owned by Don Cornelius of *Soul Train*. We stayed in a hotel (my first) and played two nights. They painted a mustache on me with eyeliner so that I would look older than sixteen. Mr. Brown kept the girls away from me. I was ready to be bad, but he protected me. I brought home about eighty dollars, but I felt like I had made a million.

By the time I entered senior year, I spent almost all day, every day, in that class. Mr. Brown would speak to my other teachers about giving me passing grades. I was treated like a star athlete, with teachers overlooking my academic shortcomings, and I did fairly well in school—at least for someone who didn't attend classes.

At high school, there was a competition between all the drummers, and Gary Herron was the king. He was amazing and could play anything that came on the radio. He was not just a drummer, he was an entertainer who played with flair. I watched his every move. He was a cool guy, and I started to emulate him, picking up a lot of his mannerisms. He smoked cigarettes so I started to smoke. I desperately wanted to be cool, to be like him. I'm not sure if I ever got there, but eventually, I was good enough that even Gary was impressed.

Late in my senior year, I was made aware that I didn't have enough credits to graduate. A teacher took me out of line while I was waiting with the rest of the class of '74 for our graduation rehearsal. He told me I would have to go to summer school and that if I walked through the graduation ceremony, they would give me a blank diploma.

It didn't much matter to me one way or another. I headed outside, and, as I was leaving school, a fellow came up to me. He had stolen my printed diploma from the school office. "Antonio,

I have your diploma," he said. "Do you want to buy it? Forty bucks and it's yours."

I gave him forty dollars, took my diploma, and went home.

"Hey, Mom," I said, "I decided not to walk with the class, but here's my diploma." She never questioned it and I never told her the truth. Best forty bucks I ever spent.

2

PURE ESSENCE

All throughout high school, I'd played in and out of bands, and after graduation, my plan was to make a living doing the same. It didn't take long, though, to learn that playing music in the real world is an entirely different experience.

During high school, playing in bands had begun for me almost by accident. I used to set up my drum kit in the basement and practice by myself at my mother's house in Madisonville. There was a window that you could see through into the backyard, and one day when I was practicing, I glanced up to see someone looking at me. I went outside to see who he was.

"I'm Russell," he said. "You're pretty good. Kind of funky. You hit the drums hard. Nobody around here is doing it like that. I'm a bass player."

He mentioned his band, and I actually knew their name. I was impressed to meet someone who was a notch up from me, playing in a real band, digging what I was doing. We chatted a bit, and I played some more for him. He told me about a cousin of his who also played bass and had a guitar player, but no drummer. He offered to introduce me. I had never been in a band. I'd never played with other musicians from outside school before. I'd only played by myself. This would be the very first time.

I joined the band with Russell's cousin Richard and another guy. We played funk music and called the band Smoked Herbs because we liked to smoke pot, though we never performed in public, only at home in the garage. We did Bobby Womack's "Woman's Got To Have It" in the first session. We learned songs by Chicago, but since we didn't have any horns, we'd play only the Chicago rhythm section stuff—or at least try to.

Russell and I became buddies. We would hang out at his house or my place and listen to music. He turned me on to Tower of Power, one mean band from the Bay Area with the cool song "What Is Hip?" and the badass drummer David

Garibaldi. One day Russell came by and asked if I wanted to go to the music shop. We jumped in his car and went to the instrument store, somewhere near where we lived, a store I'd never been to.

As we got out of the car and headed into the store, he handed me a guitar case. "Just carry this in," he said.

Once we got into the store Russell took the guitar case from me, and while I checked out the keyboards and drums, he went to the guitars and basses. We were in there for about twenty minutes when he came over to me, ready to leave, and handed me the guitar case as we walked out. It seemed heavier.

By the time we got in the car and drove off, I realized there was a guitar in the case, a guitar he'd stolen. He had made me an accessory to the theft, and I was not cut out for that. I never thought of stealing anything, let alone a guitar.

"What are you going to do with it?" I asked.

"I'm going to sell it," he said.

"Okay, but you're going to give me some of the money, right?" I said.

He looked at me but didn't say anything. His body language clearly said no. My attitude about Russell changed on the spot. Suddenly I didn't think so highly of him. I stopped hanging out with him after that. I would see him in passing, but I was no thief and I didn't want to be around one.

I found out only later that robbing music stores was his thing. He would visit the stores during the day and leave a window unlocked, then come back at night. Eventually he got caught. The irony is not lost on me—the guy who really gave me my first push into the music business turned out to be a thief.

As a band, Smoked Herbs never amounted to anything, and throughout high school, making a living from music seemed like a dream. I dove into music at school because it drew me.

I didn't think about a career in music. I was just a kid smitten with rhythm. I continued to play drums by myself at home, but after all that jamming with the Smoked Herbs, I wanted to play in a real band.

When I was about fifteen, and still going to Hughes High and studying in Mr. Brown's class, Russell did hook me up with an even better band, the Generation Gap, which turned out to be my first real professional group. I went over to audition for the band in Kennedy Heights, which was considerably more upscale than Madisonville. These were rich kids. They drove their parents' cars. They had great equipment. They had expensive amps. They played Telecaster guitars and had Fender Precision basses. I'd never seen money like this before, and I noticed the class distinction. Coming from the lower middle class, we owned our house and were by no means poor, but these guys were clearly more affluent. We didn't even go to school together—they went to Woodward High, which was in a better neighborhood back then.

Despite all that, I joined the Generation Gap—it was my first real band and these guys could play. Steve Hunter was the bass player; he also sang. Delbert Williams was the guitar player, and another guy named Greg was amazing on the organ. We had a couple of horn players. It was serious—I was with real musicians now. We played local clubs and parties, played the funk songbook from Funkadelic to Tower of Power. The band played high school proms, a few talent shows, and once did a fashion show. We had a regular gig at the Clock Bar on Burnett Avenue in Avondale, where all the pimps and hookers hung out. It was street. The guys wore loud colors and big hats and drove Cadillacs with chrome grills and TV antennas attached. One pimp named Lavender had the finest girls and kept a big knot of cash in his nylon socks, which he would take out to pay for drinks.

We decided to join forces with a singing trio and renamed our band Mama's Pride; this was the band I was in when I finished with high school. We did everything from the Spinners, the Temptations, and the Four Tops to the Doobie Brothers. We started drawing nice crowds. Our three vocalists didn't dance much, but they could sing. They brought harmonies and sophisticated ballads to the bandstand—"You Make Me Feel Brand New" by the Stylistics, "Superwoman" by Stevie Wonder. Mama's Pride was more than simply another funk outfit, although the band didn't stay together long.

After high school was over, Mr. Brown came by one of the Mama's Pride rehearsals in the basement of my girlfriend's house. He had quit teaching during our senior year to concentrate on his own singing group. He told us that day about a new thing that was going to change music—video. He said people were going to make little films of people playing songs and that would be the next new wrinkle. The music scene was rapidly changing in exciting ways, and we wanted to be part of that future.

From the crowds at our shows, and our regular gigs, it seemed like we were going somewhere. The Mama's Pride lead vocalist was Dwight Tribble, who remains one of the best singers I've ever heard. He had this amazing voice, a range that never seemed to stop. There was never a note he couldn't hit with his natural voice. He could sing like Stevie Wonder or Donny Hathaway. Or he could sing jazz. He was also a handsome lady-killer. I liked to kid Trib about it—we called him Trib. After a show one night at the Club Diplomat in Cincinnati, I made a little joke. "You're not the only one the girls noticed tonight," I said. "Some of the girls noticed the drummer."

"Well, you can have all of them," he said. "This is our last show."

I had no idea what was going on, but that was it: the band

broke up that night. The Mama's Pride singers never really got along with the guys from the Generation Gap, and there was some kind of tension in the band that went over my head. I wasn't the leader of the band. I was only the drummer.

It was disappointing—that band had seemed destined for success—but I'd gotten enough of a taste that I decided to make my life in music. I had been swept up by the experience of playing drums with my first professional group, a band I thought could be successful, and once the idea of making a living in music had taken root, I didn't look back. I had no strategy in mind and didn't know what I was doing, but I wanted to try.

Some of the Generation Gap guys called me to try out for a different band. They liked me and we ended up bringing in musicians I knew from school. First, I brought in my friend Kayo to play bass. More guys came and went, and before long, all the Generation Gap people were gone and all the Mama's Pride singers had left, and I found myself with Kayo, some other players I knew from high school, and a couple of other guys. I didn't know what I was doing, but I refused to give up the game.

We formed Pure Essence, which was more of a funk band that did only originals and covers of Sly and the Family Stone. We started out in my girlfriend's mom's basement every night at seven, but before long, we were rehearsing at whoever's house every night until midnight. After practice, we would hang out and talk until the middle of the night and sleep until noon.

The guys in the group came from all over. The lead vocalist, named Jerome Richmond but known as Mouse, was leader of the band, the motivator, the loud talker, the guy in the locker room getting everybody fired up before a game. He patterned himself after Sly Stone, so he was not exactly an original. Kayo was my best friend and the bass player. Steve Tucker Walters—we called

The Pure Essence band logo (designed by Designology), Indianapolis, Indiana, 1979

him Tuck—was one of two guitar players, a little older than the rest of us and our spiritual adviser. Tuck was a heavy thinker. He studied transcendental meditation. He taught us the difference between mediocre and great, between KC and the Sunshine Band and Funkadelic. He showed us how to write songs that had multiple meanings and layers. He wanted the band to have depth.

The other songwriter was the second guitarist, Larry Middleton, a sexy, good-looking guy with a growling baritone in the mold of Marvin Gaye. He'd dropped out of Hughes High when I was still there, but I could remember him coming to Mr. Brown's class with his acoustic guitar and killing Marvin's "Distant Lover." Larry was already a regional star. He belonged to Combined Forces, whose "Colors Are Real" was a local hit, so when Larry joined our little group, we knew it was getting serious. Larry was also the guy who gave me my nickname. It was at a rehearsal during the 1975 World Series with the Cincinnati Reds. I was wearing a Los Angeles Dodgers jersey as a kind of protest. Larry looked across the room at me. "OK, LA," he said, "you count it off." It stuck.

To this day, these are all my friends.

Pure Essence was my first group that played only original music (with the exception of the Sly covers), and because of that, the group represented a coming of age for me, a time when I began to notice life on a deeper level, a new era of consciousness for me. Musicianship began to fascinate me. Whether playing original music with my band or listening to records, I wanted true musicality, intellectual depth, songs with meaning. Chord progressions needed to be complex. While our band wasn't the most musically sophisticated, we listened only to music we felt could enlighten us. From the start, we were all determined to make a musical mark with Pure Essence.

I had discovered rock music in junior high school. I'd known about soul music, but when I started listening to rock, it opened my ears to a wider world of exciting music. I still remember the first time I heard Led Zeppelin. Drummer John Bonham was a hero to me. My high school was right across the street from the campus of the University of Cincinnati. The street was filled with head shops with black light posters and weed pipes. Hippies would sit around the sidewalk playing folk music on their guitars. I went to rock concerts at the college to see bands like Grand Funk Railroad and Edgar Winter with his brother, Johnny Winter.

When we started Pure Essence, the '70s rock scene was at its full glory. As we wrote our own music more, rock music became so compelling to us that we drifted completely away from the black music scene. We studied FM radio that played music by the Eagles, Led Zeppelin, Jimi Hendrix, and all the other rock heroes. We would read every issue of *Rolling Stone* magazine cover to cover religiously. To us, dancing was a no-no and corny lyrics were out of the question. We smoked a lot of weed and went from dressing slick to wearing blue jeans. We played long sets and every musician did lengthy solos. My entertaining, extended drum solos were earning me the reputation as the top drummer in town. We were a bunch of black hippies at the dawn of the disco age.

With the exception of Stevie Wonder, I pretty much stopped listening to much black music. I got into all kinds of rock music—the hard rock of Black Sabbath, the progressive rock of Yes. I was into Carlos Santana. I dug the horn bands—Chicago; Blood, Sweat, and Tears; Tower of Power. I even liked the supercommercial pop thing like Three Dog Night. But as I branched out, it wasn't just about rock; I also got into jazz fusion with Weather Report, Return to Forever, and Herbie Hancock. And I loved and paid special attention to drummers Billy Cobham, Steven Ferrone, Lenny White, and Steve Gadd. I liked a piano player named Deodato. There was an artist from Canada, Gino Vanelli, who was like a jazz singer. The Stones got my attention with their disco hit, "Miss You."

As we experimented with our sound and influences, we realized that in order for our band to be taken seriously, we needed to make a record. Our vocalist, Mouse, knew the Pittsburgh Pirates baseball star Dave Parker, who had grown up in Cincinnati, and he talked Dave into paying for some studio time. I had been in the recording studio only once, me and Kayo with Mr. Brown, who had hired us to play on a jingle for Keebler cookies, "Keebler's Makes Uncommonly Good Cookies." For the Pure Essence session, Mouse booked studio time for the group in a cut-rate studio in Chillicothe, outside Columbus, Ohio.

In 1976, we went in and cut two sides, "Wake Up" and "Third Rock," both in about two takes, which was important since studio time was valuable. Although we did not have any real studio experience, we were able to create a sound that was funky yet progressive. We pressed up the first single, "Wake Up," and took it to local black radio station, WCIN. It was an okay song, but we got no airplay.

About the same time, Kayo and I played a session with another local act called Larry and Vicky. Vicky was a high school friend from class with Mr. Brown, and she had real star quality along with a very sweet voice. We cut two sides with them produced by another guy. "How I Wish" by Larry and Vicky came out and went straight on WCIN and turned into a local hit. That was bittersweet after our Pure Essence record bombed.

I always tuned in rock music radio and was driving in my car listening to WEBN one day when I heard the disc jockey announce that the station was looking for recordings by local talent for a compilation album. I had a cassette in the car of the other song from the Pure Essence session, "Third Rock" (a little nod to Jimi Hendrix), and, without telling anyone else in the band, I stopped and dropped it off at the station. The program director phoned a few days later to say he wanted to include the track on the album.

I called the guys and told them the good news. Most of them were happy, but not Mouse, the bandleader. He felt I had gone around him and had been insubordinate, but the other guys quickly squashed that with their enthusiasm. WEBN started playing the song, and the station phone started ringing. We had a local hit on the radio, alongside Boz Scaggs, Steely Dan, Pink Floyd, and all the other rock radio favorites of the day.

Suddenly, one record we were on was getting played on rock radio, and Kayo and I were on the black station with Larry and Vicky, not to mention the national commercial we played for Keebler cookies. We were starting to feel some momentum and see exciting possibilities, but we were also figuring this out as we went along. With the record on the rock station, Pure Essence started to attract more of a white college crowd, which led to us playing many fraternity parties. Bit by bit, it was happening for us.

We were working gigs around Cincinnati, frequently at the Club Diplomat, the hot spot for local talent. We would rent out the club, buy commercials on local radio, and pack the place. We were having a great little run. Our plan was working. We were making a little money playing music, even though we all

Preforming with Kayo and Mouse at Club Diplomat, Cincinnati, Ohio, 1977

still lived with our parents. Also, we were getting better and better live, everything was going great, drawing crowds, playing our asses off—but it all came crashing to a halt one Sunday morning only a few short weeks later.

I got a call that the club we used for rehearsals had burned to the ground with all of our instruments and equipment inside. We lost everything. We had no insurance and no money, and, now, no instruments and no equipment with which to make money. We were able to borrow some gear to do a couple of gigs, but that didn't last more than a couple of weeks. Without income, the pressure started to get to us.

I was determined to find my way in music, but I needed to make money. I'd never made my own living in my life and didn't even know where to begin. My mother was getting frustrated with me staying home all day and going out at night, but not working, not gigging, just wasting time. She told me she had a gentleman for me to meet who would help me get a job. I told her I wasn't cut out for labor work. I flatly refused to even meet the guy, just to prove my point that my life belonged in music. She said, "Fine, but you better hope music can find you a place to live," because she was done supporting me.

I was twenty-one years old, still living with my mother, and I no longer owned a car. (I was such a horribly oblivious driver, Mom wasn't keen on me using hers.) I had no real prospects in the music business, but that didn't occur to me. I knew that if I wanted to get back on the bandstand, I needed to take every little step. I went out and looked for work.

I found a job at a factory that made paper bags. There was a strike at the Duro Bag Manufacturing Company over the river in neighboring Covington, Kentucky, and the company didn't mind hiring a bunch of kids from Cincinnati foolish enough to cross the picket lines. My job was working on the dock, loading trucks with huge bundles of paper bags. It was a dirty job, but I did it until I met Winston Twe, a slightly older African gentleman studying for his PhD at the University of Cincinnati who didn't ever seem to be working hard.

For the most part, he kept to himself, but I met him in the cafeteria and we discovered that he lived on the same street where I had taken an apartment with my girlfriend, Pamela. He spoke proper Queen's English, not American ghetto slang, and his job at the plant was to patch the bundles of paper bags if they broke, which they rarely did. So mostly he stood around all day. He took a liking to me, spoke to someone, and soon I was working/not working alongside him, patching bundles.

Winston started teaching me things. He gave me books to read. He introduced me to Bob Marley's music at parties at his home. We would hold long discussions, and he would ask me crazy questions, such as, Why are stoplights red?

"Psychologists made the stoplight red," he told me, "because red is a jarring color and it makes you stop. In Chinese theater, the performers always wear red because you can see them from any point in the theater."

I'd always felt guilty that I didn't have a formal education, so I devoured the books Winston gave me. I loved listening to him speak in his velvet tones and elegant language. With his help, I started to see, for the first time, that I was smart.

In about six months, I had saved enough money to buy a new drum kit and quit the paper bag factory. The other guys did the same and we put the band back together. We started practicing and writing songs while looking for work. Sadly, our bandleader, Mouse, had turned to heavy drugs and was strung out on heroin. He was never the same after that, although he stayed in the band.

I wanted desperately to get back to playing music, but even though I had a new drum kit and the band was back together, it was a dark time for me. To pay the rent, I had to take a job working the graveyard shift at a convenience store called King Kwik. The relationship with Pamela had been straining both of us and I'd already been feeling trapped when we learned that Pamela was pregnant. Her mother showed up one day and started in on me after checking out the décor of our little apartment.

"Why do you have the pictures up so high?" she asked— apparently I knew nothing about interior design. "And how are you going to take care of my daughter? And I heard that you was running around with this other girl, and if I hear about you running . . ."

That was way too much for me. I cracked. I called my friend Toby and told him to come get me, but I couldn't even wait. By the time he picked me up, I had already walked three or four blocks up the street. I got in his car and drove away. I knew she was pregnant, but I was in no way ready to start a family. I was a reckless, irresponsible twenty-two-year-old who wasn't ready to face a future of King Kwik and give up my dream. I was a piece of shit. I always did what I could to help, but it would be years before I could bring my son into my life completely.

Just as I was trying to get my music career back on its feet, my uncle Albert, who had inspired my love of drums, and my grandmother died in a freak accident, suffocating from carbon monoxide while they were holding a conversation in his car parked on the street. He never married and didn't have any children, but he had felt especially close to me, so he had left me his drum set and the car they died in. I was too poor not to take the car, a 1972 Ford Galaxy—my first car.

After their funeral, I went to band practice and I played harder that day than I had ever played before. I kept dropping sticks, I was so nervous, but I felt like the only way I could represent my uncle was to play harder, commit more time, practice more. He took me seriously and encouraged me to always improve myself, not just on my instrument, but to study and read and continue my education. He'd inspired me to drum in the first place and ushered me into that fraternity of musicians; now that he was gone, I was determined to put his drum kit to work in a way that would have made him proud.

Relaunching the band, we faced problems. It was 1977, and in semicosmopolitan Cincinnati, disco had taken hold and local bands were being replaced by disc jockeys. We could find work only on the weekends. In Indianapolis, a hundred and fifteen miles away, the clubs generally booked bands five nights a week, Tuesday through Saturday, but there were also several clubs that had live bands all seven nights.

One day in 1978, I took a drive to Indianapolis with a friend to check out the scene. The first stop was a club on Thirty-Eighth Street called the Zodiac Lounge. I walked in and asked for the club owner. The gentleman I asked turned out to be the owner. I explained that I had a band and was looking for work. He asked a few questions and told me he would hire us for $800 a week to play covers, if we were good. "You guys can start next week," he said, "but if you aren't as good as you say, I'm sending you back to Cincinnati."

I went to the next spot, called Ricky's Lounge. Ricky was much nicer than the tough, gangsterish guy who owned the Zodiac. Ricky also told us he would give us a shot at playing covers. Now I had two weeks of work booked for nearly $2,000, and back in Cincy, I held a band meeting to discuss the plans, but Mouse announced he would quit the band rather than go to Indianapolis and sing covers. Instead, we found another member of our high school music class who was a singer. Tony Coates wasn't a good-looking guy, but he could sing his ass off. He was more R&B than funky, but we needed somebody right away and gave Tony the gig.

It didn't take long for us to see that Indianapolis was a very different kind of town—slower, more laid-back, less cosmopolitan, but the music scene was serious. It was a real music town. The musicians were far more developed and committed than those in Cincinnati, playing music full-time for a living. The bands played like pros because if you play six nights a week, you get good. Many of them had recording deals and local hits. We had a lot of catching up to do.

We streamlined the band's name to simply "Essence" and hit the circuit. Our first few weeks were rough, as we were used to

A rare occasion—me singing—at the Zodiac Lounge

playing only original songs in Pure Essence. We had to learn the current chart-topping hits quickly, and though we played them well enough, we were not nearly as good as the bands in Indy. We drew a decent crowd most nights, but nothing to write home about. Just up the road was the more posh nightspot called the Mark 4, where we caught bands like Manchild, Midnight Star, and several other lesser-known bands, all really impressive. We especially liked Midnight Star, who were also from Cincinnati.

We moved to Indianapolis and stayed for three years working in those clubs. We didn't make a lot of money, but we made enough money to pay the rent and eat. We were playing music for a living. We were learning our craft. Playing the same cover material grew old quickly, but we definitely improved as musicians, since we had to compete with the other Indianapolis bands, who could play anything, from jazz fusion to pop. Indianapolis wasn't really a funk town, so we played black music, whatever was hot at the time. We did some disco songs. Rick James had a funky style of disco music and we could play that. Mostly, however, whatever the Top Forty songs were, we would learn twenty and play those.

Living conditions were grim in Indy. The entire band lived in a two-bedroom apartment on Thirty-Eighth Street. Eight guys, one bathroom with a broken door. We played four forty-five-minute sets every night with very few days off. We would practice during the day, learning new material, and gig at night.

Times were tough and we established a house rule with the band: no free fucking. None of us were allowed to spend the night sleeping with a girl somewhere else if we didn't bring something back—cash, clothes, food, cigarettes, something. Sometimes somebody would bring breakfast back. We quickly got trained to get money out of girls. Our conquest wasn't the girl. Our conquest was to get them to pay the rent or buy some food. Which one could we borrow a car from? We worked it like that.

One time I got into a fight with this girlfriend I had. I would never hit a woman, but I guess I raised my hand while she was ironing. I scared her and she took the iron and hit me on the temple with it. I had a show that night. She put makeup on the mark on my temple to cover it up. We were playing the show when the keyboard player saw the blood and started laughing. The music started sounding funny because the whole band was picking up on it and laughing. We used a word among ourselves—"does"—to stand for "domestic problems." "LA is having does," he said. "He has blood."

I was playing at Ricky's Lounge in Indianapolis when my cousin Rhonda, Kayo's girlfriend who lived in Cincinnati, called to tell me my son had been born. That weekend, after the shows were over, I went back to Cincinnati to visit Pamela in the hospital. I walked into the hospital room and she was holding him.

"This is your son," she said. "I named him Antonio." Looking in his eyes, I saw my life stretch out before me. It was hard for me to comprehend—this was my son. I was happy, but I still was in no way ready, so I went back to Indianapolis.

The band landed a monthlong booking in faraway New Orleans through a hustler cousin of our keyboard player. We rented a U-Haul truck, packed up our gear, and strapped it down to prevent movement during transit. We piled in some mattresses for the band to sleep on during the freezing-cold fourteen-hour trip to New Orleans in mid-February. Fumes from the exhaust mixed with the air we breathed. We had no real cash, very little food, and only a little weed to take the edge off. We ate packets of ketchup we lifted from a fast-food restaurant. Talk about struggling—a bunch of black men rolling through the South in the back of a truck.

When we arrived in New Orleans and got out of the back of the truck, we were swollen, starving, and smelly. The promoter rented us a house for the month. The first gig was at Pratt's Alhambra, a local bar near the French Quarter. No one showed up. That city is the most unusual city in America. It was hard to figure out; we felt it as soon as we were there. We played to a nearly empty room. We weren't that bad, but the club was dead. After one night, we were fired.

A week later, the promoter found us another gig and things started to look up. We played a few shows, but we didn't seem to connect with the New Orleans crowd, who preferred a different kind of music than we played. After our last gig, we went to the house to pack up to leave and found our clothes on the porch, the doors locked. We had been kicked out. No money, no food. The promoter had disappeared with whatever money there was. The only thing we had was the U-Haul truck that we hadn't paid for, so technically all we had was a stolen vehicle.

I had met a girl who worked at a nearby grocery store and went to her for help. We had had a moment while I was in town. I asked her to loan us some gas money to get back to Indy. She kindly gave whatever she could. Since she was married (although separated), I never got her phone number or address. I never gave her anything back, and I regret that I didn't know how to reach her. She saved our lives.

We packed the truck and made it back to our place in Indy only to find the same thing. Doors locked. Keys changed. No money, no food, and now no place to live. One of the guys had a girlfriend who let us crash at her apartment until I could find our landlord and beg him to let us back. He did, but only after he gave us two weeks to pay the two months' back rent.

Indianapolis was still buried under two feet of winter snow. I set out on foot to find work for the band. I went to all the spots where we had worked before with no luck. I went back to Ricky's and managed to get another two-week run with a cash advance of $200. We were again back on our feet for another round of local gigs. We played Ricky's and another popular spot called the Night Flight. This club was a discotheque, but it had a lounge downstairs where the club owner let us play for the door. That lasted a few weeks, but we never made enough money to pay the rent.

Finally, I went back to the Night Flight to speak to the owner. I asked him to advance us a few dollars against our next gig; what I got was a life-changing conversation that I will re-member forever. Walt told me, first of all, that he wouldn't give us an advance, because we were fired. "The band sucks," he said, "and didn't draw a crowd." He called us dated and uninteresting. "This band will never make it," he said. He eventually coughed up a hundred-dollar bill and told me to remember this and to do the same for someone when I got the chance. His exact words were "Pay it forward."

That club owner taught me a lesson I never forgot. The years in Indianapolis had been excellent musical training, but we had failed, no matter how well we were now playing. Clearly something had gone wrong, and the man from the Night Flight helped show me what.

That would have been the bitter finish to Essence except for one last desperate try. We made a deal to buy this sweet custom-ized van from a nighttime deejay on WTLC in Indianapolis, Vicki Buchanan. We hooked up a U-Haul trailer and went off to the South to play a string of dates in itty-bitty towns such as Ashburn, Georgia; Tifton, Georgia; Sylvester, Georgia; and Eufaula, Alabama.

First we stayed in a house in Ashburn, Georgia, and then moved into a trailer the promoter gave us in Albany, Georgia. One of the guys in the band picked the lock on a trunk in the trailer and found a collection of sex toys, so it turned out to be a place where guys brought women to have sex. That was a complete turnoff—we lived in the whores' chamber. My mom had no idea. I would call her and tell her how great everything was going. I didn't share any of the struggles with her. To me, that was just part of the deal. Losing the instruments had been depressing. Not being there for my son hurt. But the rest of it was the dream, and my optimism was as high as the heavens. I never had a doubt for one second.

We finished the tour and came back to the trailer. The next

morning I went to the promoter's house to collect the money and he was sitting there with this long face and no money. He offered me gas money for the drive back to Indianapolis. I understood. We played to empty houses. He took a gamble, we took a gamble, and everybody lost. When we got back, we still hadn't paid for the van, but Vicki told me everything was cool and to come by anyway. As soon as she saw me, she snatched the keys out of my hand and took the van back.

That was the end of Essence, but oddly enough, I didn't feel defeated. I was beginning to think I could do this. Even though I'd invested a lot of time into the band, I didn't see what had happened as a failure, because it was an experience I could learn from. When I'd arrived in Indianapolis, I had been exposed to a higher level of musicianship—those club bands could play Mahavishnu, Miles, all that badass jazz, along with Earth, Wind, and Fire, Rick James, the funk. But while their musical talent may have been superior, these Indianapolis groups seemed to lack direction, focus, and concept. And the longer we'd been in Indianapolis, the more we'd become just like those bands. We had lost our way in that city, playing those clubs, trying to get the rent paid. We had no vision, no concept, no idea. We had concentrated on playing. The fact that I could now recognize the difference between talent and vision gave me confidence—it energized me. It was the first time I realized that success in this business had as much to do with learning from what hadn't worked as it had to do with making hit records.

Drive was just part of the equation, though. If I hadn't figured out exactly where we had failed, maybe I would have lost heart, but thinking over how things had gone for Essence, I put my finger square in the socket: our band wasn't entertaining. We were serious about being musicians. We knew how to play. We knew how to sing. We even knew how to write, but we didn't understand entertainment. I knew what we needed to do—that one conversation with the owner of the Night Flight had made that painfully clear—but I just wasn't sure how to do it. Although I didn't know what my next step would be, I was not lost. I was found.

3

THE REAL DEELE

W hen I came on the scene, Cincinnati had been turning out funk for years. Of course, James Brown had begun it by recording for King Records in Cincinnati and making the city one of the secret hot spots of funk in the country. But over the years, what he'd started had just kept going.

In 1970, Bootsy Collins was a nineteen-year-old bass player working around town in a band called the Pacemakers when James Brown fired his entire band over a pay dispute and hired the Pacemakers on the spot as his new backup group. A year later, Bootsy returned to Cincinnati to begin his solo career when he decided to join Funkadelic instead. Similarly, Roger Troutman and his brothers used to gig around Cincinnati before changing their band's name to Zapp and being discovered in 1979 by George Clinton of Parliament-Funkadelic.

After everything fell apart with Essence, I was determined to take charge of my musical destiny, and with Cincinnati's funk history, the first step was getting back there, which took a couple of months. There was never any official discussion about Essence breaking up—everybody simply went their own way. The other guys left for Cincinnati immediately, and Kayo and I stayed in Indianapolis. We lived in our girlfriends' houses. Candy hid me in her parents' basement, and we would have to wait for her mother to come home and give her a couple of dollars to go buy some eggs for dinner.

I was in Indianapolis for a couple of months, sleeping here, sleeping there. I stayed on the living room sofa of Candy's friend Brenda. All the time, I was writing songs. I'd actually started writing when I was about twenty-one years old, late, but I'd never shared my songs with the band, because I was too shy. Now that the band was done, I just wrote on my own. I didn't have my instruments, but I wrote on a pad and hummed the tunes to myself. Brenda had a copy of the new Diana Ross record, "I'm Coming Out," and I listened to that record over and over. That record made me realize that music was changing. We were coming out of the disco era. I could hear it. That was disco music, but disco music with a rock flair. "I'm Coming Out" came from someone I think is one of the most talented writer-producers in the world, Nile Rodgers. I slept on Brenda's couch and listened to "I'm Coming Out" for days until Candy told me I had to leave. It was all coming to an end. It was time to go home.

I bought a round-trip Greyhound bus ticket for fourteen dollars. I cashed in the second half of the ticket when I got to Cincinnati so that I could help buy food for my one-year-old son, Antonio. I was doing what little I could to help support him.

Once we were both back home, Kayo and I started meeting in his mother's basement, where she let us set up our equipment. One day I sat at the little makeshift bar down there reading an *Ebony* magazine story about Lionel Richie and the Commodores, how a groupie went all over the country on their bus with him. Talk turned serious and I expressed my strong feeling to Kayo about our need for a handsome, charismatic lead vocalist.

"What about Darnell?" he asked.

I can't say I knew Darnell Bristol that well in high school. We lived in the same Mount Auburn neighborhood. He used to walk past my house on his way home from school and would always wave. He was one of the Backstabbers in choir class and he could sing. He was tall, good-looking, and skinny, with good hair and light skin. I had always been impressed with him, but I also wondered if he could go the distance. Revisiting it that day with Kayo, though, I thought he might be exactly what we needed, the perfect balance of talent and appeal. Kayo called him.

They talked on the phone and Kayo hung up. "Darnell is interested," he said. "He's going to come over."

"When's he going to come?" I asked.

"He's going to come out today," said Kayo.

While we hung around and waited, I worked on a song. Darnell walked in. I hadn't seen him since high school. He was the young adult Darnell, not the kid I knew in school, and he looked amazing. And so cool. He had on jeans and boots, and a Members Only jacket, which was hot at the time. He had the Jheri curl, long, shiny ringlets of hair, and he had a striking resemblance to Prince. He hadn't been playing music professionally—he was working at a car wash with his father—but he had been singing as a hobby and keeping up with all the latest. In fact, he seemed a lot hipper than we were, more in touch with what was happening, his finger more on the pulse.

While we had been waiting on him, I had finished a song that Kayo and I had been writing about President Reagan called "Mr. Clever" (those two would call me Mr. Clever after that for a while). After we talked for some time with Darnell, I pulled out my lyric pad and asked him if he would try the song. He sang the hell out of it.

With Kayo and Darnell in the fold, along with Larry and Tuck from Essence, we added a saxophone player and put together a new edition of Essence. We rehearsed in the basement of Darnell's mother's house for a gig we booked in Louisville, Kentucky. At the gig, some of the guys never showed for sound check. The show was a disaster. I knew this group of guys wouldn't last. It meant so much to me and so little to them. I didn't even bother to say anything. I simply told Darnell—whom we had taken to calling Dee—and Kayo, "Fuck these guys. Come with me."

A couple of days later, when we were back in Cincinnati, Kayo and Dee came to my mother's house, where I was living. She had moved from Madisonville back into the inner city. She had bought herself a little two-bedroom house in Mount Auburn, small but perfect for her and my little brother. Understandably, she was not happy about me coming back at age twenty-four. I didn't have a dime and had no real plans. I must have seemed like the biggest failure in the world.

One day, when she was at work, Kayo, Dee, and I held a conversation about our future. We talked about how we wanted to put together a serious band, a commercial enterprise with genuine appeal, a group that could land a record deal. That's when Dee named the band. "Let's call the band the Deele," he said.

The Deele would be where I learned everything I needed to know about the music business. This was where I came to understand songwriting, record production, the importance of image, how record companies worked, and what managers did. The Deele was my college education.

Right from the start, I knew our band needed a strong concept behind it. Dee was a huge Prince fan and wanted our band to be similar to the bands that were breaking out of Minneapolis. Prince and his crowd—the Time, Vanity 6, André Cymone, Jesse Johnson, producers Jimmy Jam and Terry Lewis—they had the funk, but they went punk with it and mixed their funk with new wave and rock. It was a new breed. They were leaders, setting the styles and rewriting the rules. They were cultural. We looked at all the fanzines and studied their style. We analyzed the way Prince wrote songs. We checked out the way the Time sported that street-smart sarcasm.

Dee suggested we call Carlos Green, another guy we knew from Mr. Brown's class in high school. "That crackpot?" I said. "Can he sing?"

I had known him as Carl Green when we were in junior high school. I went to school with his sisters. We used to play football together. He was a funny guy, always cracking up everybody, but I didn't take him seriously and had no idea if he was talented. But when he showed up at my mother's house, he had the same energy as Darnell. He was tall, slender, good-looking, had the right hair, the right attitude, and was a Prince fan. It was all there.

We brought back guitar player Steve Tucker—Tuck from Essence—and rehearsed for a few weeks, working up a bunch of songs we had written. Even though I'd been writing for a few years, I was still nervous about my work. The other guys could really write, so I was always a little embarrassed to let them hear what I was doing. I probably wrote fifty songs that nobody heard.

Each one of us took turns letting the band practice at his mother's home. We went house-to-house after each new mother got tired of hearing the racket. Everything changed. We went from being this drab funk-jazz band to being a kind of Prince knockoff band. We started dressing the part. We played our own original songs. Our only covers were Prince.

I called the owner of the Zodiac in Indianapolis, where Essence used to play for never more than a few people. I told him I had a great new band and I needed a week's work. "All right," he said. "Bring them down. I will give you one week. I'm telling you right now that if this isn't any good, don't ever call me again. I'm telling you that because I put up with your shit for so long and if this isn't it, that's it."

He gave us a date and we went back to Indianapolis. The first night the Deele played in the Zodiac Lounge, it was about half full. Second night, three-quarters. Third night, the club was packed. Fourth night, the club was filled, with people standing outside. By week two, we were a sensation. We cut back from four shows a night to three and raised our price with no complaints from the club owner. Indianapolis was different this time. Crowds came to see us. The club owner was nicer. The girls were prettier.

The Zodiac was the center of our life. Josie fed us burgers from the kitchen. The Thirtieth Street Big League, the local

For people who only need a beat

street enforcers who also frequented the club, were our friends. George, the big gangster who worked the door, would always let us in free. If the owner was at the door, he made us pay. We took a week off while the club featured a third-generation version of the Ohio Players, one that included the original sax player, Satch, but not the star guitarist Sugarfoot. George slipped us in to catch the act and we couldn't keep our eyes off the Sugarfoot replacement on guitar.

He was tall and handsome, had the hair, played wild and crazy, and was all Princed out. We instantly knew he could be our Keith Richards to Dee's Mick Jagger. We introduced ourselves to him. His name was Stanley Burke, but everybody called him Stick. We talked with him a little bit, and, because he was clearly a better fit, we asked him if he was interested in taking Tuck's place in our band. He finished the week at the club and never went back to the Ohio Players. We took him over to Kayo's girlfriend's house, where we were all living by then, and he joined the band.

We quit the club and concentrated on songwriting. We bought a four-track tape recorder with our earnings. A friend let us set up our gear in his basement, and I stayed down there for hours, learning how to work it. Stick knew how to record on the four-track. After playing for the past four or five years in a Top Forty band, I knew nothing about recording, but we started turning out demos when we weren't playing at the club. I started to become a master of drum machines and to figure out recording. Stick sent some of our demos to a friend of his, a postal worker in Cincinnati who had a few dollars, and he agreed to pay for some studio time.

We went back to Cincinnati and into the studio to begin working on recordings, but we needed a keyboard player. We were like a rock band—two guitars, bass, and drums—and that didn't work. At the Zodiac, we'd hired a sideman called Hollywood to play keyboard. Back in Cincinnati, we brought in another friend, Bo Watson, the whiz keyboard man with Midnight Star. He played on our track "Turn It Out" and liked what we were doing so much, he told Midnight Star's manager, Pablo

Davis, who came to the studio to listen with Reggie Calloway, the leader and producer of Midnight Star. They loved the music and told us they wanted to sign our band to their MidStar Productions. Reggie told us if we were signed to a major label, he would produce our album.

The next day, I went back to the studio to watch Midnight Star record, and that's when I connected with Kenny Edmonds, who would eventually become my songwriting partner and a performer in his own right known as Babyface.

Prior to seeing him in the studio that day, I'd known Kenny a bit, and we'd circled each other a couple of times. When I was in Indianapolis, his band Manchild had a record deal out of Chicago and a regional hit, "Especially for You." I went to see the band with my friend Toby, who pointed out the dark-skinned, left-handed guitarist at the side of the stage. "The little black motherfucker on guitar is great," Toby said.

I used to spend time befriending Manchild's manager, Sid Johnson, and he would play me these incredible demos Kenny made. Sid always told me he was going to introduce me to Kenny, but he never did. When Kenny came to see the Deele at the Zodiac, I recognized him. He was a member of a much more successful band, so seeing him there in the front of the club was a big deal to me. I went up and introduced myself after the set, but we didn't exchange more than a few words. I didn't think he liked me.

The next run-in I had with Kenny had come when I was back in Cincinnati and I'd received a call at my mother's house from Hollywood, our keyboard sideman at the time. He was sitting in a Flint, Michigan, hotel room with Kenny. I played them our demo of "Turn It Out" over the phone. At the time, they were working in a Top Forty band called the Crowd Pleaser full of middle-aged musicians who still thought they had a chance of making it even though they were working at clubs in out-of-it Upper Michigan. The Deele had all gone "breed"—the term we used for the new style out of Minneapolis, an androgynous look that had the men in the Deele wearing makeup and leggings. Next to us, Kenny looked like a square.

Hollywood said Kenny wanted to talk about joining the Deele. "Kenny's really talented, but he's not breed," I told Hollywood. That was the last time I had crossed paths with Kenny.

I walked into the studio in Cincinnati that day just as Midnight Star was beginning to cut a demo for a song called "Slow Jam." The studio was dark and the singer was barely visible from under the shadows of the vocal booth. I couldn't make out who it was, but, man, could that cat sing. When he finished the take and walked out of the booth, I recognized him.

It was Kenny, but now he was full breed. He had the London Fog overcoat. His hair had grown out more beautifully than mine. He looked like us.

The Deele—full-on '80s androgeny!

"That was amazing," I told him. He remembered me and told me how much he dug the track I'd played him and Hollywood over the phone. This time, we hit it off immediately.

Kenny was twenty-four years old—three years younger than me. He went to North Central High School in Indianapolis and came from a family of brothers. His mother, Barbara, supervised a pharmaceutical factory, and Kenny had been committed to a career in music since he was in the eighth grade and his father died from lung cancer. Kenny was also signed to MidStar Productions, and they were developing him as both a songwriter and as a potential future solo artist. All of us spent the next several weeks writing songs with the guys in MidStar, including Kenny, who was great with the Teac four-track recorder and produced our demos. He was also one of the best songwriters and guitarists in our crew. Kenny had learned how to overdub background vocals by himself. He made the demos sound like records.

Kenny and I struck up a friendship. We had chemistry. We liked talking to each other, liked being around each other. In this free-flowing writing environment, Kenny was clearly far advanced as a songwriter. Kenny was different, though—he was special—that much was obvious to me. He was so talented, so superior to the rest of us, that I was secretly shocked he liked our stuff as much as he did and that he wanted to work with us. He watched me at one writing session and told me he liked what I was doing and that we should write together. It was his suggestion, and I was somewhat surprised. I knew I wasn't on his level as a songwriter, but I was eager to work with him and figured I could learn a lot writing with Kenny.

The session began with him playing me his songs. His demos sounded fantastic; they sounded like masters to me. Only later did Reggie Calloway explain to me there wasn't enough dynamic range on the demos to match the other masters. But even his simplest demos were brilliantly produced. He had been writing for a long time and had stockpiled a lot of material, so at first he was playing me things he had already finished. Eventually, when he would play me something that wasn't finished, I might offer a suggestion. I might say something like "I love this track, but right at that bar it should have gone to a bridge." Kenny began to take my ideas and embellish them. Our writing together started as me listening to his music and finding the hole that needed to be filled. He began playing me everything he was working on. It was the beginning of our parallel journey.

We had lived in the same town for five years, worked the same clubs, knew some of the same people, but it wasn't until we came together that we hit the fast lane and things began to click. Our first big break came when we both signed deals with MidStar Productions.

Although I didn't notice it at the time, this might have created some tension with the other guys in the band, because after all the years I'd spent with Kayo, Dee, and Carlos, suddenly I was giving Kenny my undivided attention. We were eating meals together, playing Pac-Man.

Kenny stayed in Cincinnati, working on our demos. He went back to Michigan and then came back down and spent a month polishing our demos and writing songs. We wrote "Baby I'm Crazy about You."

Our living conditions had come a long way from the apartment on Thirty-Eighth Street in Indianapolis. The management company rented us a three-bedroom house, and we set up a demo studio in the basement. It hummed like a factory. Songs were being written at any time of the day by someone. We recorded around the clock. When we weren't working at the house, we were over with the Midnight Star guys writing with them. They had the rehearsal room, which was like a studio, and everybody's bedroom had a keyboard, a drum machine, and a tape recorder. We lived in this culture of writing songs. Once during a party at the house, I snuck off to work on a song. I even sang the demo while the party was going on. I fell asleep, but when I woke up, the guys were standing around my room listening to my voice on the tape. I was startled to have them hear my non-singing. We had food, a van, and a little pocket money, and we were surrounded by a newfound bunch of really talented, like-minded people.

We were teaching ourselves songwriting—it was like record camp. Encouraging and inspiring—and sometimes competing with—one another made us an intensive study group in the fundamentals of the craft. As I worked with the other guys, I could feel my confidence grow and discover more that I had to contribute.

We got the demos done and Kenny went back to Michigan. He was aiming for a solo deal, and his involvement in the Deele was up in the air. He would work with us on music, but when we held band meetings, he would have to leave the room. There had been some discussion as to whether he should pose with the other guys for the band photo to go with the demo, but, in the end, he posed separately and we were photographed without him.

When Midnight Star completed production of their new album *No Parking on the Dance Floor*, their manager, Pablo Davis, and bandleader, Reggie Calloway, went to Los Angeles to turn in the album to Solar Records. While there, they planned to shop our six-song demo for a major deal. Within days, Pablo called and said he had two record labels interested—Quincy Jones's label, Qwest Records, and Solar Records, run by Dick Griffey. As much as I respected Quincy Jones, Solar felt like home, not only because of Midnight Star being on the label. My high school music teacher Mr. Brown's group, the Mystics, had moved to Los Angeles, changed their name, and signed with the label. As Shalamar, the group had gone on to become one of Solar's big acts, although, sadly, Mr. Brown developed the deadly disease lupus, and he never recorded with the group.

Solar Records had been in my sights for a long time. Years earlier, I had sent a demo to Solar and had gotten a rejection letter that I kept as some kind of badge of honor. Even though they turned me down, the fact that I got the letter made me feel like I was in the game in some strange way. Solar was the place.

The first person I called was my mother. I was never a mama's boy, but it was all about her for me. It mattered to me that she knew I was making it. The second call was Kenny. I reached Kenny on the phone in Midland, Michigan, where he was playing with the old guys, and told him the band had landed a record deal. "We want you in the group," I said.

It hadn't been easy. I had to cut a deal with the other members. Kenny asked what he would do and I had to tell him that the offer came with one stipulation—he couldn't sing any lead vocals. He could play keyboards and help out with backgrounds, but no lead vocals. The matter had been much discussed while Kenny was away in Michigan. Dee and Stick, as singers, were protecting their turf. Carlos, who never saw himself so much as a lead singer, didn't care, and Kayo had been a hundred percent with me about bringing Kenny on board from the start. Once it was agreed that Kenny wouldn't sing, everybody was for it.

As I explained this caveat to Kenny, I reminded him that he would be making his own solo album someday and he didn't need to sing in this band. Kenny had put plenty of work into the tapes that had gotten us the deal, and he was as proud of the music as we were. He had never been the lead singer in any of the groups he belonged to and was happy to play guitar and keyboards, doing background parts. He was glad to know he would be part of the adventure and we wouldn't be leaving him behind. He was never a guy to get too excited.

"I'll be there Sunday," he said.

Super producer Reggie Calloway in his office at the board

When Kenny arrived in Cincinnati, we immediately started production of our first album. We had enough material for the entire album, but we all continued to write. Reggie Calloway took the helm as the song picker and producer. The first piece he picked to record was a song I wrote with Melvin Gentry of Midnight Star called "Body Talk." I still wasn't a great writer, but I did have some good instincts, and the guys always liked my taste and energy. Kenny thought more of my writing than anyone else did. I never did know what he heard in me, but strangely enough, I wrote the band's first hit. It was just something I was humming when somebody else pointed out that it was a pretty good tune. I finished the song and brought it to the studio the next day.

When we made the demo, Dee didn't like the song and refused to sing on it. So Carlos, in true Carlos fashion, stepped up and said he would sing it, even though, strictly speaking, he wasn't the lead singer in the group. Funny how things work out.

When "Body Talk" came on the radio for the first time, I danced around like my crazy uncle Albert did when I was a child. It sounded so good—drums were sharp and tight, Kayo's bass sounded wicked and funky. And, of course, that was Carlos's voice coming out of the radio. The song started gaining traction when it was released in January 1984 and climbed all the way to number three on the R&B charts.

The phone rang in my apartment and I answered. A deep voice on the line spoke to me. "Antonio, Dick Griffey," he said. "I wanted to call and offer my congratulations. You guys have a hit record."

The Deele and friends—curls activated

Chills went down my spine. I had never met or spoken to Dick Griffey before. I certainly knew who he was. Before he was the head of Solar Records, Griffey had been the talent coordinator for TV's *Soul Train*, the popular show created by the impresario Don Cornelius. Griffey and Cornelius started Soul Train Records before Griffey split off to start his own label, Solar. He was kind of a junior Berry Gordy at the moment—Solar was like a little Motown, spitting out hip, cool hit records by Shalamar, the Whispers, Lakeside, Dynasty, Klymaxx, and our pals Midnight Star. *No Parking on the Dance Floor*, the Midnight Star album that Pablo and Reggie had delivered when shopping the Deele demo, went on to become the first long-playing record by a black act to sell more than two million copies, although the record was little recognized outside the black community. "Freak-A-Zoid" was a runaway smash single. The gold record award they gave me for my contributions to that album was the first plaque I received, and I immediately gave it to my mother.

In addition to his deep voice, Griffey spoke with authority—you could tell he was a serious guy. He asked a few questions about how the recording was going and said he looked forward to meeting me in person. As it turned out, I took my first airplane ride and went to Los Angeles to complete production on one unfinished track, to polish off the mix, and to master the album. It didn't occur to me that I hadn't been on an airplane until I actually got on one, and I guess I was a little green. Carlos tricked me into pulling down the oxygen mask before takeoff, which caused a minor scene with the stewardess. I met Dick Griffey at the Solar offices, where I also ran into Howard Hewitt, the lead vocalist of Shalamar, as he was leaving the building.

"Body Talk" opened doors for us, most notably an offer to be an opening act for Luther Vandross and DeBarge on a forty-city national tour. Outside of those first few weeks at the Zodiac, our band really hadn't played live. We concentrated on songwriting

The Deele performing at Bogart's in Cincinnati, Ohio, 1984

and making demos. The opening dates were at Market Square Arena in Indianapolis. Back home. Only, the worst winter ever hit in 1984, and freak snowstorms caused the first shows to be canceled. When we did finally take the stage, nothing worked. Stick went crazy. Kenny couldn't breathe. The whole thing flew by in a dizzying blur.

We had been working on our image. On the album cover, we were a bit more street, wearing tough-guy leather with an air of confidence and testosterone that rock bands always had. For the show, we wore these cheesy sequined jackets in bright colors that more closely resembled some pop act like the Sylvers or something. We also wore too much makeup. We had been aiming for the androgynous look that Prince and the Minneapolis crowd practiced so well, but Stick and Dee decided to take it a step further. Not only did they cake on the makeup, but they also smeared bright red lipstick on their lips.

After the terrible show, one of the producers took us aside and threatened to throw us off the tour. "I just got word from the boss that if you don't take off the makeup and lipstick," he said, "they won't do one more date with you. We are not doing a Dynamic Superiors." (The Dynamic Superiors were an openly gay band at the time.)

Kenny and I were the only ones who knew how bad it was, but we kept our disappointment from the other guys. We talked about it privately. Unfortunately, on that tour, we never got any better. We could play, but beyond "Body Talk" we didn't know how to perform. We didn't know how to win over an audience that wasn't giving any love. You have to figure out how to get to them. We had no idea.

In particular, Stick didn't know we were bad. He always played out of tune and all over the place, but with a confidence that worked. As we struggled, though, Stick developed more and more of an attitude. He was frantic and unpredictable onstage. In Little Rock, Arkansas, Stick decided to try another kind of makeup. He covered himself in whiteface. "You need to change that makeup," I told him. "You can't go on the stage with that makeup."

He didn't even listen. "Stick, you need to change that makeup," I repeated.

"Fuck you, LA," he said.

He did the show with the makeup. He wandered backstage after the show with a girl he picked up from the audience who must have been six months pregnant. He was drinking heavily and passed out on the long bus ride to Houston. We couldn't wake him. He wasn't breathing right. Something seemed a little crazy. He looked really sick. We took him to the hospital and they kept him overnight.

We did that night's show without him and had our first good show. Other people on the tour noticed, too. We held a meeting in Stick's room to check on his condition.

"We don't know what is going on with you," we told him. "You've been acting erratically and going off on people and what we think is that you need to take some time off. If you have some issues, we want you to go work them out and then come back."

Stick felt bad. He knew he had fucked up. He mumbled something about how he was going to get better. He went around the room and gave everybody a hug, but when he came to me, he paused. "Fuck you," he said. He never came back. You can't say that to me.

Touring with Luther Vandross and DeBarge was a life-changing experience. We had graduated from the chitlin' circuit and were now fully professional musicians. We were doing a nationwide tour with one of the greatest singers ever, and we were watching, learning, making friends, and joining this new fraternity of successful artists. We had our own team around us and were on the road. We had found our own style—it landed us a record contract, a smash hit single, and a national tour—but we had made the mistake of tampering with it, and, after a quick course correction, we got back on track. Once we established our groove onstage, we were rolling.

After the forty dates were over, we returned to Cincinnati. We went home to our apartments and relaxed. But when I asked our manager about how much money we had made after five months on the road, the news wasn't good.

"You guys didn't make any money," he said. "You did it for exposure."

We came back broke. It was heartbreaking and infuriating. I didn't know what to tell the fellows. We were going to have to move back in with our families. We held a meeting and came to a decision. I would take over running the operation, and our manager, we fired his crazy ass. I knew nothing about managing, but I figured I couldn't do any worse.

I called our booking agent, a young buck about my age, who told me he could find more work. "The roof's still kind of hot," he said.

We went back out on the road. I paid the expenses for the tour out of our money and I took the rest of it and brought it all back home. I rented three apartments on the edge of a golf course in suburban Cincinnati, country club living, and installed two band members in each apartment. I thought I had it made.

We went back to writing and making demos, starting work on our second album. When Midnight Star came back from touring for almost a year—and selling way more records than we did—Pablo told them they were broke, too. They sued him and, as a result, wanted nothing to do with us anymore. They had lost interest in us anyway. Reggie had a way of working in the studio that undermined our confidence. He told Kenny he couldn't hold his notes long enough. He made record production seem like rocket science, saying things like, "You need to think it through," and, "I don't know. Maybe. It's not an easy thing."

We'd never been on our own in the studio and didn't know what to do. We kept writing songs and sending demos to the label. I got a call from Dick Griffey asking when production was going to start. I told him we were having difficulty with our producers. He told me he would work to resolve the issues and come to Cincinnati. The mountain was coming to Mohammed.

This would be the first time someone of Griffey's status had ever visited our apartments. I was proud to show off the new digs, my palatial two-bedroom apartment, and equally nervous with anticipation. When he walked in, I offered him a beverage. He asked for a glass of white wine. I filled a glass with ice and poured the wine over. He shot me a condescending look and I knew instantly what I'd done. *Never serve wine with ice.* I needed a few lessons in how to host millionaires.

We went upstairs to my room to listen to music, where I had my studio set up. My bedroom was a cocktail table, my studio equipment, and a sofa bed I rolled out to sleep in at night. Reggie came with him. We played a few songs without much fanfare until they heard "Stimulate." I caught Griffey and Reggie giving each other the look—*That one was pretty good.*

Griffey leaned back in the chair. "Who produced the demos?" he asked.

"We did it ourselves," I said.

"Well, you can produce your own next album," he said.

That was the beginning of my musical production journey.

4

THE SOLAR SYSTEM

was surprised to receive a phone call at my apartment from the Cincinnati funk legend Bootsy Collins after I got back from tour with the Deele in 1984.

"LA, it's Bootsy, baby," he said. "I heard you got that funk. Why don't you hook me up with some?"

I ran upstairs to my makeshift studio in the bedroom and laid down a beat, threw on some keyboard, added bass. I pumped out a track for Bootsy—the first time I had written by myself since those days of writing in Indianapolis and listening to Diana Ross—and rushed a cassette over to the studio where he was. He took it home, wrote a song to it, and called me back.

"I think I got something," Bootsy said. "Let's set up a session and get this thing done."

We went into QCA Studios in Cincinnati, where we had recorded the Deele's album, to cut the track. I put down the drums first. Bootsy was playing his own bass part when Kenny walked into the studio, dropping by to check on me and see what was happening. Bootsy looked up from where he was sitting, his bass across his lap.

"Babyface!" he said without missing a beat.

Kenny didn't laugh. In fact, he gave a slightly sour look, but it stuck with me. That weekend the Deele did a gig in Richmond, Virginia, and when it came time to do his part, where we would usually introduce him as "Kenny Edmonds" to polite applause, we announced "Babyface" and the place went nuts.

We'd shifted his identity. At the time, it seemed mildly inconsequential, but when it led to louder cheers, I realized we had done something significant. The name completes the package.

After the show, the girls all wanted to meet Babyface. With nothing more than a simple name change, he went from being mild-mannered Kenny Edmonds to being

The legendary Bootsy Collins

a star. I think it gave him more confidence in some crazy way. We had spent a lot of time trying to come up with a nickname for Kenny, but nothing had worked. All of us had nicknames—LA, Dee, Carlos, Kayo—and, after that one crazy moment that afternoon in the studio with Bootsy, now Kenny had one, too.

Babyface and I would unlock the mysteries of record production together. We were two young, hungry musicians eager to move forward, ready to expand our roles beyond that of being sidemen in a group, and we found in each other almost immediately a shared sense of purpose and an enthusiasm for learning.

I still worked with Kayo, but Kenny and I were becoming the team. We liked the same things, had the same work ethic. On the road, when the other guys would chase girls, Kenny and I would go back to the hotel room and write. I liked girls, but I liked music more. In Kenny, I found a kindred spirit.

Kenny liked to work during the daytime. I was more of a nighttime person, and I would often finish things at night that he'd started when the sun was still out. Kenny did tons of songs by himself, nothing to do with me, because he was a complete accomplished songwriter. He was a self-contained unit and could start and finish songs without any help. I, however, have always been a collaborator and didn't often write songs from beginning to end by myself. Sometimes I might sketch out the skeleton of a song top to bottom, but for the most part I did embellishing and producing. Kenny was the poet, while I was more concerned with what a song would sound like.

In public, Kenny was quiet and shy, but privately he loved to debate. Kenny was patient. He always had time to sit down and talk about something. He was never too busy and there was nothing that wasn't worth discussing. It was great for me to always have someone to talk with. And he had that golden voice.

And we would need it, because the Deele's second album would be crucial to the band's fate. The first album by the Deele sold a strong three hundred thousand copies, and "Body Talk" had been a big enough hit on R&B radio that the band's next record would get a good shot. But we were a long way from made men.

The Deele went to a studio in Columbus, Ohio, to do the second album. I was nervous sitting behind the console as the producer for the first time. Dick Griffey passed me the baton, but there wasn't any real reason behind that other than I had produced the demos and it was my band. He simply made me the producer. There was a skilled engineer next to me, but I didn't have confidence. I never asked the guys—I simply took the job—and really didn't know how they felt about it. As we went through the process and the songs turned out better and better, they grew more comfortable with the situation.

During the sessions, we got a message from Dick Griffey that he had heard the demo to a number Kenny had written called "Sweet November" and he wanted us to do the song. It wasn't a song that either Dee or Carlos could sing, and when Dick heard the tapes from the sessions he called again, asking why he didn't hear "Sweet November." I told him we didn't have anyone who could sing it, and he was confused.

"But isn't that Kenny's voice on the demo?" he asked.

"Yes," I said, "but he isn't the lead singer."

Dick obviously didn't have time for something that stupid. "This doesn't make any sense," he said. "You guys need to get this worked out."

We held a meeting and Dee and Carlos refused to allow Kenny to sing. I called Dick Griffey and told him the band voted down the song.

"If you want to make a record for me," he said, "it better have 'Sweet November' on it or there won't be any record."

I hung up the phone, secretly pleased that he had overruled my foolish band. I was getting closer to Kenny than those guys anyway.

We spent most of the day in the studio working on the song, trying to cut the track. For some reason, I decided to play live drums on the track. Oddly enough, I had not done that since Essence. All the Deele demos and records had been cut using drum machines. I owned every kind of drum machine and had become a master of programming drum sounds and adding live overdubs. I could make drum machines sound better than I could play. I made my beats sound any way I wanted. If I wanted a marching sound, I could create that. If I wanted an ensemble sound or the effect of a single percussionist, I knew how to use the machines in different configurations to create that.

But playing live drums on the "Sweet November" track that day, I couldn't perform as a musician up to my standards as a producer. My ears had outgrown my ability. I kept speeding up, slowing down. Finally we gave up and I put the song together with drum machines.

I was sitting back in the control room, still shaking with frustration from recording the track when Kenny started to sing. It was like heaven opened up. We had been on tour with Luther Vandross and we had been watching the master of the soul ballad every night. We were inspired in the production of the song by Luther songs like "A House Is Not a Home," but Kenny was magical. I snapped out of it as I listened in awe to Kenny, overdubbing his vocals and making the song into what I knew would be a hit record.

Once we broke the wall that Kenny could sing, the second album took on a completely different complexion. He sang another song he wrote, "You're All I Ever Known," and the most memorable numbers on that album happened to be his two songs.

Not even Kenny's voice was enough to help the album, unfortunately. When we put out the single of "Material Thangz" in May 1985, it stiffed, so basically the album didn't sell. The second album barely cracked a hundred thousand.

While we were in Columbus, we got a call from Dick Griffey, asking us to produce Carrie Lucas, a singer with a couple of dance club hits who also happened to be his wife. It was the dumbest song, a parody of "All This Love" by DeBarge. Kenny wrote it about Greg falling in love with Ginny, characters on the daytime TV soap opera *All My Children*, a favorite show of Kenny's. We thought the song was a joke, but Dick Griffey heard it and thought it was a smash. We flew to Los Angeles through Chicago and did the session—the first time we were brought in to work with another artist. Now we were officially producers. Now we were Jimmy Jam and Terry Lewis.

When we started the third Deele album in 1986, we were still living in Cincinnati. Dick Griffey asked me on the phone one day what I was still doing in Cincinnati. It was our hometown, I told him.

"You can make more money by accident in Los Angeles than you can on purpose in Cincinnati," he said. "Why don't you move to LA?"

Two days later, the game was on. I took my credit card—my first American Express card—bought airline tickets, and moved my band to Los Angeles. We also brought Daryl Simmons, who had been around so long we called him Silent Partner. Daryl and Kenny were childhood friends and had started out playing music together in Indianapolis. They'd both belonged to Manchild, before Kenny hooked up with the Deele.

When the Deele started touring, Daryl came along to play keyboards and extra percussion. He soon worked his way into writing and playing on the records. By the third Deele album, he was indispensable.

We landed at a Holiday Inn in LA, where I seduced the desk clerk and she took care of everything until I went to the desk at one point and they took my credit card. By then we had picked up some scraggly manager named Dollar Bill Wallet from Cincinnati. He was always a hustler and, for a minute, we thought he was a pretty good manager. But he could never somehow manage to handle the $12,500 credit card bill. I needed my credit card back. He did nothing. We dumped him and called the record company to explain the situation.

The record company put us in an apartment complex called Highland Terraces on Highland Avenue off Hollywood Boulevard, dead center in Hollywood. We had been living in beautiful town houses in Cincinnati we rented for $500 a month. Now the entire band—except for Kenny, who was living with his wife, Denise, at a friend's place—crammed into one three-bedroom apartment that cost $1,300 per month. But this was *Hollywood*. And when you're in Hollywood, you're in the game, the music industry, the film industry, the television industry, ground zero for the entire glamour profession. Every day I walked down Hollywood Boulevard from our apartment to the studio and drank it in. The rent seemed like a fortune, but I felt proud. I felt like I was living a pretty decent life. I didn't have a car, but the studio and record company office was within walking distance. We set up our recording gear in the apartment and wrote every day.

We still didn't have much money, and Dick Griffey offered me $5,000 to sign a contract as producer. He saw Kenny more as an important songwriter and encouraged him to develop a solo album. He put me to work producing other Solar acts like

Dynasty and Shalamar. It was a kind of divide-and-conquer master plan, but Kenny and I saw too much strength in our collaboration to be pulled apart.

We were beginning to see ourselves as a team that was capable of finding songwriting work outside the Deele. The Whispers approached Kenny about recording some of his songs and having him produce the sessions, but he told them he wouldn't do it without me. We wrote "Rock Steady," copping the title from the brand of keyboard racks we had in our home studio, and never consulted with Griffey about the session. *And we begin to rock/Steady rockin' all night long* . . . The Whispers acted as their own executive producers and cut their own deal with us.

When Dick heard "Rock Steady," he knew what it was. We knew what it was the night we made the record. We knew that the record was superior to anything we'd ever recorded. We spent the night in the studio laying down the rhythm track, drums, bass, keyboards, and guitars, and then brought in the Whispers to sing background vocals. Right then, even before we cut the lead vocal, we knew we had a monster. I sat between those speakers and listened to the sound coming through and I really couldn't believe what we'd done. We made songs daily, but this one was something different. It felt like God was in the room, and from then on, I'd seek out that feeling every time I was in the studio. Only during truly special sessions, though, would I find it. When it was released in June 1987, "Rock Steady" became our first Top Ten pop hit and was a number one R&B hit. It was the biggest hit of the group's thirty-year career. To this day, you can't go to a black wedding reception without hearing it.

I kept looking for a manager for the Deele because the band was an ongoing concern and my hands were full with writing songs and making demos. I ended up hiring a manager for the Deele named Don Taylor, a Jamaican guy who had handled Bob Marley. In fact, when assassins broke into his home to kill Marley, Taylor threw himself across Marley's body and took five of the six bullets in his back. Marley escaped with a flesh wound to his arm. Taylor survived and moved to Los Angeles, where Dick Griffey introduced him to me. He signed both me and Kenny, but he was another tough guy. It didn't last long.

He gave me grief over changing Kenny's name to Babyface. When Taylor showed me the artwork for the album at his office, it said "Kenny (Babyface) Edmonds" on it.

"It's supposed to say 'Babyface,'" I said. "What are you doing?"

"That sounds kind of crazy," he said. "We should make it Kenny 'Babyface' Edmonds."

"Listen, motherfucker, I said it's Babyface."

I spoke plainly and loudly, in full shot of secretaries and other people working in the room. He stepped back and looked at me. I didn't care. All I was thinking about was that I wanted his name changed to Babyface—*I'm the art guy; you manage the business.* He gave me a long, hard look and walked away, but he called me that night at home.

"I'm sending somebody over to get your little ass," he said.

"You pay the rent, so you know where I live," I said and hung up.

Nobody ever showed up. I sued him—because I was a crazy young man. That lawsuit tied things up for a while, until Dick Griffey stepped in, settled the beef, and made everything good.

Dick Griffey was a lot of things to me: a father figure, a tasteful gentleman, a charming ladies' man, a tough guy you didn't mess with, a passionate record executive, and a smart businessman. He used to share business strategy with me, explaining legalities, management tactics, and music publishing.

He was Griffey U. I learned about artist imaging by watching him and observing the decisions he made. He was careful to sign only good-looking groups. He knew that while one band may play better than another, the one who could get on television had an advantage.

Early in my career, Griffey ingrained in me the ability to discern which artists could be telegenic and which would not. Of course, real music has nothing to do with what you look like, but there was a tendency to find someone who could play the part and come up with the fake music. As you raised the bar on beauty, you lowered it on music.

He could be funny, too. I remember complaining that five guys couldn't live on the money he was paying us.

"Young man," he said, "the record business doesn't pay by the pound."

It was through Dick that I came to be really comfortable in the studio, because he let Kenny and me use his Galaxy Studios downstairs from the record company office. That was where we got our advanced degree in how to make records. At Galaxy, we worked with a great engineer named John Gass, who taught me about the studio in a way that I hadn't quite understood before. He showed me about expanding sounds, equalizing and mixing records, really understanding the dimensions of a mix: the highs, the lows, separation, panning—in other words, what gives a record punch and what makes it lush. Night and day, I attended these postgraduate seminars at that console in Dick Griffey's studio next to John Gass.

Dick liked me. He laughed at me one time in his office when "Two Occasions" was on the charts. "You're never satisfied," he said. "Your record is number nine on the charts and what do you have to say about that?"

"It's not number one," I said.

Mr. Griffey was my teacher and my role model, my supporter and protector. I patterned myself after him. I studied him carefully and could imitate him flawlessly. I would call up the guys in the band and pretend I was him. "Dick Griffey here," I boomed over the phone, and the guys would quake in their boots before I broke into laughter. "Hey, it's me, LA."

We were having fun and we were learning how to make records, but it all came at a cost. Solar Records was a limited universe. We had to work within a system with only a few acts. Griffey had me tied up with an exclusive contract as a producer, but not Kenny. Griffey saw Kenny as a songwriter and an artist (his first solo album that we did on Solar, *Lovers*, came out in October 1987). Our reputation was growing, but we couldn't get anywhere with the other labels, who were all afraid of Griffey's exclusive contract, whether Kenny was signed or not. Nobody would touch us. What's more, Griffey never even paid me the $5,000 he promised me.

Griffey was a tough businessman. Kenny once asked him why we didn't get money for our publishing up front like other writers did.

"You're lucky because Berry Gordy took all of the publishing," he said. "At least you get some of your publishing. All this shit isn't free, Kenny."

He was telling it how it was. I learned a lot from Dick Griffey, but it made me angry to be shut down by him. As I grew in the business and produced hit records, I started looking around.

About a year after I moved to Los Angeles, in 1988, I quit the label, and then worked hard to get Kenny released. Griffey wasn't happy to see us leave and there were certain contractual entanglements that needed to be straightened out before we could. That took some time, but I was able to make it happen. It turned out to be the breaking point in my relationship with Dick Griffey, and while that disappointed me personally, I knew it was the right move for us professionally. It was what Babyface and I needed to take our success to the next level.

For the first time, we were on our own.

5

GIRLFRIEND

With Babyface and me starting to find work writing songs for other acts, the guys in the Deele drifted back to Cincinnati, and we weren't able to work on the band's next album with any regularity. Kenny and I stayed busy with our own material, writing and looking for places we could sell songs. We started doing some work with MCA Records and were meeting with an artist and repertoire executive named Cheryl Dickerson, who showed us a photo of a very pretty lady.

"I have this girl that I want you guys to meet and see if you're interested in working with her," she said, handing us the photo.

Neither Kenny nor I expressed much interest. She looked good, probably decent talent, but she appeared sweet, not the kind of thing we were into—bad girls. But Cheryl was insistent. She asked us as a favor to meet with her at the studio. "You're going to love her," she said.

By this time, Kenny and I had done many sessions at a lot of different studios around town, but when we went in Studio Masters on Beverly Boulevard that day, neither of us had seen anything like it. From the moment we walked into the room, we could tell that this was different. There were flowers and a big fruit plate, and everybody was drinking champagne out of flutes. Everything was prettier—including the girls in the room.

The girl from the photo came up and introduced herself. I looked at her and realized I was staring straight at the finest thing I'd ever seen in my life. I was instantly taken. I couldn't keep my eyes off her.

She was down to earth and put us at ease right away, chatting happily about current musical styles, asking our opinions. She played us some of the things she had been working on and they sounded like hits to me. I was more than happy to be engaged in conversation with this beautiful woman, and we clearly clicked. We exchanged numbers in a friendly way—I didn't have anything in mind. I didn't know anything about the girl, whether she was married or whatever.

Kenny and I wrapped up the meeting and walked outside. He gave me a long, serious look. "If you get her, I'm going to be pissed off," he said with a smile.

Kenny may have had a crush, too, but, of course, he was living with his wife, Denise, whereas I was single. In fact, the girl I had been seeing had recently dumped me and moved to Minneapolis to be with the producer Jimmy Jam. Kenny knew he didn't have a chance, because he could tell she was a bad girl and he caught the spark between us.

The next day, Kenny and I headed into the Solar Records parking lot in his Chevy Nova to do more work at Galaxy Studios. As we pulled up, a shiny black Porsche glided into the lot beside us with a license plate that said PEBS2. Behind the wheel was the girl I'd met the day before—Pebbles.

She and her girlfriend got out of her car and walked over. She was very friendly, acting like we'd known each other forever, and she told us she'd dropped by to see what we were doing. We took the elevator to the studio and the girls sat on the sofa, making occasional comments, but staying out of the way. At the end of the session, she invited us to dinner.

We drank more champagne—she loved her champagne—and talked. She knew our history. It turned out we had a mutual friend in the Deele's road manager, Leon Burnette, who used to tell us about her. It all started to come back to me. We did know about her, and she certainly knew about us. She was bright and very knowledgeable about music. We traded stories and talked over a long dinner. We became fast friends that night, Pebbles, Kenny, and me. She wanted us to produce her album. Her brand of danceable, light funk was right up our alley.

Around the same time, we developed a relationship with Ed Eckstine, the son of the singer Billy Eckstine who was running

Pebbles at the premiere of Beverly Hills Cop II *at Mann's Chinese Theater in Hollywood*

Mercury Records and had recently started the Wing label. He introduced us to Vanessa Williams, the former Miss America who had been stripped of her title after some beautiful photos of her posing in the nude had surfaced. She wanted to start a singing career, and we made arrangements to cut some demos with her. I met with Vanessa alone in my apartment, where I was working, and I played her a song I had written and was preparing for her to record. That night at Galaxy Studios, Kenny played me another track he had recorded, and we wrote the lyrics and cut a demo of this new song we called "Girlfriend."

I played it for Ed, Vanessa, and her manager-husband, Ramon Hervey, and they all loved it. We made a deal for the song and shook hands. Vanessa was more than six months pregnant, so the timing could have been better, but they were going to pay $12,500 for the song.

A couple of days later, Kenny and I went to Silverlake Studios to listen to Pebbles sing. We fell in love with her voice; she had this magical tone. She wasn't a crooner or a belter—she was a pop singer. Her voice was perfectly designed to sing hit records on the radio, and we knew it. Kenny started talking about "Girlfriend."

" 'Girlfriend' isn't Vanessa," he said. " 'Girlfriend' is Pebbles."

I had already promised the song. Money hadn't changed hands, but I didn't want to go back on my word. I told Kenny we couldn't play the song for her. Kenny was adamant. When Pebbles heard the track, she wanted the song. She asked how much Vanessa Williams was paying us and offered us $18,000. "Plus I'll throw in two cars," she said. "I have two cars at home. I have a Mercedes and a Jaguar. Which one would you like?"

I hadn't realized it before, but suddenly it dawned on me: she was married and they were well off. Sure, there had been sparks between us, but whatever was or was not going on between us could take a backseat. It was a momentary fever that would pass. It was more important to get this music done.

I called Ed with the bad news. He was understandably angry. He didn't say much, but he was upset. Vanessa Williams never spoke to me again.

Kenny and I went to pick up our cars in San Francisco, where Pebbles lived with her husband, a big deal real estate developer named George Smith, one of the leading black entrepreneurs of Oakland. He was a great guy. We spent the weekend with them. They lived in a mansion, ate at expensive restaurants. She had clothes, jewelry. They were rich people. We drove home in our cars. I took the Mercedes. The paint job was a little beat up, but it was my first good car. I soon had it repainted.

When we took Pebbles into the studio to cut "Girlfriend," her sassy vocals were perfect for the tone of the song. She nailed it. Cheryl Dickerson, the A&R gal from MCA Records, showed up to listen with Louil Silas Jr., the star A&R guy at the label. They went crazy, kept playing it over and over. And Louil liked to listen to music loud. They immediately proclaimed the track her first single.

Pebbles was more ahead of the curve than we were. The Deele had never done a music video. We watched in fascination as she did her video and the photo shoots. Not only did she have her own stylist, she had a special relationship with her photographer. She looked hot—perfectly curly hair, the exact lipstick, and the right tight black catsuit. We were learning and we were becoming friends.

"Girlfriend" was the last track on her album. The rest of the record she recorded with Charlie Wilson of the Gap Band. Pebbles had grown up in San Francisco and had worked with Bay Area funk artists like Bill Summers and Con Funk Shun. She had this song, "Mercedes Boy," that she may have written about a former boyfriend. It was one of those things I didn't need to know, so I didn't ask—but I could tell she was going to be a star.

She kept a plush condo on the Wilshire Corridor. I still lived at Highland Terraces, but Kenny and I visited her place frequently, getting to know her friends, hanging out. The three of us became inseparable, seeing each other every day. She went home to San Francisco on weekends. Sometimes her husband was around. He took us all to Las Vegas for a weekend to go to a fight and gamble, my first time, and we had a ball. Pebbles and I went on dates with Kenny and his wife. I had never gone on dates before—I had had girlfriends, but I never went to the movies, out to dinner, or anything like that.

The chemistry between us was getting to be obvious. One of her girlfriends took her aside and told Pebbles she could see what was going on between us and that she should put a stop to it. When Pebbles told me what her friend had said, though, it didn't have the intended effect of stopping things. Instead, something happened and we really started to fall in love.

One night in her apartment, after everybody else had left and it was just the two of us, I started playing the new album by Alexander O'Neal, produced by Terry Lewis and Jimmy Jam, and kept playing the same song over and over, "Never Knew Love Like This." The song was about everything I was feeling. Here I was, lovestruck and happy, with this beautiful woman who was going to be a big star. I planted the kiss, one thing led to another, and the greatest thing happened.

I was driving home afterward down Santa Monica Boulevard in my funky Mercedes with the illegal chip phone listening to a cassette of an instrumental track Kenny had recorded a couple of days before. Suddenly I pulled over, and, sitting in my car by the side of the road, a song spilled out of me, these words just poured through me, "Every Little Step." I'd never experienced anything like it before, and I'm not sure I've experienced it since—sitting there in the car, the dashboard in front of me, my hand scribbling furiously across the page. *I*

Bobby Brown—the King of the Stage

can't sleep at night, I toss and turn/Listenin' for the telephone. I couldn't hold the song or the feelings back anymore. I was living what I was writing and writing what I was living, feeling the words like never before. The next morning I was up early knocking on Kenny's apartment door—it usually worked the other way, with Kenny knocking on my door—and sang him the song in my non-singing voice over the track. He sang the demo.

A few days later, Louil Silas Jr. called and asked if we would like to work with Bobby Brown. We were huge fans of New Edition and had briefly met Bobby on tour with the Deele. He had left New Edition and released an unsuccessful solo debut. He hadn't had a hit, but we knew he was something. We met with him at Silverlake Studios and the first thing we played Bobby was "Every Little Step."

Kenny and I clicked with Bobby. We liked that he was a bad boy, edgy, had attitude, was unpredictable, but in the studio, he worked like a complete professional. He came to the studio on time every night and took suggestions well. I could sing Bobby a line in my awkward way and he'd sing it back to me and sound incredible. His voice had power and confidence. Because Bobby had edge, I could have edge. Kenny could have edge. I could make my drums as hard as I wanted to make them. Kenny could play guitar as mean and aggressive as he wanted. It was still the same guys—Kenny, Kayo, Daryl, and me—from the Deele, but we were always harder-sounding on the Deele records than we were on Babyface albums. With Bobby Brown, we never had to dial back and make it pretty.

Around the same time, I met Paula Abdul when she was working as a choreographer with Dan Ackroyd for the Blues Brothers movie at Galaxy Studios. She was a Laker Girl and she didn't have a record deal yet, but she was well known as a choreographer who had worked with Janet Jackson and others on many music videos and movies. We asked if she would choreograph a music video for Kenny—we were putting the finishing touches on his second Babyface solo album—and she said she would trade us for a song.

We wrote "Knocked Out" for her and we took her into Studio Masters, where it took a long time to cut her vocal. We sold the record to Virgin Records, a label that had only recently opened a new American division, and they included the track on a sampler distributed to radio stations to introduce the new label. Some disc jockey in San Francisco picked up the cut and Virgin decided to make an album with her, *Forever Your Girl*, which went on to sell more than twelve million copies.

We didn't work on the album—Pebbles saw to that. Paula and I started to be friendly. We didn't have a relationship, but one night Paula came to my house and it was after midnight. We stood on the balcony together listening to "Man in the Mirror," a song from the new Michael Jackson album, and we had tears of joy in our eyes from how good the music was. Paula had a long history of working with the Jacksons. Jackie Jackson had been her boyfriend for a while.

The phone rang. It was Pebbles, wanting to know what I was doing. I made some excuse, got off the phone, and went back to talking with Paula. Suddenly somebody was knocking on my door, hard. I opened the door and there was Pebbles. Never taking her eyes off me, she walked past me into the kitchen, grabbed a broom, and shattered all my glass furniture. It was like slow motion, tearing shit up. I smiled and loved it. She never looked at Paula, who was trembling in fear. Finally Pebbles turned and looked at Paula.

"I think it's time for me to leave," Paula said.

It was very sad for Paula. She hadn't done anything wrong. She was gaming and was innocent. Paula didn't speak to me for years. She signed with Virgin, made the album without us, and went on to become a huge star.

Despite not getting to write or produce on Paula's record, Kenny and I were becoming much more in demand. When the Pebbles record released, it quickly became a hit—"Girlfriend" was a Top Five pop smash when it was released in October 1987—and while she went off to tour, Kenny and I started to get approached about working with other artists. We began to see that even though there was a lot we still didn't know about the music business, the Deele was a complicated and inefficient way for Kenny and me to use our talents. We could make more money songwriting and producing than we could with the band. Spending time with Pebbles had given me a glimpse of the good life, and it all seemed within grasp.

In many ways, we'd chosen exactly the right moment to get involved making music for other artists; we'd become producers and songwriters almost by chance, but we couldn't have planned it any better if we'd tried. A big part of the reason that our work was attracting a lot of attention inside the industry was that the rhythm and blues world had drifted into a smooth, polished sound in the wake of all those massive Whitney Houston hits. R&B was going through changes, and more people in the music industry were noticing this shift. Kenny and I had tastes that matched these changes, and with this style and direction, we were poised to capitalize on the popularity of this new pop-R&B hybrid.

We took a meeting at Warner Brothers Records with an A&R executive named Benny Medina, who would years later become one of my best friends. But that day, when we walked into his office, he took off his watch, laid it down on his desk, and told us, "You have ten minutes."

I had seen this kind of Hollywood stuff before and didn't take it seriously. When he went over the list of artists on the label, we stopped him at Karyn White. I knew her from a song called "The Facts of Love" that she sang with Jeff Lorber, a modest hit I had heard on the radio. She was going to be doing a solo album. Benny arranged for us to meet with Karyn. Kenny and I went back and started writing songs for Karyn, even before we'd met her.

She also came from the Bay Area and had a little different taste in music, but I loved her voice. She is still one of my favorite vocalists I've ever recorded. We ended up doing almost her entire album for Warners. Every time we finished a song, they would ask for another. We gave them "Superwoman," "The Way You Love Me," and "Secret Rendezvous."

Eventually it got to a point where Kenny and I were constantly recording. Between Bobby Brown, Karyn, and others, we sometimes kept three studio rooms running at the same time. Kayo would be working on tracks in one. Kenny would be laying down keyboards in another, and I would be cutting vocals in the third. We were constantly writing. We started "Don't Be Cruel" for Karyn, but decided it would be better for Bobby Brown and finished the song with him in the studio.

In spite of all the success Kenny and I were having on our own, we were reluctant to let go of the Deele. The band was still our home base, even though it was increasingly becoming a side project for both Kenny and me.

It didn't help that making the third album was becoming a long, complicated affair. Part of the problem was that because the other guys didn't like Hollywood that much and couldn't hang, they kept going back to Cincinnati. As a result, we were unofficially broken up, but Kenny, Kayo, Daryl, and I had made all those records without the other guys before, so we arranged for them to come in from Cincinnati when we needed them to sing. Because Kenny and I were constantly doing work for other people, we weren't always both there for the sessions with the Deele. In fact, I was in another session the day the Deele recorded the song "Two Occasions" and listened back for the first time only at the apartment later that night.

I did not think the bridge was right. I asked the guys to go back in the studio and redo the part. Dee and Carlos both refused. They were going home.

"I've got a Halloween party at my house and I can't stay," Dee said.

Kenny and I looked at each other like, *Can you believe this? A party?* We needed to finish this record, but they went back. Kenny and I went to the studio and Kenny sang the bridge. That vocal part made him famous. It was a massive pop hit, and those guys didn't even stay to finish the record.

We brought in this superstar mixing engineer, Barney Perkins, who mixed incredible Steely Dan records and all of the Anita Baker records. The first time he mixed the song, he made the bass too loud. He was kind of intimidating, but I called him up and asked him to come back. He came back with some attitude ("What's wrong with it? Let me hear . . .") and took the headphones to listen. By the time he finished the second mix, the song sounded amazing.

When the guys returned from Cincinnati, Carlos brought a couple of songs, including "Can-U-Dance," which we picked as the first single and watched it flop. That was when Dick Griffey stepped up and picked the second single "Two Occasions," which became a Top Ten smash when it was released in April 1988 (the follow-up, "Shoot 'Em Up Movies," didn't do badly either).

On the back of our success, Kenny and I got the Deele together to tour behind the album. Since we were making some money, Kenny and I underwrote the tour. But before we left on the road, Kenny talked to me seriously about my relationship with Pebbles. Not only did he think it was distracting me from music, he thought it was wrong because she was married. Kenny took his marriage seriously and he thought my messing around with a married woman was a bad idea. He was gentle but firm. He spoke to me man-to-man. At this point in my life, the kind of friends we had become, he was the only person who could speak to me like that.

"You can't do this," he said. "You've got to end this relationship. It's not good for you. It's not safe. It's just not right. You've got to stop this."

Hard as it was, I knew he was right. However, since the band was about to leave on tour, I realized I had the perfect out. I called Pebbles and told her we needed to end the relationship. "But I love you," she said.

I told her I couldn't be with her unless she was divorced, and I wouldn't ask her to leave her husband. Her career was off and running, I told her, we had been good for each other. The Deele had their own record now. It was time to part.

Kenny and I flew back and forth, always first class, between dates on the Deele tour and sessions in Los Angeles. We were in Dallas, Texas, when I received a phone call at my hotel from a cousin of Pebbles named Cherrelle, who was also a singer with hit records produced by Jimmy Jam and Terry Lewis. I knew her a little bit, but I was somewhat surprised to be hearing from her.

"You've got to fix this thing with Pebbles," she said.

"There is nothing to fix," I told her. "She is married and I can't be with her."

"But, LA, she loves you," Cherrelle said.

Almost as soon as I hung up the phone, there was a knock on my hotel room door. I looked through the peephole and it was Pebbles. She had flown in to find me.

"I left him," she said.

My heart did not exactly leap for joy. I was a little happy, but part of me was also sorry she took me seriously. She told me she had rented an apartment on the floor above me in Highland Terrace. It was all too much for me. I remained friendly but distant. I said she could come to the gig that night, but she couldn't stay with me. She went to the show and didn't stay with me that night, but she came back to my room in the morning before she returned to Los Angeles.

"I'm very serious," she said.

As if the Pebbles situation wasn't confusing enough, the Deele tour did not go well. The band was never very good live, largely because the other guys refused to practice, and Kenny hated that. It didn't help that the band resented the success that Kenny and I had outside them. Because we flew in and out of the tour, the band called us "jet-setters." For my part, it was difficult to sort out my priorities, but I knew I was less sharp on drums—in fact, drumming had become almost impossible for me. Not only had I lost my chops, as my demand for studio perfection had let me know, but my hands were killing me. I had developed arthritis from years of playing. My hands were so tender I could barely hold the sticks. I wore gloves to soften the impact. I didn't tell anybody, but I couldn't carry luggage, it was that bad.

We didn't even make the last date on the tour. Kenny and I missed a connecting flight and showed up at the gig more than an hour after we were supposed to have played. They did the show without us. They could cover for Kenny on keyboards and vocals, but I was the drummer. When we walked in backstage, they glared at us like we were motherfuckers. That was the end of the Deele.

When I got home, the strangest sight greeted me. Pebbles had been in my apartment and changed all the linens on my bed, put new towels in the bathroom, had her perfume on the counter. She packed up some clothes my stand-in girlfriend had left behind and took them to where she worked at Solar Records. Pebbles had her own cars, but now that she was a big star, she took a limousine to the record company office to deliver the clothes. She chased off that girl and I never heard from her again. Now Pebbles lived in an apartment upstairs and had semi–moved in to my place. I surrendered.

After the Deele, I never played drums again. But I didn't look back on that for a minute. Being a drummer had gotten me to where I was—if it hadn't been for that passion, I still would have been in Cincinnati. Now it was time to move on from that part of my life, to realize that I was creating music in a new way. In my mind, just because I didn't have sticks in my hand, I wasn't any less of an artist. My ear for what I wanted to do had grown beyond my skills. Being a drummer had taught me how to make a hit record, and I'd need all of those lessons going forward, but my passions had led me to something bigger. Once I'd thought I was going to be the next John Bonham; now I didn't want to simply play on hit records, I wanted to discover them, I wanted to make them, and I wanted to watch them become a reality.

6

THE DIRTY
SOUTH

The Deele might have been over, but as far and Kenny and I were concerned, we were just getting started.

In 1988, the industry had discovered us. Our records simply exploded that year. By the end of the year, we had two Top Ten hits with Karyn White and two Top Ten hits with Bobby Brown. Ultimately, we ended up with five Top Ten songs on Bobby Brown's album *Don't Be Cruel*, which hit number one on the album charts, sold more than twelve million copies, and was the best-selling album of 1989. We made number one on the R&B charts with a group called the Mac Band for MCA. We wrote and produced "The Lover in Me" for Sheena Easton, another Top Ten hit. We did "Dial My Heart" with the Boys on the Motown label and made the Top Twenty. We were cutting hits with another member of New Edition, Johnny Gill, and had more projects lined up than we could do. We were making culture.

After all that, we were officially the hot new songwriters on the scene. Pebbles and I moved out of the Highland Terrace into a little house in West Hollywood with three floors, a sauna, and an elevator. I bought all new furniture. I was beginning to feel like a citizen. I had a couple of cars now, and so did Pebbles. We were starting to live well. Her daughter Ashley spent a lot of time with us, and then Pebbles got pregnant with our first child.

We were hitting our stride, but then, in the first six months of 1989, three large earthquakes rocked Los Angeles. Neither Kenny nor I had ever been through anything like that, but Kenny in particular was really affected. He was frightened enough that he wanted to move. At the same time, Pebbles and I were having our own issues with LA, which had nothing to do with earthquakes. Suddenly, Los Angeles seemed like a small town and we felt hemmed in. Our success gave us the confidence to think about other possibilities—because of how we'd gotten into the business, we didn't feel tied to any city. We started to talk about relocating, so that Kenny and I could begin our own label.

Kenny, Pebbles, and I brought a map into the studio and pinned it to the wall. Where would we go? How about Texas? Nice homes were affordable in Dallas and Houston, but it didn't seem right for the music. We thought about the Bay Area, where Pebbles was from, but quickly rejected that idea too. Indianapolis, Kenny's hometown? Scratch. Cincinnati? Scratch again. We talked about New York City, but hadn't had much luck making records in that town. The only time we recorded there we made "Refuse to Be Loose" with the great Siedah Garrett, who'd written "Man in the Mirror" for Michael Jackson; it was the only record we made during that period that wasn't a hit.

The three of us stood there looking at that map, and I do not remember which one of us said Atlanta, but after that, nothing was the same.

Atlanta was not on the pop music map. It was a large Southern city, but it didn't feel like the old South. It was the birthplace of the Reverend Martin Luther King Jr., and the city where civil rights leaders Andrew Young and Maynard Jackson had been elected mayor. Atlanta had this robust history and an upwardly mobile black community. It felt like a city full of dreamers, a place where things could happen and a place that hadn't been born yet musically.

It was a city that, in many ways, reflected what was going on with our music. Postdisco rhythm and blues in the MTV world had taken on a pop sheen, losing much of the raw, ghetto funkiness of the music I grew up playing. Like the black community itself, our music had taken on elegance, class, and dignity, without sacrificing any of the essential black ingredients—grit, sass, and soul. The more we thought about it, the better the idea of Atlanta sounded. We could own that town in a way we never could Hollywood. We would have first shot at all the talent and instantly be the biggest tree in the forest. It wasn't some fully formed strategy. None of us were from Atlanta or had relatives there. None of us had even really spent any time in the town, but Atlanta it was.

For a while, Kenny and I had spoken about having our own record company. It seemed like the obvious next step. It would give us control over our creative decisions, instead of being at the mercy of A&R executives. We never really considered the business side of the equation, other than assuming we would make more money if we had our own label. We came up with the name LaFace while driving down Sunset Boulevard and talking about how all the hot new restaurants in town were "La" something—La Place, La Dome, La Anything. We made a contraction of our names into LaFace. Forming our own label seemed obvious to me, and Kenny went along.

In our years of working together, Kenny and I had learned everything about how to write, record, and produce catchy songs. Because of everything we'd been through together, we had a lot of confidence that we could translate those skills of making catchy records into discovering sticky talent for ourselves. Until now, we'd been following the lead of others, producing and writing what they asked us to; at LaFace we'd be following our own lead—we were about to get a crash course in the art of discovery, with ourselves as the teachers. I have no idea what made me think we could do it, but I didn't have any doubts.

We had made a lot of our hits for MCA Records, so the next day I called the president of MCA, Irving Azoff. I told him I wanted to move to Atlanta and start the Motown of the South, LaFace Records. He loved the idea. I asked for $600,000. Not only did he say yes to the money, he also offered to book the travel, arrange the hotel rooms, and introduce us to Joel Katz, Atlanta's international power broker. Two days later, the money was in our account.

I had never really been to Atlanta, other than passing through on tour. As I drove around the town with a real estate agent and saw the place, I started to grow fascinated. We could have some pretty decent lives here. We found this ritzy, gated subdivision in North Atlanta built around golf courses called Country Club of the South that felt right. Kenny found his house, and Pebbles and I got a place. Kayo came along, as did Kenny's friend Daryl Simmons.

The stucco house that Pebbles and I bought was quite grand. The great room had twenty-foot ceilings, and a sweeping stair-case led upstairs. The eight-thousand-square foot, five-bedroom house sprawled over a corner lot, occupying an acre and a half with beautifully landscaped gardens. We used a decorator from Atlanta and did the place in a combination of California shabby chic mixed with Southern charm. We finished out the terrace level with a movie theater, an exercise room, an extra bedroom, and a beauty salon that opened to the pool.

These were richly emotional days. Pebbles and I ran off to Las Vegas and got married. We were young and in love. She was pregnant with our son, Aaron. We brought her daughter Ashley with us to Atlanta, and Antonio Jr. came down from Cincin-nati to live. I had always sent his mother money and did my best to stay in touch, but I had been largely an absentee father and I hoped to make up for that in some way. He started high school that fall in Atlanta. After all these years, I was finally in a position where I could buy some things. I was glad to buy my mother a house in Cincinnati, and she never had to work again. She and her sister Katrina were constant visitors at our new home in Atlanta.

Between Pebbles's career and Babyface's solo work, we were big-time for Atlanta. There was a splash in the *Atlanta Journal-Constitution*. TV news covered us. When we moved, we rented one of those giant car carriers that auto dealers use to transport new cars and filled it up with our cars; Benzes, Range Rov-ers, Porsches. I remember that thing pulling up in the Country

Club, a seriously uptight, exclusive little enclave. Back then, I didn't give it a thought, but now I wonder, what the hell did the neighbors think?

My life had completely changed. I was running a record company and living in a mansion with my new family. I wasn't rich—I went to Atlanta with $40,000 in the bank. We moved into this giant place that didn't have curtains up yet. We felt like we were living in a fishbowl. That first night, Pebbles, Ashley, and I went out to dinner, and a terrible loneliness descended on us. We had moved to a city where we knew absolutely no one. What had we done to ourselves? And what were we going to do?

The first thing was to get the record company funded. Our intended deal at MCA fell through when Irving Azoff grew bored running a label and quit his job. Our industry godfather Clarence Avant, the same man who steered producers Jimmy Jam and Terry Lewis to the top, took us to see Mo Ostin at Warner Brothers, Herb Alpert and Jerry Moss at A&M Records, and even arranged a meeting with David Geffen, who sent a car to the studio one Sunday afternoon to take us to his Malibu place for lunch.

I walked in and was greeted by a tall guy wearing an apron. "Hi, I'm David," he said. I thought he was David Geffen. He pointed us to the deck and went back in the kitchen. When a short, casually dressed man came out and said hello, I looked puzzled and asked him who he was. "David Geffen, you schmuck," he said.

Over lunch, Geffen was the charming host. He regaled us with tales of the record business and concluded by saying he wanted to make a deal with us.

A couple of days later, Clarence called to tell us David had changed his mind. "There's one last meeting I want you to take," he said. "I want you guys to meet Clive Davis."

Clive Davis? I read his book when I was eighteen years old.

He was the man behind Sly and the Family Stone, Miles Davis's *Bitches Brew*, Herbie Hancock's *Head Hunters*, Chicago, and Blood, Sweat, and Tears. He had made Janis Joplin a star. I knew he was the guy.

We went to Clive's Beverly Hills Hotel bungalow, where he had the air conditioner set to full chill. Everybody else had wined us and dined us, but we went to meet Clive around noon and he had a plate of cookies out. Where the fuck was lunch? We told him we were hungry and he ordered some sandwiches.

Clive was running Arista Records and had Whitney Houston and Kenny G, both at the height of their careers; otherwise, the label was not making an impact on youth culture. That didn't matter to us—we loved him. He played us some records, we talked shop, held a nice, friendly meeting. Clarence called back and told us Clive wanted to make the deal. He would pay the million-dollar advance we wanted plus cover our overhead while we built a staff that the record company funded. I felt official for the first time.

A tlanta was not quite ready for us. There was no music business. There was no place you could rent a luxury car. Hell, there weren't even rehearsal studios or equipment rentals.

We looked at every studio in town—and there weren't many—and sort of settled on Cheshire Bridge Studios, where we'd cut Bobby Brown and Johnny Gill. The studio owner paid a visit to my home, where he let me know what a top dog he was while he flicked his god damn cigarette ashes on my Oriental rug. When Kenny suggested building a studio on my property, we got the builder together with a studio designer and made a two-bedroom guesthouse that was a replica of the main house with a studio, named LaCoco Studios, after our Lhasa Apso puppy, Coco. We were up and running in four months. The first thing we did was finish Pebbles's next record, which had been going slowly because she was pregnant. Meanwhile, Kenny and I kept flying back and forth from Los Angeles, finishing his next Babyface album.

Once we had the studio built, the house turned magical. It became the castle of my kingdom, a busy hive of creative activities that went on day and night. My label was my life, and as it was a small, family-size company, we blended our social and professional lives seamlessly. I wanted to be around that kind of energy, right in the middle of it.

I made my home the center of everything. We kept a chef on duty around the clock in the main house. The terrace level was always humming with people watching movies, shooting pool, using the small demo studio, or hanging out in the beauty salon. It was our little recreation center, and we drew around us not only the artists and musicians, but the trainers, the hairstylists, all the kinds of creative people we needed. When the neighbors complained I was running a business in their residential community, I told the fellow they sent to interview me that I was a musician and I had a studio. My neighbor is an accountant— does he have a calculator? They left me alone after that. There were a lot of people coming to the studios, cars parked around and activity, but I never worked on weekends. I needed to make that commitment to my family and it was a strict rule.

After we'd set up shop, we quickly started checking out the local scene. Joyce Irby of Klymaxx, whom I knew from Solar Records and who had moved to Atlanta several years before, introduced me to Dallas Austin, a nineteen-year-old wonder boy I met at Cheshire Bridge. We instantly became good friends and started to spend a lot of time together in the studio. He already had a couple of hits, and when we opened LaCoco, Dallas came around a lot. He had a very different style from ours, hipper than we were. By this time, our sound had saturated radio, and I knew we had to broaden what we were doing. We'd had something like fifty songs on the radio; what we were doing was no longer new. Meeting Dallas was a breather, and it happened at the perfect time. With Dallas, we got another swing at the ball. I was already scouting for new sounds when we found Dallas. The first thing he did for me was a remix for a Pebbles song called "Backyard" featuring Salt-N-Pepa. When I heard what he did, I realized he was the hot young guy and I was now the older cat. I became the teacher who was really the student.

We were pulling together a clique, and Atlanta was getting to be our town. About the same time, Bobby Brown moved to town. He was officially Bobby Brown and quite the celebrity. We got him to make an appearance on a Babyface video we shot in Los Angeles. Babyface also finally scored his first hit record on his own. *Tender Lover*, our second Babyface album, released in July 1989, was an across-the-board smash, launched by Top Ten pop hits, "Whip Appeal" and "It's No Crime."

Before we left Los Angeles, we had signed a group called After 7 to Virgin, although we wound up recording them in Atlanta. The group was built around two great vocalists, Melvin and Kevon Edmonds, who also happen to be Kenny's brothers. We made a Top Twenty hit in August 1989 by After 7 with "Heat of the Moment," a song I wrote about seducing a secretary in my office bathroom.

To get things out of the house, Kenny, our assistant Sharliss Asbury, and I rented an office space in Norcross. We hung the LaFace logo on the wall and opened for business. I dressed in a suit every morning and went to the office, feeling special about life. Everything was great, except one thing: I knew nothing about business. Outside of Uncle Rueben's barbershop and my stint at Duro Bag, my entire life had been spent playing and making music. My business skills were nonexistent; I had never

A meeting at the LaFace office in Atlanta

given a thought to the *business* side of the record business. All I knew how to do was make records. I had never worked at an office—what the fuck do they do there? One day, I dictated a letter to Sharliss and she stopped in the middle. "If you want a copy for your files," she said, "you're going to have to get a Xerox machine." Step by step, we figured this stuff out and started to build an administrative staff.

I never stopped to consider what I knew or didn't know about what I was trying to do. I assumed we would figure everything out as we went along, as I always had. I had the confidence of ignorance, and what I didn't know wasn't going to stop me. I was running on instinct and had started a record company simply because I thought that it was the next step up the ladder.

The first act we signed was Damian Dame, a male-female duo that we moved from California to Atlanta and recorded in LaCoco. It was a good album with tracks I really liked; "Right

Down to It" and a heavy rhythmic number called "Gotta Learn My Rhythm." We took a small team to New York to present the album to Clive's entire group. Our presentation to the Arista staff was a moment of immense pride for us. We did the entire album—the photos, the cover design, the video, everything. We had their photos blown up on poster boards. We took great pains to make sure this event went off completely professionally. This was LaFace's first release—a celebrated moment at Arista. We played the album and the video and we left. We turned it over to Arista to do the promotion, marketing, and sales. "Exclusivity" was a big R&B chart-topper when it was released in July 1991.

Around that time, Clive asked me and Kenny to produce Whitney Houston. She was making her third album. She was undoubtedly the most popular female vocalist of the day and the biggest-selling act on the label. She had a string of number one hits, but Clive felt she needed to strengthen her grounding in contemporary black music and ease up on the pop songs. So he called LA Reid and Babyface.

Whitney flew to Atlanta and the limo service failed to pick her up. I made the forty-five-minute drive in a mad rush from Alpharetta to the airport, and I am not that good a driver under the best of circumstances. I had never met Whitney before, so I didn't know what to expect. I was looking around the terminal for maybe a mini-entourage, maybe an assistant, when I saw a lady sitting on a bench alone in sunglasses and a scarf.

"LA?" she said

I made my apologies and whisked her off in my car, only now I was even more nervous. There was nothing in my playbook about driving around with the stars, and I was driving around in my car with Whitney Houston. I small-talked and played the radio. We hit it off instantly. We sang along to the songs on the radio together. That forty-five-minute ride felt like about five minutes.

When I got back to my house, the first thing I did was introduce her to my wife. She and Pebbles started gabbing about shoes and shopping, making that girl pop star connection immediately. We had written "I'm Your Baby Tonight" for her, and Clive found this song, "My Name Is Not Susan," that he wanted us to produce with her. She knew the songs from the demos and had done her homework. We walked over to LaCoco, and before she stepped into the vocal booth, she stopped.

"Baby, we want to go shopping," she said. "How long do you think before the mall closes?"

Now, "I'm Your Baby Tonight" has a lot of parts and is a bitch to sing. There was no chance she could finish her singing in the forty-five minutes before the stores closed. "I know the song," she said. "I don't know the bridge yet—you guys have to write the bridge—but I know the background parts and I know the lead parts. Let's do that."

She went into the studio, cut the lead vocal for the chorus and stacked her vocals, doubling and tripling her original vocal perfectly. Then she laid down the first track of background vocals, the second track of backgrounds, the harmony parts. We stacked them up and flew them through the track. That took her about twenty minutes. I was blown away. That voice coming through my speakers on one of Kenny's and my songs—we'd produced a lot of records by then, but I had never heard anybody sound that good, ever. Not even close.

"Baby, I really want to go to the mall," she said. "Let's get to the lead vocal."

She got behind the mic and belted that song, nailed it on the first take, right up to the bridge, which we still needed to write. "Okay, baby, give me another try," she said.

She did it again and nailed it a second time. "Okay, what else you need?" she said.

"I guess we need to write the bridge," I said, and off she and Pebbles went to the mall.

While they were at the mall, I went down the block to Kenny's house and we wrote the bridge. When the girls returned from shopping, Whitney went back into the studio and polished off the bridge. Whole song, top to bottom, vocal time spent: one hour.

We finished that song and "My Name Is Not Susan." Whitney went back to New York. We wrote a song for her called "Miracle," and Clive wanted us to do another one he found called "Lover for Life." Whitney came back to Atlanta one week later and she knocked out these two songs like they were nothing—*pow, pow*—only now we were used to it. Talk about a superpower. The girl would work to the point of exhaustion.

She came back a third time to do some fixes. Aaron had been born and Pebbles was out touring behind her new album. Whitney called from her hotel to tell me her room had been broken into and she felt uncomfortable at the hotel. Could she use the guesthouse? She showed up with her manager and running partner Robyn Crawford. It was late. I put on a movie in the theater to watch and the phone rang. It was Pebbles, who quickly became upset when she learned Whitney was there.

"Whitney's in my house?" she said. "We're not having that. My husband is not going to sit in my house late at night watching a movie with another girl."

I tried to explain, but she threw a tantrum and I started to get angry. I told her she had nothing to worry about, this was completely safe, platonic, and just us musicians. I got loud and Whitney overheard.

"She's trippin', huh?" she said.

Whitney offered to leave, but I told her my responsibility was to take care of her and everything would be fine. "I don't want to be in the middle of y'all's mess," she said.

Pebbles kept calling back and finally I took the phone off the hook. I was embarrassed. I pride myself on being a professional. I was starting a business, and was now working with— and entertaining—major celebrity superstars. I didn't need this bullshit. Whitney went to the guesthouse to sleep.

The next day, Pebbles came home and had attitude with me. She tried having attitude with Whitney, too, but Whitney put out that fire in, like, two seconds. I don't know what she said, but everything quickly was cool. Whitney invited us all—me, Pebbles, Babyface and his new girlfriend, Tracey (he and his wife had divorced)—to her place, so we all piled on a Delta jet and spent the weekend in New Jersey.

After I submitted the mixes, Clive sent me a five-page letter detailing what he thought was wrong. Clive is Clive and he knows what he is talking about, so you have to take it seriously, but the difficulty was understanding what he was talking about—*the range and ambience surrounding her voice*, stuff like that. I tried everything, but it still wasn't right. I told Whitney to come back to Atlanta and sing it again and, this time, I made the vocal a little louder. Clive loved it. I was going through all this and he wanted the vocal more prominent. I ended up using her original vocal, only louder. Clive taught me that with a pop singer like Whitney—as opposed to the R&B ones I had been working with—you have to put the vocal way out in front. That's her money, her sweet spot.

Whitney spent the next three days staying in the guesthouse, hanging out with my wife. I was glad to have her, but all the work was done; why was she still there? The third day, the phone rang and it was Bobby Brown.

"Whitney there?" he asked. "Let me speak to her."

She trotted to the phone. "Hi, baby," she said.

I had no idea that these two had a relationship. I don't know what he said, but when she hung up the phone, she was giddy as a kid—happy, sparkling, excited. She was no longer just a shining superstar. Bobby made her a person.

"Bobby's on his way," she said. He showed up a half hour later in his blue Mercedes station wagon and whisked her off. The girl had been hanging around at my house for three days waiting on Bobby to call.

She had fallen in love with Bobby Brown under my roof. As I watched them ride off into the sunset, the realization sunk in. I became fascinated by this. It seemed so unlikely, but, at the same time, so right. Bobby was a street-smart bad boy and Whitney was an R&B angel. You never would have thought it, but when you saw them together, they fit like puzzle parts. They were R&B royalty.

We went from producing the regal Whitney Houston to making the next record with one of the royal family of R&B, Michael Jackson's older brother Jermaine. While we were working on Whitney's record, Arista had suspended the funding for LaFace because we were technically in breach of contract by not working on LaFace. It didn't matter that Clive had been the one who asked us to work on something other than LaFace. Kenny and I had to go in pocket to cover our overhead while we worked on Whitney's record, which left a bad taste. So when Clive asked us next to work with Jermaine Jackson, another act on Arista, we told him we would be happy to work with Jermaine, but he would have to become a LaFace artist. Clive arranged to transfer his contract.

Jermaine rented a house in Buckhead and moved to Atlanta with his family. He would come over to the house and work out with me. He wanted me to jog, eat better, to live better. I loved the guy. We started working on his album, talking with him, trying to get ideas of what he liked, writing for him. Then his brother Michael called.

Out of the blue, we received a call from Michael Jackson's manager, who told us Michael wanted to arrange a meeting to talk about working together. This was Michael Jackson in his moment. His latest album was *Bad*. This was great, except what

With Kenny and Jermaine Jackson, Atlanta, Georgia, 1990

were we going to tell Jermaine? We decided to avoid it altogether, simply telling him we had a session in Los Angeles and
quietly slipping away for a bit.

A helicopter picked us up at Burbank Airport and took us to
Neverland. It was a choppy ride, scary as hell. When the helicopter landed, someone drove up in a golf cart. The first thing

he did was hand us confidentiality agreements to sign. Nobody got to see Michael without signing one.

We were taken to his library. The shelves were full of books about fairy tales, but the place hardly looked like a child's house. It was done very tastefully, not like some first-year basketball player's house with the black leather couches. We sat nervously waiting when Michael entered through a secret door behind us. "How was your flight in?" he asked.

"It was a little choppy," I said.

"You were afraid," he said. "I can tell. It's in your eyes. You were afraid." He put his hands up to his mouth, gasped, pointed at me, and started laughing.

That broke the ice. We had never met him before. We didn't know if we were going to be meeting a weirdo or what, but right away, he was this fun-loving guy, joking around. We laughed from the first moment on. That was his way of relaxing us— pulling a joke on us—and it worked. We felt at home right away. Michael was very childlike, easy to be around. We started talking about music. He asked us what we liked. I don't even remember what we said, but I asked him what he liked.

"I love Janet's album," he said. "You know that song 'The Knowledge'?" He named four or five songs from Janet's album, which was produced by Jimmy Jam and Terry Lewis. I kept looking at Kenny, wondering why was Michael talking about Jimmy Jam and Terry's songs to us. Does he know who we are or does he think we're Jimmy Jam and Terry Lewis?

"Those songs are great," I said, "but we didn't do them."

"I know that," he said. "You asked me what I liked. You know what I love that you guys made? 'It's No Crime.' I love the drums on 'It's No Crime.' I love the whole *Tender Lover* album, Babyface. You're amazing."

He liked our drum sound on one specific song? How could I have been so wrong? He knew who we were. He knew *ex-*

actly who we were. Michael took us on a tour of every nook and cranny of his incredible Neverland. "You want to have some more laughs?" he said.

He took us to a screening room and ran a short clip of a James Brown concert at the Wiltern Theater in 1983, when Michael was called out of the audience and danced a few steps, mesmerizing the audience in an instant. In the clip, Jackson then whispers in Brown's ear that Prince is also in the audience, and Brown calls him up, too, only Prince can't make his guitar work, frantically stripping off his shirt and trying tricks with the microphone stand and making all these poses. After Michael's dazzling star turn, Prince fell as flat as he could, and Michael enjoyed laughing at the video. After that, he put on a scene from Prince's movie *Under the Cherry Moon*, the artsy, black-and-white bomb he made after *Purple Rain*, and he laughed some more at Prince.

He drove us in his golf cart to lunch, where his twin chefs served bowls of pasta for lunch, only Michael's pasta was all cut in the shapes of Disney characters.

Michael didn't want to buy a song. He wanted to pay for our time and have us work with him for three weeks. It was an unusual deal, but it appealed to us.

We went back to Atlanta to continue working with Jermaine and we didn't say anything. Now we needed to figure out a way to get out of town for a few weeks to work with Michael after Jermaine had moved his family to Atlanta to work with us. Tucked back deep in my mind, I sensed that this could be a headache, so we decided to keep quiet. We worked with Jermaine for a couple more weeks and gave him the news that we needed to go to Los Angeles for three weeks to finish a few projects we were working on. He was cool.

Intimidated beyond belief, we sat in a couple of Los Angeles studios, trying to come up with something for Michael. But sitting there working for Michael, it was impossible to escape the idea that this was the guy who did *Thriller*, the biggest-selling album ever. How do you top that? How do you hope to match that kind of magnificence? It towered over us. How do you write a song he will like? At the time, Kenny and I were on a roll, but we couldn't figure this out. Michael would come by and listen. He would like a little bit of this, a little bit of that, but nothing was blowing him away. We kept working.

He would visit. "Just keep playing me everything," he said. "Play me music."

He wanted our sound. We owned the charts. Our sound was the hip, cool, hot thing, and Michael wanted to use us the way he did songwriter Rod Temperton of Heatwave after he'd heard Heatwave's "The Groove Line." That was how Michael had made his classic breakthrough solo album, *Off the Wall*. We were so fascinated by him, so intimidated by his talent and stature—Michael Jackson at the absolute height of his Michael Jackson–ness—that we couldn't get it right. We spent three weeks working night and day, so we had plenty of time to get over any initial jitters. The significance of the assignment simply overwhelmed us. We managed to put together a song called "Slave to the Rhythm" that Michael liked enough to lay down a finished vocal, and he never sang a song he didn't believe in—he didn't even bother to try if he didn't.

I sat across the other side of the glass and watched in what was almost an out-of-body experience as Michael sang our song, top to bottom, twenty-four times in a row, and each take was better than the last. When he was done, I couldn't tell track eight from track twenty-four—that's how perfect his performance was. God was in the room and He looked just like Michael Jackson.

During another one of these sessions with Michael, I was called to the phone. I went down the hall and took the call in an office. It was Jermaine. He went crazy on me.

"I heard that you guys were in LA working on Michael's album," he said. "I'm sick of this. I came all the way to Atlanta to sign with your company and have you guys do my album. I hired you, and then Michael shows up and steals you. I'm sick of this guy stealing my producers. What kind of guys are you that you would even do this? I want off the label."

I tried to reason with him a little, calm him down. Leaving the label seemed a little drastic. "No, I'm calling my lawyer," he said. "I want off the label." *Click.* Fuck.

Michael walked in. Kenny had been sitting there while I was on the phone. "What's the problem?" asked Michael.

I told Michael that it was his brother Jermaine, who was unhappy that we had left him in Atlanta to come out to California to work on Michael's album. "He'll get over it," said Michael.

"That's not really the problem," I said. "The problem is that he wants off the label now."

"Did he sign a contract?" said Michael.

"Yes," I said.

"Then he'll have to live with it because those are the rules," Michael said and walked out.

That Michael Jackson was one shrewd man. He was not wrong, but you didn't expect that from Peter Pan. You expect a little compassion or something. No. Cold as ice.

We finished only the one song, "Slave to the Rhythm," during those sessions where Michael laid down lead vocals, and it wasn't released for another twenty-five years. We had another track nearly done, but he never finished it.

We went back to Atlanta and needed to patch up things with Jermaine. We went over to his house and apologized, explaining that it was a lifetime opportunity for us, because, after all, this was Michael Jackson, at that moment the greatest artist alive. We couldn't turn that down. We told him we didn't realize there was any sibling rivalry, but that we now understood how he felt and we only wanted to go back to work with him.

Jermaine was okay with it. We went back to work and what was the first thing Jermaine tells us?

"I want to make a song about my brother," he said. "I want to talk about how he's treated me through the years, like how every time I find producers like you guys, he takes my producers. He doesn't care about his family or anybody but himself. "

He was the artist. We pulled out the lyric pad and drum machines and dialed up some beats. We ended up with a clever song, "Word to the Badd!!," but we kind of lost our nerve and redid the song to make it more about Jermaine and some girl, not his brother.

We got a call from Clive. He had heard the original version and wanted to put that out.

I wasn't proud of the record. I was ashamed. As producers and writers, we didn't write for people; we wrote from our emotions. With Jermaine, our job was to dig into the artist's mind and try to get his emotions on the record. We had done that, but, in this case, it was Michael Jackson we were talking about. I lost that fight. The big Los Angeles radio station Power 106 started playing the track and it caused a shit storm. Their New York City sister station Z100 jumped on it and, after that, stations across the country picked up on it. Jermaine was dissing Michael on a record—it was hot news for a second. The song was getting requested on radio. It was all over the papers.

I still kept my apartment in Los Angeles, which is where Michael reached me by phone. "You have to stop this," he said. "You're the head of the label. You have to kill this. This isn't good."

It wasn't my fight and I wasn't going to referee a fight between the Jackson brothers. I told him that it didn't matter if I agreed with him, the matter was between him and his brother and I couldn't help. Jermaine was insistent that his record be released. Apparently Michael and Jermaine held a meeting at their mother's home at Havenhurst. I wasn't there and I don't know what happened, but when they came out of the meeting Jermaine called me.

"We resolved it," he said. "The record stays out."

Then Michael called back. "Jermaine and I had our conversation," he said, "but I'm telling you, you really need to stop this. This is not good."

Two days later, the record disappeared off the air, as if it had never been there in the first place. I don't know what Michael did, I don't know if Michael did anything, but it went away in a flash.

7

END OF
THE ROAD

We had no way of knowing this back then, but LaFace arrived in Atlanta at the perfect time. New sounds were hitting the charts, as hip-hop and rap made inroads into the mainstream. The city was turning into a major metropolitan area quietly, without anyone much noticing outside the South. The new One Atlantic Center in Midtown had marked the beginning of high-rise construction that was suddenly booming. There was a fresh, vital energy that you could practically smell coming off the sidewalks. The city was brimming with possibilities. Atlanta was on the make, and the record industry wasn't looking there. The musicians in Atlanta were hungry and we were eager to serve them.

We needed to sign our own acts, and there was no telling where we were going to find them. We didn't really know where to look for talent or even how to look for talent, but if we were going to build our label from the ground up, we were going to have to figure those things out. We started looking everywhere and following up on every lead. The path to finding and putting together the biggest-selling girl group of all time started, of all places, in my living room.

One afternoon, my home audio specialist was lying on the floor, plugging in wires for the sound system he was installing for every room in the house, when he asked me if I knew Ali Hassan. The name meant nothing to me.

"He said he used to be a friend of yours," he said. "They called him Dee Dee."

Dee Dee? My best friend from junior high school, whom I'd worked on the riverboat with, was now Ali Hassan and was the sound technician's barber. We got back in touch immediately and Ali started coming over to my house every Sunday to give me a haircut. Pebbles, who didn't have a hairstylist in Atlanta, asked Ali one day if he knew any beauticians. He recommended a lady named Marie Davis and offered to have her come over to the house, but Pebbles said she would rather visit her shop.

While Pebbles was at the shop having Marie do her hair, she met Marie's darling little assistant named Tionne Watkins. She told Pebbles she belonged to a group called 2nd Nature, and Pebbles invited her to bring her group over to audition.

The three girls came over—Tionne, Lisa Lopes, and Crystal Jones. Babyface, Pebbles, and I were there, as was a guitarist and friend of ours named Reggie Griffin. We went into the gym and the girls auditioned one at a time. Tionne, also called T-Boz, sang the Teddy Riley song "Wanna Get with U." She impressed me with her tomboy look and deep masculine voice.

Then Lisa started rapping and making sound effects with her mouth. These two girls were about the same height, cute as hell. Pebbles, Babyface, and I exchanged looks. The third girl, Crystal, wasn't as good, but we loved them, and Pebbles had already named them TLC from their first names—Tionne, Lisa, and Crystal.

About the same time, I went to a dance rehearsal for a Damian Dame video at which one of the dancers in the background kept making eye contact with me. After the rehearsal, she came up to me.

"I'm Rozonda and I can sing," she said.

"What do you sing?" I asked.

"I sing like Anita Baker," she said, and right there she started singing "Sweet Love" like Anita Baker. She sounded pretty good, too.

"I've got some people I want you to meet," I told her. "Come with me to my house."

I called Pebbles and told her I had just met the third member and I was bringing her over. Lisa, who was also known as Left Eye, and T-Boz, were there. Crystal was already gone. We walked in and it was like they had known each other a hundred years. I threw her in the room and left. When I came back, they had asked her to join the group and had changed her name to Chilli so they could still be TLC.

Oooh . . . on the TLC tip

As naturally as it came to me at the time, this was practically my first experience with discovering talent and creating recording artists. The fact that I was new at this didn't occur to me, because I was only trying to find talent for the record label and was doing what I thought any A&R person would do.

TLC became Pebbles's project and she swooped down on them. She didn't have an official role at the record company, but she was the unofficial adviser on everything. She still had her own recording career, but she began to make plans to enter talent management on her own, separate from the LaFace operation. She signed TLC to her production company, Pebbitone, in February 1991. They were always spending time together at my home in the beauty salon downstairs, talking, writing, and being girls.

We took them to a concert by Bell Biv DeVoe, a group consisting of the three leading members of New Edition, where we ran into Dallas Austin. We loved Michael Bivins of Bell Biv DeVoe. They had a new style, almost hip-hop-meets-R&B. TLC was like the female version. I told Dallas I wanted him to produce the group's album and he was all over that. What I didn't see was that it was love at first sight for Dallas and Chilli that night.

Dallas started recording TLC while Kenny and I were in Los Angeles with Michael Jackson. When we came back three weeks later, Dallas came over to play me the TLC tapes. I don't know what I expected, but it was like striking gold when you're barely beginning to dig. He had "Ain't 2 Proud 2 Beg," which would be their smash debut release, "What about Your Friends," and another called "His Story." All really good. Hit records.

Halfway through the sessions for the first TLC album, Pebbles told me she was thinking of taking the girls to Giant Records, instead of signing them to LaFace. I would be damned if I was going to let TLC leave my house with my producer and my wife to sign with Giant Records. I told her that if TLC left, she could leave, too. I drew a line in the sand. It wasn't that big a fight. She may have been only messing with my head—she liked to do that—but she signed the group to her company and we made a deal with her. The girls never actually signed to LaFace;

our deal was with Pebbitone. Eventually, Kenny and I came in and did two songs for the album, "Baby-Baby-Baby" and "Shock Dat Monkey," but Dallas was always the architect behind the TLC sound.

With those girls, there was always backstage drama. Pebbles and Chilli stopped getting along, and Pebbles, who ran the group, fired Chilli, although that is not how Pebbles remembers it. We went so far as to hold auditions for her replacement at the house, but Pebbles was out of town on tour. We looked at a cattle call of about fifty girls one afternoon and didn't find any-

TLC in concert

one who worked, but it was a nice party. Chilli was reinstated. All this happened before the first single was even released in November 1991. The group went out as an opening act on MC Hammer's Too Legit to Quit tour. "Ain't 2 Proud 2 Beg" was the first of three consecutive Top Ten hits off the album, followed quickly by "Baby-Baby-Baby" and "What about Your Friends," as TLC exploded on the scene.

TLC wasn't simple pop—it was edgy, dangerous, and daring music coming from unapologetically emancipated females. They were young, sexy women, but they turned the tables on male stereotypes. They took B-boy style and made it their own. Their influences were men more than women. The lyrics that Dallas wrote came from a female point of view, but they were about power and superiority; the girls were never victims. A lot of thought went into this by the people making those records, and the group struck a huge cultural chord. They were so pro-female they became heroes to their audience.

T LC was only the beginning. That same month I signed TLC, a man who worked for Clive called about a group the label had signed called the Braxtons that Clive was dropping. "I think you and Kenny should see them," he said.

They were five sisters—Traci, Tamar, Trina, Towanda, and Toni. They came to Atlanta and we auditioned them at one of the local nightclubs. When the girl on piano started to sing, Kenny and I looked at each other. We knew that was a special voice. She sang in a lower register, almost an alto, but I sensed something more in her. We told them we wanted to sign the group, but we really only wanted the piano player, Toni. As we worked out the contract later with their manager, I told him we really only wanted the one, and we wanted to offer her a deal with LaFace Records.

At dinner with Toni and my brother, Bryant, Miami Beach

Toni now had to decide whether to take the contract or stay with her sisters. For years, I didn't know this, but it turned out that her mother went crazy on her—*How dare you leave your sisters? They are your sisters. You've been singing together your whole lives. You go to Atlanta and these men want to separate you. And you want to do it? How dare you?* She made Toni feel terrible about it, but Toni signed as a solo performer with LaFace Records.

We made these two signings in February 1991, but the label still hadn't made a true hit. In the eighteen months since we had moved to Atlanta, we had made big records with Pebbles, Babyface, Johnny Gill, Bobby Brown, and Whitney Houston, but they were all for other labels. We were recording the first TLC album, and we thought Toni Braxton could be something. But it was up to me to get the label going. Kenny was mainly involved in composing and recording. I was in charge of running the day-to-day affairs of the company. The label was my dream, not necessarily Kenny's.

I needed a breakthrough strategy. It kind of started with a dinner I had with Toni Braxton and her manager at a restaurant called Pricci in Atlanta a couple of weeks after we signed her. The manager asked me what my plans were for Toni. I didn't have any plans, but I started talking, and pretty much on the spot, I devised a plan: We would go find a movie soundtrack that would feature Toni Braxton. That would be the launching pad for her career, and then we'd make her album. They loved the idea. I had no idea where I came up with it. We finished a lovely dinner, said goodnight, and I never thought about it again.

A few months later, I had still forgotten all about what I told Toni and her manager when I called Cassandra Mills, who worked with Irving Azoff, to ask how could I get a soundtrack deal. She told me Eddie Murphy was making a movie called *Boomerang* to be directed by the Hudlin brothers, Reginald and Warrington Hudlin, premier black film directors.

"You should call them," she said. "They'll take your call. They know who you are. Tell them that you want that soundtrack. It's perfect for you."

I reached out to them and they invited me to New York City. I flew up by myself and went to meet them at a screening of the Tupac Shakur film *Juice*. I met Diana Ross at the screening, as I hung around the lobby after the movie trying to meet up, but I didn't know what either of the Hudlin brothers looked like. I asked Andre Harrell, who had his own label, Uptown Records, and whom I had chatted with before the movie. "That's Warrington over there," he said, pointing.

We arranged a meeting for the next day. They told me that

With the First Lady of LaFace, Toni Braxton

the movie was about to start production, a romantic comedy starring Eddie Murphy, Halle Berry, and Martin Lawrence. They were receptive, but had reservations about LaFace and wanted me to arrange a meeting with Arista to make sure we had their support. It took a while to reach Clive—he was attending some convention—but he agreed. I set up the meet at the ultrahip Royalton Hotel, and when Clive assured the Hudlins that Arista Records would back the play, we landed the deal.

Kenny and I came up with a wish list for the soundtrack, and at the top of the list was Anita Baker. Not only was she the coolest new singer on the scene, but her demographic fit perfectly with that of the movie. We watched the dailies in New York and would take notes. In this one scene, Halle Berry turned to Eddie Murphy and said, "Love—what do you know about love? Love should have brought your ass home last night."

Kenny and I traded that knowing look.

We went back to Atlanta and started writing songs. We picked up another piece of dialogue—"There you go again"—and wrote "There U Go" for Johnny Gill. We wrote four songs that we thought would be perfect for Anita Baker, including "Love Shoulda Brought You Home." We asked Toni Braxton to sing the demos.

We wrote another song, "End of the Road," which Kenny sang on the demo, and sent them to the Hudlins and Anita Baker. I got a call back from her.

"These songs are really good, but they're not for me," she said.

My heart sank. "We wrote the songs specifically for you," I said. She didn't budge.

"I believe you," she said, "but it's just not for me. I don't want to offend you guys, but I'm going to have to say no."

Devastated, I called Reginald Hudlin and told him Anita turned us down. "Well, who's the girl singing on the demo?" he said. "Let's keep her. She sounds great."

We kept Toni on the record. Her vocals were perfect—nobody missed Anita Baker—but we gave one of the songs, "End of the Road," to a hot boy band out of Philly called Boyz II Men.

When I showed up at the writing session that produced "End of the Road," in a little hideaway house we kept in Buckhead near Kenny's apartment, Kenny and Daryl Simmons had already finished about 90 percent of the song, but there was this one little part that needed filling out, a space in the lyric that was missing. I walked in and filled the part. If I hadn't showed up when I did, they would have filled it without me. It was another song we wrote after watching the dailies, writing songs for specific scenes. Kenny, Daryl, Kayo, and I cut the demo at LaCoco and played the finished demo for the manager of Boys II Men, four teens who were riding high with a big hit record, "Motownphilly," by Dallas Austin.

Kenny, Daryl, and I flew to Philly and met the guys in the studio at about eleven in the morning on a Sunday. It was one of those memorable days that live in your mind forever. We started by recording their background vocals, all four of the guys at one time. We spread the background parts throughout the track, and it was time to cut lead vocals. First up was Nate Morris, always the guy who started their songs, and when he opened his mouth to sing the first verse, what came out was gold. The song had sounded good with Kenny singing on the demo, but Nate transformed the song in the first bars.

Shawn Stockman took his place behind the mic to sing the second verse. "Do you mind if I play with this a little bit rather than singing exactly the way Kenny sang it on the demo?" he asked.

I told him to go for it, and, as he slid into Kenny's melody, he massaged it, squeezed it, manicured it, and gave that verse a whole new sound. That hadn't happened much with us, somebody singing something that differently from the demo, but when Boyz II Men sang the song, they found their own beauty in it.

When we got to the bridge, Wanya Morris, their take-it-home singer, took everything to church. "*This time instead / Just come to my bed / And baby just don't let me go.*"

We staggered out of the studio in Philly around five in the

afternoon and flew back to Atlanta, where I stayed up all night with our engineer Barney Perkins at LaCoco mixing the song. My trainer showed up at eight o'clock Monday morning for my workout and I was still in the studio when he found me.

"Do me a favor," I said. "Can you clap on the beat?"

The two of us went into the booth and laid down about four tracks of handclaps. Barney and I mixed the ending so that we faded down the instrumental track and left Boyz II Men singing the chorus, Wanya wailing over the top, and the only thing you can hear is the handclaps by my trainer and me.

As much as I liked the song, I didn't truly know how good it was until Clive Davis came to Atlanta to listen to music and I played him four or five things, including "End of the Road." I saw him and his number two guy exchange a look when that song played. I hadn't seen that look before, but I knew immediately that it was the look of a hit. He had seen God in the room. You know when that's it.

"That song right there, 'End of the Road,'" Clive said, "that's a very special song."

We used all our relationships for the *Boomerang* soundtrack. We got Johnny Gill to do "There U Go." We gave a song to Keith Washington. Grace Jones was in the movie, so we asked Dallas Austin to write a song for her and he came up with "7 Day Weekend." We flew her in to record. She had demands up to here and we needed to put one of our girls on her case full-time to make sure she got everything she needed. We found this group called PM Dawn who gave us a great song, "I'd Die Without You," and we got "Hot Sex" from hip-hop legends A Tribe Called Quest. We finished the album and the Hudlins cut the songs into the movie. The first single was "Give U My Heart" by Babyface and Toni Braxton, the closing-title love song that was supposed to have been a duet between 'Face and Anita Baker in June 1992.

If you hear any noize, it's just me and the Boyz II Men.

The record started to catch steam and turned into a hit. Next up, we put out "End of the Road," and it skyrocketed. The damn record held down the number one spot for thirteen weeks, breaking a record set thirty-six years earlier by Elvis Presley's "Hound Dog/Don't Be Cruel." "End of the Road" won two Grammys the next year. The third single, "Love Shoulda Brought You Home" was the best of the bunch, and it *instantly* established Toni Braxton. Her new album was anticipated and her career was launched, just as I told her it would be.

The *Boomerang* soundtrack sold more than three million copies. The first TLC album, *Oooooooohhh . . . On the TLC Tip*, did more than two and a half million albums. Now LaFace was established, too. With the successes of *Boomerang*, TLC, Toni, and Babyface, everything was coming together—Atlanta, LaFace, the music scene. We were in a town that couldn't feel the pulse of the music industry. It wasn't a media center like Hollywood or New York. We were successful, but we couldn't feel it. Not only did we establish LaFace, we put Atlanta on the music map.

8

ANOTHER SAD
LOVE SONG

With our massive twin successes of TLC and the *Boomerang* soundtrack, it's hard to say when I first noticed that Kenny and I had been drifting apart. It was an incredibly busy time, and the distance between us was small at first. What I do know is that it didn't happen all at once. It began gradually, but once it gathered momentum, it was impossible to stop.

Early on, it was little stuff. He started finding reasons why he didn't like Atlanta anymore. The houses were cheap. There was no culture. The city was too unsophisticated, its citizens didn't take well to fame. Those superficial complaints revealed other signs. He became less communicative—I could feel him inch away, resist, question in ways that he never had. It came out of nowhere and I didn't understand why it was happening, but I could feel it.

It didn't help that he was simply around less. After he married Tracey in September 1992, Kenny started spending more time in Los Angeles. His new wife didn't like Atlanta, so Kenny soon sold his house and moved back to LA, earthquakes or not, although he kept an apartment in Atlanta.

While geography kept us in different parts of the country, in truth, that was just an easy excuse. After our initial run of success, LaFace didn't have Kenny's full attention. He felt he had to keep his presence as a writer-producer with mainstream stars like Madonna and believed it helped all of us if he stayed hot. I didn't disagree, but that kept him from concentrating his energies on LaFace artists. As a result, a divide began to form.

The first real split in the road came with Usher, whom I had signed to LaFace as soon as I could after his sensational first audition in early 1993. I really wanted Kenny to work with him, but that was when I realized there was this undercurrent of tension between us. I asked Usher to come back and do a second audition when Kenny was there. He and Daryl Simmons were not overly impressed with Usher. They preferred Tevin Campbell,

Usher and I posing for a photo at the Ritz Carlton in Chicago

another teen soul singer Kenny had recently started working with in Los Angeles. Campbell was a fourteen-year-old vocalist whom Quincy Jones had taken under his wing, and who sang the vocal on the lead single from Jones's 1990 Grammy-winning album, *Back on the Block*. Benny Medina signed him to Warner Brothers and Babyface agreed to write and produce for him without me. Tevin Campbell was cute, but he was no Usher.

The growing gulf between Kenny and me was not the only problem at LaFace. TLC fired Pebbles. When TLC returned from the group's first tour as an opening act on the 1992 MC Hammer tour, their album had sold almost three million copies and they found they did not have as much money as they expected. History has taught me that nobody makes money touring as an opening act. When they first came home, the girls came to the office and Pebbles had presented each of them with a new car. They all wore long faces and didn't have their typical bubbly attitudes. I didn't understand it at the time, but it wasn't long before it all came out in the open.

They focused their resentment on Pebbles. It was girl drama—three girls in a group and a girl manager. Pebbles could be heavy-handed with the girls, very protective, making them go to bed on time on work nights, that kind of thing. These were unruly teenagers with very little life experience, so Pebbles took the lead. TLC was very much her vision, and she was hands-on with the music, their looks, the videos—everything. She played a large role in their success.

In the end, they were unhappy about the amount of money they'd made, and they fired her not long after returning from the MC Hammer tour. I never fell out with TLC. I had many uncomfortable days, but I always stayed close with Left Eye and T-Boz, and I loaned my Miami apartment to her during all this disruption. Although she had kept her condition a deep secret, T-Boz suffered from sickle cell anemia and had been in and out of hospitals since she was seven years old. The secret came out when she collapsed during the first tour and had to be hospitalized. Lisa and Chilli stayed with her and they canceled a few shows, but she soon bounced back. She was my favorite, my eyes and ears on the street, my little muse. Living next to the ocean at my place in Miami was beneficial for her condition. Chilli and I were never close, although we were accused of having an affair many times. It was up to me to broker a deal, which put me in a difficult position with my wife.

Despite what the girls thought, Pebbles hadn't seen a dime. Arista Records hadn't paid us yet. They had been covering the label's overhead and recording costs, but there was a nine-month waiting cycle for royalties. Also, the girls didn't write the songs, so there was no publishing money. Before Pebbles had a chance to properly compensate the girls, they fell out. Pebbles is a lot of things, but she is no thief.

The TLC debacle haunted us—Pebbles, Babyface, and me— for years. They didn't get ripped off. They started screaming bloody murder prematurely. They would have been smarter to ask for an advance instead of going ballistic. It wasn't payday.

I was caught in the middle between my wife and my record company. I felt I needed to protect TLC, our first big act, and to protect the label. Many times I took their side over my wife's, but I also think that her relationship with the girls was a tough one to manage. I had to navigate those shark-infested waters. I don't think Pebbles felt supported by me at all. I consciously avoided arguing about it with either party, because I didn't think I could win that. Hell hath no fury . . .

I took dirt for it, too. The girls went public with their case. People thought I hadn't paid them. But, truth be told, we didn't pay any of our artists at that point, because we didn't have the money. We were selling tons of records for Arista, but we were not seeing the money. I always had other ways of making money from songwriting and production royalties, but I was naive about the business end of the industry and didn't really understand the control Arista exercised over our finances. Our setup was still not sophisticated. We didn't even bring in our own finance people at the label for another year. It was the last thing we learned, because we never did it for money. We did it because we loved music and we wanted to do something special in music. I knew how to make hit records; now I needed to learn how to run a business. About that time, I signed up for a crash course at the Harvard Business School in their Advanced Management Program.

Success was proving hard to handle. The more success we had, the more complicated our relationships became. Money changed everything. When we were starting out, everything seemed simple, but as the stakes rose, distrust and envy entered the picture. We were no longer the same crazy gang that had moved together to Atlanta. The happy family had turned into several battling camps.

And yet we were still making hits. Nothing slowed down. The first Toni Braxton album hit the streets in June 1993 and blew up immediately. After two hits off the *Boomerang* soundtrack, the world was primed for her debut album. Kenny wrote "Another Sad Love Song" initially for TLC and was going to give it to Chilli, but Dallas Austin took the group in a different direction, so Toni cut that one. Kenny wrote another unbelievable song called "Breathe Again," and Kenny and I did a song with Daryl called "You Mean the World to Me." My brother, Bryant, found writers and producers like Teddy Bishop and Tim Thomas, who did "Love Affair," or Vincent Herbert, who gave us "How Many Ways." Kenny and I wrote "Seven Whole Days," which remains one of my favorite records I ever made and which also, sadly, turned out to be one of the last songs we wrote together. *Toni Braxton* was a number one hit album that went on to sell more than eight million copies. We called her the First Lady of LaFace.

Toni and I connected musically. I love her voice. Of all the singers I have recorded, Toni remains my favorite. Though Toni and I had a special connection, it was always purely platonic.

We would play-flirt, but she was seeing my brother, so she was hands-off. I pushed her and was able to pull out something special. We found her superpower.

We promoted her everywhere. Toni had a signature hairstyle, adopted from a cut originally worn by Halle Berry. We did beauty salon promotions. We went to the Bronner Bros. Hair Show, the big convention for black hairstylists. Hairstyles are a big deal in music. The target audience for an artist like Toni was the women who go to the beauty salon. That album won Toni an amazing three Grammy Awards over the next two years, Best New Artist in 1994 and two consecutive Best Female R&B Vocal Performance awards in 1994 and 1995. We were ecstatic. Toni was truly the First Lady of LaFace, and LaFace was now a Grammy-certified record company.

The same month in 1993 that I found Usher, Pebbles introduced me to a producer named Sleepy Brown at her office. He was part of a production team called Organized Noize. They brought an act over to my office called PA, which stood for Parental Advisory, but Pebbles wanted to sign them to the label she had started, so I passed. Next they brought me another act. These two seventeen-year-old kids—one named Antwan, one André—who called themselves Outkast. They stood to the side of my desk and started rapping. They were so nervous, they wouldn't look at me. I didn't really know anything about rap. I went by my gut instinct.

"I think you guys are really good," I said, "but you're not ready yet."

They came back a couple of weeks later, stood in the same spot, and went at it again. This time was better.

"I think you still need some work," I told them, echoing what had gone wrong with Pure Essence all those years earlier.

"You've got to work on things like sex appeal. It's not the singing business or the rapping business, it's the entertainment business, and you have to entertain."

A little later, the leader of Organized Noize, Rico Wade, called.

Rico and his two partners, Ray Murray and Sleepy Brown, were young Atlanta producers who had studied the New York hip-hop scene. They were the songwriter-producers of a local collective called the Dungeon Family, named after the basement studio in Rico's house where they recorded. They had started Organized Noize in 1992.

"The guys don't want to come to your office and audition again," he said. "They want you to come to a studio. They're going to do their audition for you onstage and we're going to invite more people this time. We want to fill up the room because we want to show you that we heard what you said. You said it's not the singing business, it's not the rapping business—it's the entertainment business. We want to entertain."

Something about their obvious dedication the first time they showed up in my office had made me have those guys back for a second audition—little more than a hunch—but they had seriously improved, and that was impressive in itself. When they called back with this invitation, it was clear they had paid attention to what I'd told them and had absorbed the information. These were artists who could grow, that much I knew. I was curious to see how that would play out. They definitely had my attention now.

I went to the third audition at a rehearsal hall called Crossover Studios in Atlanta. When they came out onstage, it was night and day from what I'd seen before. Not only were they great, they had presence—they knew how to entertain. During the set break in the bathroom, I overheard someone say that Polygram Records was in the house. I was not going to have

Polygram Records sign an act under my nose. I went to Rico that night and told him that I was ready to sign the group. Like finding TLC and Toni Braxton in the same month, I landed Outkast and Usher only days apart.

Without Kenny's support, I needed to develop a different approach for Usher. I decided to pursue the same strategy that worked so well with Toni Braxton. Soundtrack albums had become big business, although it was not yet common to introduce new artists on movie soundtracks. Toni Braxton was one of the first unknowns to ever break out of a soundtrack, and it couldn't have set up her solo debut better. Usher seemed like a perfect candidate for the same treatment.

I heard about a soundtrack for a movie called *Poetic Justice* starring Tupac Shakur and Janet Jackson, and I wanted Usher to be part of that movie. With those two stars, the movie was a ghetto story directed straight for the young black mainstream audience, Usher's natural constituency. I happened to know the director, John Singleton. I had been in a restaurant the night he and his family were celebrating his graduation from USC film school, and there was so much joy at their table, I paid for their dinner. It was just a spontaneous gesture of mine at the moment. We became friends. His first movie, *Boyz n the Hood*, was a big hit, and he had been nominated for an Academy Award, making him, at age twenty-four, the youngest director and also the first black person ever nominated for Best Director. *Poetic Justice* was his next project.

I arranged for a meeting with John in my villa at the Peninsula Hotel in Beverly Hills, where a winding staircase leads down from the upstairs bedroom. I hid Usher upstairs while John and I talked business downstairs in the suite. He wanted TLC for the soundtrack and I assured him that would not be a problem, but there was a young unknown I wanted on the soundtrack. I put on a track we cut with Usher called "Call Me a Mack," and

Usher slowly made his way down the stairs, lip-synching the song, performing his way down. When he finished, John looked at me. "You're a real showman," he said.

That number from the *Poetic Justice* soundtrack became the first Usher single in August 1993. I hired F. Gary Gray, who had done a video with insane special effects for "Natural Born Killaz" by Dr. Dre and Ice Cube and would go on to become a major Hollywood director (*Straight Outta Compton*), to direct the music video. Usher was on the map.

Still, I found myself in a strange predicament: Usher's single was mine and not Kenny's. I had done it all without him. The label, which, admittedly, was my dream, not his, may have been exploding, but it had become plainly obvious that Kenny and I were not in it together in the same way. We didn't have the same connection that we once did—in fact, we really didn't have much of a connection at all.

Kenny grew increasingly remote. Finally, on one of his rare trips to Atlanta, Kenny told me he wanted to meet for dinner. Over the meal, he said he didn't have as much money as he should and he wanted to conduct an audit. That didn't make any sense to me. We shared the same business manager. We didn't split everything fifty-fifty. We split fees evenly, but not songwriting royalties and his performing royalties. Still, he insisted. The audit came up with nothing, but it turned out that Tracey had gotten into his head. Something or someone had clearly driven a wedge between us.

The worst moment came when Kenny came to Atlanta to record Tevin Campbell on a song called "Can We Talk," a song I fucking loved, and the first song he wrote and produced without me. It would have been perfect for Usher, but Kenny brought Tevin Campbell to Atlanta and recorded the song at Doppler Studios in the room next door to where I was working with Usher. That was no accident.

Tevin Campbell was an incredible singer, but he was, like I said, no Usher. Tevin had a great voice, perfect for radio, a voice that went places where usually only females could go. But Usher had a more complete package; he could sing, he was a ladies' man, handsome, flirty, masculine, full of swagger. Usher was going to be a star.

Usher didn't understand why Kenny was working next door on this song with someone else. He was confused and hurt. I was crushed.

Shortly after that, Kenny called me and told me he didn't want to work together anymore and he wanted to make it official. We put out a press release in late 1993 saying that we would no longer be working together, although we would remain partners in LaFace Records. It wasn't clear how this would work, but the songwriting production team of Babyface and LA Reid had come to an end.

We never stopped talking. Kenny clearly had mixed feelings about the breakup too. He didn't want to do his next album without me, even though we weren't producing partners anymore. A couple of months after the press release, Kenny hired me as a producer of his third solo album, *For the Cool in You*. He gave me my producing fee and travel expenses, but capped the amount so I wouldn't overspend on hotels and luxuries. Now I was working for Kenny, not with him. It was a very good album, perhaps not as poignant as *Tender Lover*. I wrote a little bit. I produced a lot of the vocals for him and did my customary thing, but it didn't feel the same anymore.

I loved Kenny. We had made so much great music together over the previous decade—the Deele, Babyface, LaFace Records, and all the success with *Boomerang* and Toni Braxton—and now he looked at me like I had done something to him. It broke me. It wasn't only that I was losing a close friend. Kenny and I had battled our way to the top side-by-side. We were different parts of something that was a whole. He spurred me to creative heights I would have never known without him, and I liked to think the same was true for him. Before Kenny, I had never really been in the record business, and I didn't know what it would be like without him.

After Kenny and I stopped working together, I never again put pencil to paper to write another song. Kenny's departure made it clear that things had changed and my job was to concentrate on running the label. I had started writing songs only out of necessity to move my career forward. I'd accomplished that, and I was entering a different phase, a time when I needed to focus on taking the success we'd built to date and turning it into something lasting.

I'd been lucky to stumble across someone as monumentally talented as Kenny, but in many ways his departure gave me the freedom to go beyond where I'd come from. Since we started LaFace, I'd realized that one of my greatest contributions came from finding new talent—I had an instinct for it, a vision for artists that I'd come to believe in. But as long as Kenny and I were working together, I'd always have one foot in the past and be reluctant to stand on my own. When he left, I no longer had a choice. It took his departure to make me realize that LaFace's legacy would be much bigger than anything I had to offer as a songwriter.

9

PLAYER'S
BALL

Every little step in my career had been taken out of need; I'd never had a master plan. Whether it was producing records in the first place because Reggie Calloway wouldn't do the Deele's second album or writing songs for the group because we needed material, every new role I'd been in had come from a need.

After Kenny left, I felt embarrassed, hurt, and afraid. I was sailing in unchartered waters. Virtually my entire career had been spent either in a band or in a partnership with Kenny. At the same time, my marriage with Pebbles was falling apart and nobody knew what I was going through. I didn't know if the artists would stick with me and I didn't know if the label would still be a magnet for talent. Kenny and Pebbles were the famous ones. I didn't know where I stood with Arista. It was a devastating time, but all this personal turmoil, fear, and insecurity ignited an inner fire of strength I didn't know I had.

Most immediately, I needed somebody to help me make the records. For years, I had been developing my relationships with writer-producers like Dallas Austin and Organized Noize because I'd known Kenny and I couldn't write and produce everything for LaFace. But suddenly, those relationships became more important than ever, because I knew I'd need even more outside producers to keep the label growing. It was time to find some new associates.

Next to the article about me and Babyface breaking up in one of the trades was a piece that said Andre Harrell of Uptown Records had fired Sean "Puffy" Combs. I needed a new A&R man, a person who knew music, someone who could bring a vision. Puffy was all that. My office manager, Sharliss, knew him, and in 1993 I asked her to arrange a meeting. I went to New York and he picked me up at the Four Seasons Hotel on Fifty-Seventh Street in a convertible BMW 325i with his pregnant girlfriend in the front passenger seat and his seven-year-old godson in the back. He took me to a Harlem hot spot and soul food restaurant called the Shark Bar and said good-bye to his girlfriend and the little boy. It was my intention to hire him for LaFace Records.

Since we didn't know each other, the meeting was awkward at first, but it quickly turned into this wonderful, eye-opening creative conversation that lasted four or five hours. I was knocked out by his commitment, determination, discipline, and imagination. He described his vision for a Mary J. Blige video featuring her on a mountaintop outlined by thunder and lightning bolts. He talked about the company he wanted to start called Bad Boy Records with the slogan "The Next Generation of Bad Mother-fuckers." He even had a poster for the label with a picture of his godson making a gun with his fingers. That is now the famed Bad Boy logo.

He explained the difference between my music and his. He even saw it in our styles. "For example, you like to do photo shoots inside," he said. "I like to do photo shoots outside. I noticed all your photo shoots are on the interior. That makes them more elegant. Mine are outside. It makes them more street."

By the time dinner was done, I had completely changed my mind. I didn't want him to work for me—I wanted to help make his dream come true. I told him I would take him to meet Clive Davis. I would see that he got his recording studio, a handsome advance, and everything he needed to achieve his vision. I had already set up Dallas Austin with a label deal for his Rowdy Records at Arista, where he would have big success with the R&B singer Monica, so I introduced Puffy to Clive, too. From that meeting, Bad Boy Records was born, launching Puffy the megastar and adding considerable institutional value to Arista Records. I wanted to see that next generation.

Puffy's superpower is to try hard; nobody tries harder than he does. We became friends. We were alone in my office's conference room one day and I played him the video of Usher's

"Call Me a Mack," but I didn't just want Puffy's opinion, I wanted his help.

"Will you take this kid and teach him your swagger?" I said. "Can you just give him some of your flavor?"

And so I sent Usher to New York for what I called the "Puffy Flavor Camp." I wanted Usher to be edgier than La-Face was. We had made a few records with him after "Call Me a Mack," but nothing I found compelling enough to release. Our music could be soft and pretty. I didn't want Usher to be pretty. I went to Puff because I loved the sound and the edge of New York. At that point, Puffy was making *Ready to Die*, the classic first album by the Notorious BIG. He was also recording his female vocalist Faith Evans. He and the team of writers and producers around him created a hip-hop-infused style of R&B made famous by Mary J. Blige and Jodeci. It was very different from the music we made, and I didn't want Usher to have our sound.

Usher was fifteen years old, but nothing about him ever seemed juvenile. I was turning him over to the wildest party guy in the country at an age when I still needed to get his mother's permission, but he went to New York for almost a year. I didn't know whether I was being irresponsible or having an epiphany. I would never be sure flavor camp worked until he came back.

Helpful as Puffy was with Usher, I still needed to get new producers and artists to LaFace. About the same time Kenny and I split, Pebbles introduced me to the first artist I wanted to produce on my own, Tony Rich. His demos sounded like Kenny. I was especially reminded of a song of Kenny's called "When Will I See You Again" that we produced. It was like a revolving door—Kenny walked out, Tony Rich walked in, and they just missed each other. For a minute, I thought I had found my Babyface replacement.

Tony Rich performing on The Tonight Show with Jay Leno

His real name was Antonio Jeffries and he had moved to Atlanta from Detroit with his wife and brother, Joe Rich, who was also a songwriter. Tony was a jokester, a little weird, kind of cosmic. He and his brother would come over to LaCoco and work on their demos. Before long, Tony was practically living there. I decided to sign him to LaFace and started producing for the first time in my career without Kenny.

Although I was still mystified about what had gone wrong between us, Kenny could be antagonistic. He hijacked a soundtrack project for a new Whitney Houston movie, *Waiting to Exhale*, that I thought I had a deal to do. One of my A&R people had come up with the idea of doing an all-female soundtrack. Whitney loved the idea. Director Forest Whitaker liked it, but Clive called and said the album had to be on Arista because Whitney was an Arista artist. He offered to work out something in the way of royalties, and I told him I don't do royalties. Kenny wrote and produced the entire album for Arista and then invited me to the studio to listen. That was not easy. I made a halfhearted attempt, but truthfully I was devastated. At least, this made me realize it was over between us professionally for real.

He emphasized this several months later during one of his sporadic visits to Atlanta. Although we were no longer working together as producers and songwriters, we were still partners in LaFace, he continued to work with Toni Braxton and others, and it still wasn't clear what role Kenny wanted to play in the company. He'd recently signed a male vocal group his mother-in-law had discovered called Az Yet to LaFace. What he wanted to tell me in Atlanta that day was that he and Tracey had started a label of their own called Yab Yum Records. He played me some things he had done with a guy named Jon B. and left me with the impression that he felt his new label was going to be superior in every way to LaFace. I did not tell him about Tony Rich. Babyface was gone, but I had already moved on.

New talent was just the start of what had to change at LaFace. I also came to see that, without Kenny, I needed to make different kinds of records. Producer Teddy Riley and others were cutting hits in the new jack swing style (Michael Jackson had switched from Quincy Jones as his producer to Riley on his 1991 album *Dangerous*), which featured computer-generated samples and electronic beats from the Roland 808 synthesizer. Our glossy pop-style R&B was beginning to look decidedly out of date (although there is always room for a great pop song on the charts), and Outkast was my first step toward fixing that.

In 1993, I had this idea to do something called "The La-Face Family Christmas." I did two songs with Toni Braxton, two songs with TLC, a song with Usher, a song from a new act called A Few Good Men—one of the few acts we had that didn't hit—and I asked my brother, Bryant, to round up a song with Outkast. It was T-Boz from TLC who first told me I needed to check it out. I always listened to her—she kept her ears to the ground. Bryant brought me a cassette of Outkast jamming, kind of a Christmas song, kind of an anti-Christmas song, but hot and cooking, produced by Organized Noize. They called it "Player's Ball."

Their producer Rico, Outkast's Big Boi (Antwan), and André gave me a copy of the final mix backstage at a gig at the Tabernacle, a nightclub in Atlanta. I immediately went out to where my limousine was parked and sat in the back, playing it over and over, really loud, going crazy. I knew nothing about rap, but I trusted my ears and my instincts with Outkast. A hardcore rap act like Public Enemy may have been an important cultural act, but I wouldn't have been able to tell which of their songs would be a hit. Theirs was a different brand of hip-hop than I understood, full of synthesizers, samples, sound effects. Outkast didn't use samples and played real instruments, Fender Rhodes keyboards, guitars and bass, and it sounded very familiar to me, like the soul music of Isaac Hayes or Curtis Mayfield. Some of the words I'm still catching up on, but I reacted to the musicality immediately.

When I finally drove off that night, the gig was over and the guys were hanging out on the sidewalk outside the club. As my car rolled by, I held up the cassette through the sunroof in the limo, yelled, and pumped my fist. I knew what we had.

But while I was convinced it was a hit record, I also recognized my own inexperience when it came to hip-hop. I hired an independent record promoter with experience in the field to work the record. When Christmas came and went and the record still wasn't a hit, I didn't give up. I sent the boys back in the studio. They changed the line "*'cause the Player's Ball is happening on Christmas day*" to "*'cause the Player's Ball is happening all day, err'day.*" Not "every day"—*err'day.* Outkast's thick regional dialect was an important part of their cultural identity to the point that even I had to get the guys to teach me how to say it.

"How do you say this now? Ery'day?"

"No. Err'day."

We continued to promote the song, and watched as it caught fire in January 1994 and burned up the charts. Our first rap record made number one on the Billboard Rap Chart. The debut album by Outkast, *Southernplayalisticadillacmuzik* went platinum.

With the success of Outkast, a real identity began to form around the new kind of Southern music that we were making. LaFace had never been a hip-hop label, more a modern-day Motown. Our artists were young and hip, even cutting-edge, but Kenny and I always made pretty, polished music. This was different. This was getting cultural. We had put Atlanta on the national music map. The Dirty South, as Khujo of the Goodie Mob called it, was rising. Our first contribution to hip-hop culture was a smash. The entire Atlanta music scene—much of it nurtured and developed by LaFace—was beginning to flex its muscles. At the same time, hip-hop was quickly becoming the most important new development in the music scene since the Beatles and the British Invasion.

The world was turning—for me, for LaFace, for Atlanta, for hip-hop, for the culture. LaFace had arrived with TLC and Toni

Braxton, but for me privately, the success of Outkast was more important. More than anything else, Outkast showed what I could do without Kenny, that I could push into new realms, that my instincts would serve me well, regardless of the sound I was looking for. Instead of supervising the recordings in the studio, I was now truly a record man, using my intuition and imagination freely, no longer tied exclusively to the kinds of music Kenny and I could make ourselves. Having a big hit rap record without Kenny did wonders for my confidence, just when my confidence was at an all-time low.

Still, I was insecure about how I might be viewed by my corporate partners. I flew to New York to meet with Clive Davis and his top guys to make sure our deal with Arista was secure. On the plane, I pored over a new business plan I had worked up that called for Kenny to still write and produce some records and for me to become more of an executive producer. I knew it was incumbent on me to act like a thorough, efficient, responsible record executive. Clive never gave the business plan a second glance. When he told me he never had a concern, he meant he never had a concern. I would say he was supportive, except that might imply that he had some concerns.

Kenny stayed in touch. He would call me from his car, but never from home. I figured out that he was probably not allowed to call me from home. I became the side bitch that you call from the car. As challenging as making the business end of the label work, the personal side was always the trickiest, the most difficult to handle.

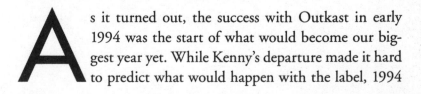s it turned out, the success with Outkast in early 1994 was the start of what would become our biggest year yet. While Kenny's departure made it hard to predict what would happen with the label, 1994

was the year that we came into our own. In rapid order, we launched Outkast, turned Usher into a million-seller, and detonated the explosive return of TLC, all in the course of the year.

Of course, that success came with its own mix of drama. In June of that year, I was supposed to start my program at Harvard Business School to enhance my understanding of the business world and the realities of finance, but I delayed it for a few days to attend a conference in Austria with executives from the Bertelsmann Group, which owned Arista and by extension LaFace. One morning, as I was packing to leave for the meeting, I got a frantic call from our nanny who was taking Aaron to kindergarten.

"Mr. Reid, Lisa's house on fire," she said.

Left Eye lived around the corner and down the street from me in Country Club of the South with her boyfriend, the football player Andre Rison, an All-Pro receiver for the Atlanta Falcons. They had a rocky relationship and the police had been called to their home before on domestic violence beefs. I looked out the window and I could see helicopters circling and a thick plume of smoke where Lisa's house was. Television news was already showing the house burned to the ground. Holy shit.

The phone rang again and it was Lisa, calling from her cousin's house.

"Fucking Andre," she said.

Pissed off at her boyfriend because he had received a shipment of shoes from Nike and there were none for her, she'd thrown a teddy bear she'd given him into the bathtub, set it on fire, and watched in shock as the teddy bear—and the bathtub made of fiberglass—exploded in flames and the entire house went up. Both she and Andre escaped without injury.

It was the first public drama created by one of my artists that I had to handle, but I knew what to do. I called Eldrin Bell, a

Outkast and our LaFace Atliens

friend of mine and the chief of police. He had already heard about my little disaster. He told me to take her to the Swiss Hotel in Buckhead and that he would post a couple of officers to guard her floor for the time being. She went to a hearing on arson charges and the chief recommended rehab because he felt Lisa had a drinking problem. We sent her to the Betty Ford Clinic and she was never charged. She and Andre got back together after she came back from the clinic.

I still went to Austria for the conference and everybody wanted to know what happened. Clive started talking about how we would now have to make Chilli a solo artist. What he didn't understand was that while she may have been the prettiest, there was no way she was a solo artist. I assured everybody the group was going to stay together, and I returned to Atlanta determined for that to happen. Harvard was going to have to wait.

This drama aside, these were largely happy days for LaFace. Our company now boasted as many as sixty employees. We were no longer a family store, but a thriving, bustling operation, poised to get even bigger. Usher was waiting in the chutes with his debut album, and work on the second TLC album had been under way for some time. Despite their ongoing negotiations over royalties, their problems with Pebbles, and now Left Eye's problems with the law, TLC had been working every day with Dallas Austin, and what I heard coming out of the studio was knocking me out.

In the wake of Outkast's success, Shanti Das, who had been running the Outkast marketing campaign, thought up the idea

With my girls T-Boz and Left Eye at my home in Atlanta

of throwing the SouthernplayalistiCookout. She rented a ranch on the edge of southern Atlanta, put up a stage, and invited the cream of Atlanta hip-hop society to our party. About two thousand guests converged on the forty-acre site that Saturday afternoon in July 1994. We hung lanterns to drive off the mosquitos, and the red clay dust swirled in the air. The rain stopped and the weather cooperated with a cool, dry day against a backdrop of Georgia pine.

Southernplayalisticadillacmuzik set the theme of the cookout. The program for the concert—Outkast, Usher, Goodie Mob, Puff Daddy, Notorious BIG, Busta Rhymes—was an extraordinary historic passing of the torch, almost like a one-day hip-hop Woodstock. At the time, Outkast was the only nationally known performer at the festival. Opening the show was Busta Rhymes, fresh out of a group called Leaders of the New School. In a short time, he would be widely recognized as one of the greatest rappers ever, but that day he was only starting his solo career. Puffy had finished the Usher album and had been working on tracks with TLC, but he was not known outside the industry. He brought Biggie Smalls—the Notorious BIG, who had yet to release his first album. I was at the edge of the crowd and Left Eye was sitting on the porch of the ranch house (her first time out in public since the fire). She came up to me and asked me who Biggie Smalls was. Even the rapper for TLC didn't know who Biggie was, although his underground reputation was well enough established that an old guy like me did know him at that stage. But not Left Eye.

Usher was about to drop his first album, and he made a clear statement that he was a superstar in the making with his performance. The Goodie Mob introduced CeeLo to the world, years before Gnarls Barkley. Outkast brought the party home with raucous live versions of tracks from the *Southernplayalisticadillacmuzik* album like "Ain't No Thang" and "Crumblin' Erb."

This was my new family, my new artists, and my new friends—a team I took pride in that could be shared with the public. SouthernplayalistiCookout was a safe, happy place where you could take your kids, and I certainly took mine: five-year-old Aaron rode around all afternoon on my shoulders. All the media were in the house: *Jet*, *Ebony*, *Source*, and *Vibe* magazines, the Miami video channel the Box, MTV. People stopped me for interviews as I walked through the crowd. The media had never evidenced much fascination with us before. This was getting good.

Usher's album was released right after the cookout in August 1994. I first heard the finished record when Puffy brought it to me in the Presidential Suite of the Four Seasons Hotel in Beverly Hills, my work office when I was in Los Angeles. Over at a table, the members of Outkast were meeting with director F. Gary Gray about their next video. Puffy walked in without a shirt like

With Aaron, in our matching custom David Rickey suits, Atlanta, Georgia, 1994

the king of the world, popped a cassette into my stereo, pressed Play, and started dancing all over the room as soon as the music began.

What was great was I didn't hear a big hit—far more important, I heard a style. I first search for style, even before songs. If I can find a style, it becomes easier to find songs, and also better to listen to, to have that composition produced so that it fits the larger body of work. I didn't want a hit for Usher from Puffy, I wanted a style. Puffy had done exactly what I wanted him to do for Usher. He gave this little kid a hip-hop-infused R&B sound full of bad boy swagger. The record embodied all the hip-hop bravado, yet he remained an R&B singer. We played it over and over, completely disrupting Outkast's meeting with F. Gary Gray.

While Outkast and Usher set the stage for the new LaFace, the release of TLC's second album solidified our ascendance into a new era. Two months after the Usher album, in November 1994, we dropped the new TLC, *CrazySexyCool*, which would become their career album. Born of tough times, for sure, the music was probably the only thing that kept us all sane. Our work ethic kept us grounded, and we all needed the music.

I never felt that I was in a fight with TLC, and we always had fun. One night in New York during the album's production, over dinner with TLC, I phoned Barneys and arranged to have the store stay open an extra hour for the girls, and I sprung for a spree. I was able to muster up the money from Arista to pay them and to make a new contract.

Work on the album took almost a year. The first song Dallas Austin had played me early that year in the control room of his beautiful studio (called DARP Studios, short for Dallas Austin Recording Projects) was "Creep," and I loved it instantly and made Dallas give me a copy. I played it in my car on the way home, I played it once I got home, and I played it all weekend.

From the first time I met Puff, I knew his vision for Bad Boy would become a reality.

I wore out the cassette. Dallas did an amazing job, but I needed more. We launched plans to make the song the album's first single, even as the group continued to make the rest of the record. I went to the video shoot for "Creep"; Tupac Shakur was on the set hanging out with the girls, where I grabbed Jermaine Dupri, who was also there, sat him down in my Land Cruiser SUV, and played him some of the things Dallas had done with TLC.

"I don't feel like I have the big one yet," I said.

Jermaine agreed to work on the album and he quickly came up with "Kick Your Game." Then I played his songs and Dallas's songs for Rico Wade of Organized Noize and told him I was still looking for the big one. He went to work on coming up with something. My only vision on the TLC album was to create a powerful follow-up to the big hit debut by challenging each producer to top the other producer, to create a competitive environment—and I have to say that worked like a charm.

Kenny and I never discussed the album—we weren't speaking about much of anything—but he wrote three songs, flew the girls to Los Angeles, and produced the tracks at his studio. Then Rico Wade called me down to Bobby Brown's studio, Bosstown, slid into my car smelling like a pound of weed, pushed a cassette into my tape deck, and played me "Waterfalls." Oh my God, it was like music from a funk dream, like Sly and the Family Stone with wah-wah guitars and thumping bass, only sung by the girls. I was awestruck and all I could do was look at him and think, *You came up with this?*

When I went home, somebody was using my studio, so I went to the little demo room we built in the basement of the main house and sorted through all the pieces of the TLC album. It sounded like a masterpiece, except one thing was missing. The title of the album was *CrazySexyCool* and I didn't have a song called "CrazySexyCool." I called Puffy and asked him to write some interludes that would incorporate the title. He brought the girls to New York and cut four pieces that tied the record together brilliantly. I took the tapes to Herb Powers at the Hit Factory in New York for mastering, which is who

you want to see for killer bass, and sat there listening back to
the completed album. I knew it was done.

When it came time to release "Creep," the problem was that
the first video we shot wasn't good enough. I convinced the girls
that we needed to do another and went back to the same director
for a whole second video for the same song, but it wasn't much
better. Now I was more than a million dollars down and I still
didn't have a hit video for my hit song. I didn't feel comfortable
going to Clive and Arista and asking for money to shoot a third
video of the same song, so I announced I was switching singles;

*TLC in a lounge area fashioned to look like an airplane during the
1995 MTV Movie Awards*

that way, I would need a fresh video budget. Nobody liked the idea. The TLC girls complained, Dallas Austin called, nobody bought it. When Clive called, I came clean to him. He asked me to show him the videos. I flew to New York, checked into a room at the Helmsley Palace Hotel, and set up my stereo set gear with the little television monitor. I showed the video to Puffy.

"Yo. I didn't think TLC could catch a brick," he said, "but they just caught a brick."

Catching a brick means you failed.

At that moment, another music video flickered on the hotel TV screen, a song called "Whatta Man" with En Vogue and Salt-N-Pepa, the combined forces of TLC's two main competitors on the pop charts—and this video looked unbelievable. Puffy noticed it, too. I scratched down the director's name, Matthew Rolston, when the credits flashed. Clive looked at the TLC videos and reached the same conclusion.

"Listen, TLC's first album was a huge breakthrough, sold over three million copies," Clive said. "This follow-up is really important. The stakes are huge here. I'll support you."

I hired Matthew Rolston, and the day of the third video shoot, Left Eye had a meltdown on the set, locked herself in her trailer and wouldn't talk to anybody. The fire at her house and all the subsequent stress had taken a toll on her. She shut down the shoot and left everybody standing around doing nothing. Finally she let me in and I talked her off the ledge. When the girls emerged from makeup and wardrobe, they were wearing these beautiful satin pajamas, each in her own color. I'd never seen TLC look like this. TLC up until this point had always looked like tomboys. This was the first time the girls were going to look like young women—young, sexy women. They brought out the trumpeter to start the scene and, as I watched through the monitor, I could tell we were going to nail it. Now we were off to the races with *CrazySexyCool*.

For the photo shoot for *Vibe* magazine, the stylist brought in a rack of clothes and included a few firefighter's uniforms. They ended up on the magazine cover in full firemen's gear. "TLC Fires It Up," said the headline. "Burning up the charts, burning down the house." Not politically correct, but the stunt launched the album and it shot straight to number one.

10

WATERFALLS

Pebbles had been beyond involved in my success. She was responsible for much of it—along with her personal hits, Pebbles had been the eyes, the taste, and the tone of LaFace for years. Kenny and I had selected the artists and the music, but Pebbles had been behind the scenes, making changes, introducing me to new talent, being creative. Even the artists didn't always know how important she was. Toni Braxton thought she had nothing to do with her records, but Pebbles was there, helping edit the videos and offering suggestions about Toni's hairstyle and look.

As important as she was to the building of LaFace, by 1995, our marriage was in a slow, glacial decay. It melted away. There was no big moment, no climactic scene—it just happened.

This was brought on by a lot of things, but chief among them were the issues between her and TLC, which made our relationship unbearable and caused the desire, the passion, and the love to evaporate.

For a couple of years, I'd been caught in the middle of the fight between her and TLC. I loved my wife, but I also loved those girls, especially T-Boz. I have always been upset that Pebbles got such a bad rap as a result of the litigation with TLC, but at the time, I felt boxed in by my position. After the release of *CrazySexyCool*, TLC still had not come to terms with Pebbles, and their new managers were not acting friendly. Eventually, the strain became too much and my marriage started to suffer. Pebbles and I started to see each other differently. I think she saw me as a capitalist who was only interested in the success of my label, and I probably saw her as being too controlling, too willing to push those girls away.

One of the final straws was a trip we took to Miami. Our families were with us, our kids, my mother, her mother, but the whole time she and I were so distant from each other, so far apart, it crushed me. On one hand, she had been my best friend and the love of my life. On the other hand, the weight of what was going on around us pushed me to the idea of being free. For years before I'd met her I'd been struggling to become success-ful. Once I became successful, I got married and had a family all at the same time, so I had never enjoyed success as a single adult.

My marriage came to an end in the middle of the night in June 1995. I knew that things couldn't continue as they were, so I left my wife, my family, and my house at Country Club of the South. I said good-bye to Ashley and went into Aaron's room, where my six-year-old boy was asleep, and kissed him on the head. I grabbed a couple of suits out of the closet, threw them into my Bentley, and drove downtown to check into the Ritz-Carlton. I didn't take a book or a record, and I never went back.

Coupled with the split from Kenny, the breakup with Peb-bles took a heavy emotional toll on me, but it was such a crazy period for the label that it was hard for me to see it at the time. Business was great, never better. Starting in July 1995, "Water-falls" was number one on the charts for seven consecutive weeks, which kicked album sales into multiplatinum orbit. I'd wanted "Waterfalls" to be the second single from *CrazySexyCool* after "Creep," TLC's first number one, but Clive wanted the Babyface song, "Red Light Special." Although none of the TLC tracks were formula, "Waterfalls" was nonetheless a departure, so Clive went with the Babyface song. It went to number two on the charts. The album had already sold more than two million when we released "Waterfalls." Clive was not enthusiastic.

"I played it for my staff and they say it's a seven," he said.

We hired F. Gary Gray to direct a stupendous video for "Wa-terfalls" with a massive $750,000 budget. The groundbreaking video, in which a running waterfall morphed into the girls, ig-nited the massive hit, and "Waterfalls" took the album from two million to ten.

"You were right, I was wrong," Clive later told me. "This is your hit."

That felt good, because I'd gone through a lot at that point. It had been a hell of a year and I needed that huge win.

Yet even as they were having their biggest hit to date, the situation with TLC's finances was growing more desperate. In July 1995, the same month that "Waterfalls" was released, the group filed for bankruptcy in order to get out of their contracts with Pebbles and LaFace. TLC claimed they were in debt more than $3.5 million and that they were earning around $35,000 apiece per year after paying agents, managers, and lawyers, but it was really only a legal tactic to get the group out of contracts. Their new manager took them to talk with other labels such as Russell Simmons at Def Jam Recordings. It got so crazy that, at one point, the girls showed up unannounced at Clive Davis's office in New York, accompanied by their bodyguards. Clive was meeting with Puff Daddy. They ordered Puffy out of the room and demanded their money from Clive, who was threatened enough to call security. They were not above creating a scene.

In the end, TLC wouldn't settle their lawsuit and dissolve their management contract with Pebbles until November 1996. Eventually they came to understand that the problem wasn't with LaFace; Arista had sold millions of records and kept the money. But Pebbles was devastated. She lost her family and left show business forever. She filed for divorce the same month TLC filed for bankruptcy, a week before our sixth anniversary. The next month, she sued LaFace for $10 million. All through their legal battles, the TLC girls continued to work on records and we remained on good terms, but the damage to my family life was done.

When we finally got divorced, I had to write Pebbles a very large check, and I had no regrets about doing it, because her contribution was huge. She had helped me when I was nothing, when I didn't have a dime. At the start, Pebbles had been the key to our success in Atlanta. She was the attraction. I wasn't famous and Kenny wasn't there much. Pebbles was the reason that everybody wanted to come over and visit, my beautiful wife, the singer, the star. Pebbles kept the house. I didn't need the studio any longer. Besides, by that time, there were other studios in Atlanta. Dallas Austin had built his DARP Studios, where TLC spent most of their time. Daryl Simmons, our Silent Partner, had built a studio called Silent Sound. Outkast had a studio called Stankonia. At that point, we were recording everywhere anyway, Los Angeles, Atlanta, Miami, even New York. The label had become established, so I didn't bother with a second studio.

I maintained appearances, but in reality, I was at loose ends. I started dating a string of actresses and models, but nothing mattered much. I asked my assistant to call the Porsche dealership and deliver me a black Porsche convertible—a midlife crisis car. A couple of hours later, a beautiful black Porsche convertible pulled up downstairs. I went down to look at it and wrote the guy a check. I remember going over to my brother Bryant's house, where he was entertaining Toni Braxton, and they were having a cookout. I was all by myself. I didn't have a steady girlfriend, a wife, or a family. I didn't have Kenny. I was living in a hotel, driving around town in my Porsche with this girl, that girl. I was overcome with a feeling of loneliness. I felt like a misfit because I was used to having my wife, but now, I was completely alone, rootless. I decided to buy a house.

My business manager warned me against buying a house during a divorce, but I told him I didn't give a fuck. He told me, in that case, not to spend too much, $400,000 or $500,000, since I would be living by myself. I bought a beautiful place for $2 million. I brought in a designer and made myself a fine home in Dunwoody, suburban Atlanta. It wasn't the same, but it was the start of something new.

With so much of my previous life gone, I dove into the music—the only true constant that remained. I spent that Christmas in St. Barts listening to the demos for the second Toni Braxton album, *Secrets*. I had plenty of company and was feeling pretty good, exploring the island, eating out with my friends, and sitting around listening with them throwing their comments in. Sifting through the songs and getting ready to make what I knew would be a special album refocused my energies after a difficult year. Although Kenny and I no longer produced together, he did a ton of songs for the second Toni Braxton album. One track, "You're Makin' Me High," I got from a writer named Bryce Wilson. He played me the track in the studio, and I sent it to Babyface, who wrote the top melody line and produced the song, but it was Bryce Wilson's track.

Though Kenny and I had never stopped communicating, the way we worked together was different now. He had always left the operation of the label to me, but now he was completely out of touch with the company's business affairs. His only interest was writing songs for some of the acts, like Toni Braxton. The songs he made, he would send to me. I'd make my comments and he'd make his alterations. I got other songs from different producers like R. Kelly, who contributed a pair of songs. Tony Rich did a cut. After we had mixed the album and put the whole thing together, I took the tracks, sequenced the album, and picked the singles. We had stopped producing together, but Kenny and I found comfort in our new roles. I became an A&R man and record executive, a coach of sorts, and I was very happy with my new duties.

I heard a piano-and-vocal demo of "Unbreak My Heart" by Diane Warren, the songwriter who wrote all those hits for Elton John, Aerosmith, Celine Dion, Cher, and Tina Turner, among others. I brought in David Foster to produce the song with me in

Hollywood. I went to his house and he played the fully produced and orchestrated track for me. I only asked for a different snare drum sound. When I brought Toni into the studio to record her vocal, I saw his true genius. I watched as he sang a riff to Toni, one riff that took the song from here to there on the end of the bridge, and he laid it out perfectly for her. He was magnificent. The only thing I contributed was to have Toni change one of the background vocal parts.

With the blockbuster sales of her Grammy-winning debut album, the second Toni Braxton album burst out of the gate in June 1996 with two consecutive number one singles—"You're Making Me High" and "Unbreak My Heart"—and went on to sell more than eight million copies in this country alone, an explosive smash.

To this day, *Secrets* remains one of my favorite albums. It stays with me, one of the few of my records that I still play. One of Kenny's songs in particular hit home at the time, "There's No Me without You." He sent me the demo of the song before I went on a company retreat in the Bahamas, and when I returned to my apartment in Miami afterward, I listened to that song over and over, thinking about my ex-wife. It made me sad, but it made me feel good at the same time. It was my version of eating ice cream.

U nsettled as I was on my own, I tried to keep busy, focusing more time than ever on the running of the label. It had been ages since I'd thought about actually producing music myself, and I figured it would stay that way. I was also at the worst stage of my creative existence.

Around the same time, I received a call from Elton John, who had lived in Atlanta since 1990. We had never met, but I had always been a fan. He wanted me to produce a track with

Toni backstage at the forty-third annual Grammys

him for a Curtis Mayfield tribute album. Although I was extremely honored, I had doubts about whether I could pull it off. I did not have a new rhythm section or new keyboard players. *Captain Fantastic and the Brown Dirt Cowboy* is one of my all-time favorite albums. I had made a conscious decision to not produce anymore, but this was Elton John calling.

I took Tony Rich and Kayo into the Bosstown Studio in Atlanta and made a track that was at least good enough for Elton to put on a vocal. I met him for the first time when he came into the studio. He was the nicest guy in the world and excited about working with me. He knew my songs and, even somewhat more surprising, he knew what my contributions had been. He didn't think I was Babyface, which had been my main concern, because I wasn't going to be writing him any big, beautiful ballads. He wanted me because he knew I was good at producing vocals.

I first learned how to produce vocals from Reggie Calloway when he produced the Deele's first album. Every vocal that was laid down, I sat in the studio and I watched him do it and saw how he communicated with our band, and noticed all the things he was looking for—the intonation, the pocket, the climax. He showed me what to look for and how to ask for it from the talent, and I became skilled at it. I produced a lot of the vocals for Whitney Houston, Bobby Brown, Johnny Gill, Karyn White, Babyface. I produced most of Toni Braxton's vocals.

You're basically a coach. You're the guy who says okay, try it again, only this time I need you to enunciate more because the words are getting lost. Or your rhythm patterns are a little bit off. Or listen to the drums—dance with it. I remember asking Toni Braxton to sing like she had a mouthful of water.

Kenny was also an incredible vocal producer, as was Daryl Simmons. Between Kenny, Daryl, and myself, we could run multiple sessions at the same time, because we all knew how to produce vocals, how to create harmonies, stack vocals and create thirds and fifths to match the chords of a song. We could tell each other's work apart, but no one else could. Kenny is such a gifted vocalist himself, he tended to coach other vocalists into singing like he did, but since I couldn't sing at all, I was more free to bring out the singer's own style. Kenny would come in and laugh. "Man, it's funny," he'd say. "You can't sing, but I hear you all over this track. I hear you in all the vocals."

But when Elton John got behind the mic on the other side of the glass that day and started singing, I was so lost in the moment I didn't know if he sounded good or not. He was Elton John. He did a couple of takes. I suggested a couple of harmony things and it was all over really quickly, old pro that he was.

"How about some piano?" he asked.

As soon as he touched the keyboard, you knew it was Elton John—that's how recognizable his style is. He wailed on the first pass, asked for another track, and laid down a second, equally astonishing piano part. I took the tapes to Jimmy Jam and Terry Lewis's Flyte Tyme Studios in Minneapolis and let the Sounds of Blackness, Jimmy and Terry's soul choir, wail all over the track, their arranger Gary Hines doing his own thing on top of Elton's version of Curtis Mayfield's old song by the Impressions, "Amen."

I struck up a great relationship with Elton. As a gift, he sent me a gorgeous light box painting by the identical twin Boston artists Doug and Mike Starn. A couple of days later, another package arrived from Elton containing some beautiful photographs. I visited his apartment and have never seen such a magnificent private art collection. Every inch of his walls was covered with carefully hung, beautiful pieces of art. We started having monthly dinners either at his place or a restaurant in Atlanta I owned called the Fuse Box.

Even though producing for Elton was a onetime gig, I searched for ways to extend my business beyond LaFace. It occurred to me that I was finding more songwriting talent than my label could use, so I started a publishing company called Hitco and hired a woman named LaRonda Sutton to run the company.

One day, she brought a fellow over to my house when I was in my Minnesota Fats mode—shooting pool in the billiard room, sipping cognac, smoking a cigar, television on in the background, Miles Davis playing *Kind of Blue* on the stereo. His name was Shakir Stewart, an Oakland native who graduated from Morehouse College in Atlanta and had been promoting parties. She wanted to hire him to do A&R for the publishing company. We hung out a few times; he was easy to like, a cultural kind of guy, always had a one-liner. I told LaRonda to bring him aboard.

One of the first people to contact me about publishing was Matthew Knowles, who called about his daughter Beyoncé. I had first met the young lady when she was around eleven or twelve years old. Daryl Simmons had a production deal at Elektra Records for a minute and had signed a group of young girls called the Dolls. When Daryl introduced me to the girls (who would change their name several years later to Destiny's Child) and Matthew Knowles, who acted as their manager, I told them all I thought the girls were too young for a record contract. Fast forward several years, the girls were sixteen years old and Matthew called to ask for a meeting with him and his daughter. He remembered what I told them. "That said a lot about you," he said.

They came to my bungalow at the Beverly Hills Hotel and played me a couple of her songs. They floored me. I knew immediately I wanted to sign her. I quickly handed off to LaRonda and Shakir to close the deal and manage the relationship. Shakir jumped all over it. He developed a close rapport with Beyoncé and her father, started placing the songs and handled the account. The sign of a great executive is if you assign them a superstar project and you never get a bad phone call—then you know they're doing their job. My phone never rang once with Shakir on the case. He would become one of my closest associates.

Through opportunities like Hitco and my continuing work on the label, I kept myself busy, but I remained lost personally.

Moving on from Pebbles proved much harder than I'd ever anticipated, and a year after we'd split, I remained confused about who I was personally and professionally. I was living alone and working all the time. My life looked so different than it had just a couple of years earlier, and a big part of me was living in the past.

Still, I did my best to hide my struggles. In June 1996, I threw a giant three-day fortieth birthday party for myself. My whole life paraded before my eyes that weekend. I was surrounded by people I loved and admired. There was an immense satisfaction in looking over the scene and realizing how far I had come, even though there was no shortage of adversity to go along with the success. It was an opportunity to savor the love and accomplishments I did have. Too bad I couldn't enjoy it more.

The first day was family and friends. My kids came over. My mother and her sister Katrina, who was her partner in crime, were there every day.

The second day was the big blow-out, seven hundred people under a tent on my tennis court with Morris Day and the Time as the entertainment and Kid Capri as the DJ. It was a cataclysmic, over-the-top extravaganza. There was a cigar bar, a martini table, various food stations. The guests came from all over. I invited all my neighbors so there would be no complaints, and we had a great time.

In the middle of the party, I left and went to my bedroom, opened the closet door, sat down, and closed the door behind me. I'd thought this would be a joyous occasion—all my girlfriends at the time were there, and they were all happy to be with me. In many ways it felt good to be celebrating the success I'd earned. I felt like the king of Atlanta for a night, and I was sharing that moment at a big party. Sitting on the floor of the closet, though, I couldn't ignore the truth: I missed my wife, and even though I was happy to be away from her, I was still lonely. I had all these girls, but inside I felt empty. Everybody had a great time, got buzzed out of their heads, but me. I was simply going through the motions.

The third day was a pool party with everybody around the pool, and the music of choice was Tony Rich. All the girls at the party kept asking me to play the Tony Rich record—I could tell it was going to be a hit. Even though I had moved out, Tony was still practically living at my old place. He continued working at my old studio. He would give me reports—the chef quit, she's seeing this guy or that guy—like my spy.

By the end of the pool party, I was ready for everyone to leave my house. In theory three days of parties were fun, but instead I realized that something was missing in my life. I needed something—what, I didn't know. But what I also didn't know was that it would come sooner than I could have predicted.

I first met Erica Holton while she was still at Clark Atlanta University and working as a hostess at one of the premier restaurants in the city, Pricci. She also worked at the Ritz-Carlton restaurant, where I would sometimes go for breakfast. I would run into her from time to time and she was always nice to me. It was always "Hi, Mr. Reid." One day in the summer of 1996, I was walking through the LaFace office, checking out what everybody was doing, something I always liked to do, and wandered into the marketing director's office. They were friends and Erica was visiting her. "Hi, Mr. Reid," she said, only this time it was a different kind of "hi."

This time I saw this gorgeous creature with these long, beautiful legs I hadn't noticed before. When I returned to my office, I asked Sharliss, who also knew Erica, to ask her to stop by my office before she left. When she and her friend showed up, there were a few people in my office talking about the Olympics.

The Olympic Games were being held that summer in Atlanta. LaFace made an album to celebrate. We did a song with

Gloria Estefan, "Reach," that became the unofficial theme song of the games that year. Consequently, I had tickets to everything. The US Olympic basketball team that year was the killer Dream Team—Charles Barkley, Shaquille O'Neal, Scottie Pippen. I asked her if she would like to go and she asked if she could bring her girlfriend.

"Of course," I said. "We can all go."

She called the next day to make sure the invitation was still on, and, when the day came, I picked her up at her apartment in my black Porsche with my pal Toby driving a second car, since mine was a two-seater. We were going with six people, but I insisted on driving my Porsche. When we arrived at the arena, I realized I had left the tickets, and, while Toby went back for them, Erica and I decided to wait at a nearby restaurant called Mumbo Jumbo.

By the time Toby got back, we had decided that we'd missed too much of the game and stayed at the restaurant to have dinner. After dinner, we went upstairs where there was a lounge and sat around listening to music when she surprised the hell out of me.

"You know, I've been to your house before," she said.

I had no memory of her being there and asked if she'd come to my fortieth birthday party. She said no and I asked her to tell me when she'd gone to my house.

"First let me describe your house to you," she said.

She started talking about the statues with candles in the entrance, the large great room, my son's bedroom downstairs. She knew every detail. It was getting a little weird. It turned out that Sharliss had been at Pricci when she got a call from my business manager telling her to hire somebody to straighten up my place before I got back in town. When Sharliss couldn't find anybody, Erica volunteered.

Anyway, Erica and I really hit it off, really connected that night. I'd seen her in passing so many times, and I kept thinking,

With Erica, cruising in the midlife-crisis-mobile

this girl's been right here the whole time—how come I didn't pay attention? I knew I was crazy for her. We were having fun and started dancing. I gave her a hug and held her close. "I bet you didn't know you were cleaning up your own house," I said.

That's the day Erica became my girlfriend.

With Erica in my life, I began to feel grounded again, back on my feet, and it couldn't have come at a better time, because in the fall of 1996, we started Usher's second album, *My*

Way, with Dallas Austin. After all his TLC hits, he had also done young acts such as Boyz II Men and Another Bad Creation, which I thought made him perfect for Usher. I bought him a Lamborghini Diablo as an advance down payment (that doesn't happen anymore in the business).

When he turned in the album, it didn't have the magic. Dallas is a genius, but for whatever reason, the chemistry between Dallas and Usher never quite happened, and the album they made simply wasn't up to standards. I was determined to take my time with Usher. Puffy had set the stage with his first album; the next album had to do even better. We knew he had talent. We knew he had charisma. We needed hits and groundbreaking music—we needed to define his importance in music—and I would keep trying until I heard what I needed to hear. I next turned to Jermaine Dupri, who was then hot with the multiplatinum teen rappers Kriss Kross. I first met Jermaine when my brother, Bryant, hired him on a remix for Damian Dame. He had done a couple of songs with TLC and he was very much a mainstay of the Atlanta music scene.

I ran into Jermaine as I got out of my car in the parking lot next to Gladys Knight's Chicken and Waffles restaurant in Atlanta. We stopped to chat and I asked him what he thought about the idea of working with Usher. He started talking about the direction he thought Usher needed and seemed to have an instant vision for it. I put them together, and, a short time later, Usher showed up in my office to play me a track they'd cooked up that he didn't like very much. I thought he was crazy—I loved the track—and went to the studio to watch Jermaine work.

He put up the track. He started singing. He wrote the bridge while I stood there. I knew Jermaine more as a rap guy. I didn't know he could sing like that. He was on fire. A few days later, I ran into him when I was leaving an Atlanta Hawks basketball game with my son, Aaron, and I asked him how the song was going.

"I actually have it in my car," he said. "Get in."

Aaron climbed in the back and I took the passenger seat. Jermaine got behind the wheel and played me "You Make Me Wanna . . ."

I had never heard Usher sound like this before. When he hit the bridge, whether it was the melody or the key or the combination, I don't know, but Jermaine had found Usher's superpower in that song. And the song was a stone smash. Usher's debut had been a success, but I knew this was the record that would make him a superstar. Jermaine cut the song in a key that gave the illusion of range, meaning that when Usher went into his high note on the bridge, it sounded like it was way up there, further than it really was—the illusion of range. He captured the climax on that bridge of "You Make Me Wanna . . ." in a way that pushed Usher into raw emotion. He made Usher a soul singer, launching a whole new phase of his career.

The next single, "Nice & Slow," went all the way to number one after it was released in January 1998 ("You Make Me Wanna . . ." stayed at number two beneath the fourteen-week reign of Elton John's remake of "Candle in the Wind" in honor of Princess Diana). With so much riding on the success of the second single, in typical LA Reid style, I invested heavily in a monumental video.

We landed the most cultural video director in the business for "Nice & Slow," Hype Williams, whose services were in such demand he could pick and choose among the hottest acts. We shot the video in Paris, and since it was Erica's birthday, I brought her with me. We pulled up on the video set and parked under the Arc de Triomphe, stepping out of the car and gazing down the Champs-Élysées at the City of Lights, a moment neither of us will forget.

I spoke to Hype Williams and asked him who the leading lady was—I am always interested in the leading lady. He pointed to a beautiful model on the sidelines, but somehow she didn't resonate with me at all. Hype suggested we try Kimora, the hot, tall Asian American model who was dating Russell Simmons. We flew her in and the shoot lasted several days, not the typical one-day shoot. Clive Davis called to complain about the budget. We had to put Usher on a milk crate for the kissing scene on the bridge, but the video was a massive hit, paving the way for Usher's first number one.

Although Usher's first album had been a hit, the massive success of his second album felt particularly vindicating to me. Though I'd taken special, patient care developing his career as a recording artist, there had been bumps. In the years since I'd found him, I'd had my moments when I didn't know if Usher was the complete goods, but I always stuck with him. At one point Puffy had to talk me off the cliff because Usher had gone through a voice change during puberty. Because I had never before worked with a boy that young, I didn't know what was on the other side of a voice change. I voiced my concern. Loudly. Too many times, to too many people. It was a moment of doubt that probably left a permanent scar on my relationship with Usher.

In spite of my concerns, I always remembered the kid who walked into my office that day, and what I saw in him as he performed. I always remembered the sight of him dropped to one knee as he serenaded the office, and how in that moment I could see the entertainer I knew he'd become. My confidence in that vision convinced me to look past my uncertainties. With this album, not only were my doubts proven wrong, but my discovery had been proven right. My vision of a superstar had become a reality.

11

NOBODY KNOWS IT BUT ME

Back in 1994, about the same time that Usher, TLC, Toni Braxton, and Outkast all ruled the charts, I had received a call from my Atlanta lawyer, Joel Katz, who told me that Michael Dornemann wanted to come to Atlanta to meet me. I said that was great, but who was Michael Dornemann?

"He's the chairman of BMG, you nitwit," he said. Bertels-mann Music Group (BMG) was a wing of the massive German-based media conglomerate that owned not only Arista, but also RCA Victor and other labels. "He's the guy who distributes your records. He's Clive's boss."

The music scene was at high tide that year. Not only were the LaFace acts selling millions and setting the pace, the whole field was bursting with exciting new music. From Seattle, the grunge rock of Nirvana, Alice in Chains, Soundgarden, and others made a huge impact on the rock scene. In England, Britpop by bands such as Oasis, Pulp, and others was blooming on the charts. Meanwhile, punk by bands like Green Day was breaking out of the underground.

The rap and hip-hop scene was quickly reaching some kind of critical mass. "Gin and Juice" from his album *Doggystyle* announced the ascendancy of Snoop Dogg and the whole West Coast school of rap, followed shortly by the sensational Tupac Shakur and his *Thug Life, Volume 1*. Puffy's Bad Boy empire was about to explode out of New York with Notorious BIG and his *Ready to Die*. Method Man was only the first solo act to emerge from the Wu-Tang Clan, whose debut album the previous year, *Enter the Wu-Tang (36 Chambers)*, rewrote the rules of hip-hop. It was a very exciting time in music, and acts I discovered and cultivated were leading the way on the charts.

I knew we were hot, but I wasn't accustomed to this kind of attention from corporate executives, so I had no idea why the big guy would want to meet me. Of course, I had to spruce up my house if he was going to visit. I called my business manager and told him I wanted to install some landscape lighting for the occasion. He convinced me to save a few bucks and only put lights in the front of the house. We decorated the house, put out flowers, and Michael Dornemann came over for dinner. What did he want to do after dinner? He wanted to go to the studio, so we stumbled out through the dark backyard where I hadn't installed the lights and listened to music in the studio. Fucking business manager. I saved something like $300.

A couple of weeks later Joel Katz called again and told me that Michael Dornemann wanted me to come to his house in Greenwich. The way he said "Greenwich" made it sound like some kind of big deal. I thought he meant Greenwich Village; I'd never heard of Greenwich, Connecticut. I went to New York and met Michael at his office and he drove us to Greenwich while we made small talk. His girlfriend served us dinner. I noticed he had a file marked "LaFace" with him. He opened it up and started going through the file in front of me.

"Your company's wildly successful," he said. "I have an idea. Not now, but I want to prime you, because I want you to become the president of Arista Records and replace Clive Davis."

Seriously? I thought. *Me?* Now, I think I'm good, but I don't think I'm that good. I listened as he talked, somewhat dumbstruck.

"We'll prepare for it, but I want to put that in your mind and let you know that's what I'm thinking."

I really didn't know what to say and was surprised to hear myself say something I had never said before in my life. It was a thought that had never occurred to me. "I'll have to talk it over with my wife," I said.

I didn't know what else to say. Isn't that what proper people say?

Dornemann, who was German and may have held somewhat more continental views of the relations between the sexes, smiled lightly. "You do that," he said.

At that exact moment, his girlfriend was clearing the table and walked by him. He reached out and patted her ass. It was like he was saying, *Women aren't important—what the fuck are you talking about, "check with your wife"?*

I stayed in touch with Michael from time to time, but he never again mentioned the subject and it quickly went out of my mind.

In the years after that meeting, I had my own issues with Clive. After years of selling astronomical amounts of records, LaFace still hadn't made any money. I lived well because I had other ways of making money as a songwriter and producer, but I could never make any money from Arista.

At our peak, LaFace employed only around sixty people. We didn't have a high overhead and we didn't have to deal with any of the other associated costs. We didn't have a promo staff or independent promotion. Arista paid for manufacturing and packaging, supposedly covered through the 15 percent service fee we paid the company. The biggest problem for us was that our contract with Arista allowed any costs to be charged back to the label. If we made a video, the entire cost was charged back to LaFace.

Because of this tough agreement with Arista, I knew that it would be very hard to turn LaFace into a moneymaker on its own; Arista was always going to have the edge over us. The only way to realize capital gains was to sell the company while the catalog still held value. I was always concerned that, in the music business, when you have a company entrenched in urban music, the valuation is always significantly lower. People really do buy more Barbra Streisand than Luther Vandross in catalog. It's more a fact of life than a racial thing. Black catalog doesn't sell as well as white catalog, largely because there aren't as many black people.

LaFace may have plenty of potential to discover talent and

create new hits, but discovering talent and creating new hits were its greatest assets. LaFace at its peak could only start to lose value, so I wanted to exit the company and get paid while the price was high. I worried that I might not ever have another hit. Some people can proceed without any trace of self-doubt, but I'm not wired that way. During the day, around the artists and the people at the label, I was confident, but late at night, by myself, I could feel deeply insecure, like maybe I had already done my best work.

The first time I approached Clive about buying LaFace, he didn't even give me the courtesy of a reply. He just looked at me and smiled, saying nothing. I told him after so many years, it was time for me to get paid. We'd had massive success together. I had brought him the Bad Boy and Rowdy deals. My contributions to Arista were enormous. He should buy the company and I would go to work for him. No reply was my answer. He simply turned his head. It didn't make me angry—I knew businesspeople acted like they were playing chess—but I did take note.

Then, in 1997, three years after Michael Dornemann first called me, Strauss Zelnick, the president of BMG, phoned. He and I had met at a conference in Switzerland a couple of weeks earlier, and he had quietly watched while Clive Davis and I talked music and played records for each other. He wanted to arrange a meeting in Atlanta. Immediately I realized it must be the Arista thing again. Despite my frustration with Clive, I hadn't thought about taking over for him since I had spoken with Michael Dornemann three years earlier.

Zelnick and I went to dinner at a fancy restaurant. "I know Michael Dornemann mentioned this to you a couple years ago," he said. "I'm basically here to tell you that we're very serious about you taking over Arista Records. But you have to prepare. I'm going to recommend that you go to Harvard Business School. We'll take care of everything. We'll get you admitted, we'll pay for it, and you'll be there as a representative of Bertelsmann Music Group."

This was the same program I had put off once before when Left Eye had burned down her house. Zelnick was a very likable guy who had graduated from Harvard himself with graduate degrees in both business and law. "If you need tutors, I'll help you with tutors," he said. "If you get stuck, you can call me. I'm going to be your guide."

With the master, Clive Davis

I had had my problems with Clive—clearly it was like pulling teeth to get money from him—but Arista was Clive's company and he was Clive Davis, one of the greats, if not the greatest. He and I never exchanged an angry moment or a single harsh word. We had differences of opinions on how to run our businesses or artists and music, but he was always cordial and gracious with me, even if money could be a bone of contention. So I didn't completely buy the idea that I would be taking over Arista Records—I still wanted to sell Arista my label and go to work for Clive—but this seemed like a great opportunity to prepare myself for whatever my future might be.

In January 1999, I arrived at Harvard Business School, enrolled in the twelve-week Advanced Management Program, with two trunks packed with clothes and gear. That was a big day for me. I brought what I considered my most conservative wardrobe, but when I showed up for the welcoming reception in blue Prada shoes, baggy trousers, and shoulder pads, I immediately felt like a fish out of water in this sea of gray flannel.

We were assigned rooms in a dormitory so small I could reach the computer on my desk while lying on my single bed. I spent the second day sending home most of what I'd brought.

The program was open to executives from companies with a minimum valuation of $100 million, the small end of big business, and I was the only person from the entertainment field. There were people who worked for British Petroleum, Toyota, and Merck pharmaceuticals, hospitals or grocery store chains, doctors who ran medical centers, and bankers, lots of bankers, from all over the world. There was one guy from the radio business and one from newspapers, but they both worked for large corporations.

One professor gave me some heat in a study group early on. "Why are you here?" he asked. "You're in music. I don't see the connection."

For a kid who barely paid attention to high school and never even bothered to graduate, the whole Harvard thing was pretty intimidating. It was also very exciting because I'd always regretted not going to college; the chitlin' circuit had been my university. The knowledge I could gain I would put to use my first day back at work. If I was going to ascend to the corporate boardroom, this was stuff I needed to know. I started out at Harvard weak, but I knew by the end of the course, I would be one of the standout students. And I was.

The classes started at eight in the morning with ten-minute breaks between them and a half-hour for lunch, straight through to dinner. After a one-hour dinner break, we went to a two-hour study group, so the school day didn't end until ten at night. Math was difficult. I found a business school student to tutor me and learned algebra and trigonometry, and started calculus. I knew so little about computers that I went to the Coop on Harvard Square and bought a giant dictionary, only to have one of my fellow students show me the dictionary button on the computer.

I got into the groove. We studied cases like the Disney/ABC merger and the competition between Nike and Adidas. We spent a lot of time on the Japanese automobile business. I took tons of notes. It was a crazy, up-and-down experience. There were definitely those moments when I would sit quietly in class, hoping the professor would not call on me, because I had no idea what he was talking about. And there were moments when I waved my hand frantically because I knew the answer perfectly.

We were not allowed to communicate with our companies. Not only were we told that, but the other executives in our companies were also instructed not to speak with us. I called Clive once. "How's it going?" he said. "We're going to send you a care package. Good-bye." *Click.*

I was a huge Michael Jordan fan, and missing all those Chicago Bulls games was disappointing. Sometimes we would take a little break at night to watch television, and one night, flicking the channels, we caught a new Usher video for the song "My Way" on MTV. I had personally overseen every detail of the LaFace creative work, from the video treatment to the final edit, every song, every mix. I approved everything, completely hands-on. Sitting in this room watching a new Usher video—which was great, by the way—at first I had this sinking feeling that I might not be as important as I thought I was if they could do this without me. But the more I thought about it, it became a good lesson for me on my way up the corporate ladder: If I was going to rise in this business, I had to learn to delegate. I couldn't micromanage everything. I couldn't always be sitting behind a drum kit, a mixing board, and a desk at the same time. If I was going to be comfortable being the head of a label like Arista, I had to learn how to strike a balance that would allow me to keep one foot in the music and the other in a boardroom.

By the end of the course, the professor who called me out in the study group for being in the music business apologized and praised my work. Erica came to the graduation and she was as proud as I was.

Although the experience was useful in improving my ability to evaluate executive talent and for the friendships I made, Harvard was really a validation of things I already knew. It translated my street smarts into technical business terms. But America is incredible—here I was, someone who largely stopped studying anything but music past the tenth grade, who never finished high school and never graduated, and now I had a Harvard degree.

The only matter traumatic enough to make me leave school was the Toni Braxton situation. After selling tens of millions of albums with her first two releases, Toni first filed a suit in December 1997 in California trying to have her recording contract voided. In January 1998, she filed for bankruptcy—like TLC—to get out of her contracts, and I was called to a judge's chamber for a court-ordered mediation. I never understood Toni's issues, because—unlike TLC—she was getting paid. Her problems were rooted in her own fiscal issues and our difficulties with proper accounting from Arista, not with LaFace.

We tried to make settlements, but she and her new manager dismissed our offers as laughable. Toni was not happy. She didn't like being dressed in fancy gowns, she said. She complained it made her look too elegant and too old. She went on the Oprah Winfrey show to take her case to the public, only to have Oprah embarrass her with questions about her overspending and money mismanagement ("I didn't know Gucci made silverware," Oprah said).

None of this made sense to us at LaFace. It wasn't like it had been with TLC—Toni wasn't signed to a production deal; she was signed directly to the label. There was nothing to impede cash flow, information, communication. Toni was our girl. At that point, she was as promising as Mariah Carey and Whitney Houston. She was heading in that direction and having that caliber of success. How could she be so unhappy?

We'd taken care of her from the moment she came to town. We fixed her up with an apartment, gave her a Mercedes-Benz, took her shopping. I have had a lot of other artists who didn't get a fraction of that when they started, even if ultimately they made big money. Toni was well taken care of from the beginning, but never seemed comfortable. I never understood why.

What can I say? Talent turns on you—that is one of the pit-falls of success. TLC turned on Pebbles. Babyface turned on me. We turned on Dick Griffey.

The situation with Toni was symptomatic of our relationship with Arista. Clive was always great, but his right-hand man was murder. You had to battle for every dime with that guy, and at LaFace, we simply didn't have the financial people in place who knew how to collect the money we were owed. What we knew how to do was make records, which was why I went to Harvard.

When I finally got out of school, I went to Clive and his guys and told them to get the lawsuit settled. I wanted Toni paid. The lawyers weren't getting anywhere. Her former managers were doing no good. The new manager wasn't helping. No one could get it settled. There was no amount of money that was enough money. It was more like an angry divorce than a business deal.

For their part, TLC had gotten past the lawsuits and bank-ruptcy and had spent two years in the studio with Dallas Austin, once again serving as executive producer. The group's third album, *FanMail*, was released in February 1999 and sold more than 800,000 copies the first week. Left Eye came up with the concept of the album—saluting the fans who sent the group letters by including all their names in the album design (Left Eye had also given both the previous TLC albums their names). Ironically, she was virtually absent from the recordings and the group had to go back into the studio and recut the obvious single, "No Scrubs," because Left Eye wasn't on the first version.

One of my producers played me the demo of "No Scrubs," which was written by a producer named Kevin "She'kspere" Briggs and Kandi Burruss, long before she starred in *The Real Housewives of Atlanta*, but was already successful in the music business and had belonged to the popular girl group Xscape. Everybody could tell the song would be a monster smash.

TLC receiving their FanMail

That one was done, but I didn't feel like we had a follow-up, because although Dallas Austin had done an incredible job being the architect of the album, I didn't hear any more hit singles. I went to one of my favorite producers in the world, Timbaland, and asked if he and Missy Elliott had anything we could use. They sent me this song called "Where My Girls At?" which I immediately gave to TLC to record.

The group refused to do the song. They told me they wouldn't take material from outside their Atlanta camp, that they wouldn't cut songs written by their competition. I knew the damn song was a fucking smash and told my little muse T-Boz, who was the group's lead singer, I would pay her the same $100,000 that I would have to pay the writers if she sang it. She agreed to do it, but called the next day and said she had changed her mind.

"You're a dick jumper," she said.

"What does that mean?" I said.

"You jump on the dick of whoever's hot. Well, we're not dick jumpers. We don't jump on the dick of whoever's hot."

Reluctantly, I gave the song back, and Timbaland cut a Top Five hit on the song with a girl group called 702. At that point in my life, I may have fucked everything else up, but I knew a hit song when I heard it. If we had had that song as a follow-up to "No Scrubs," the album would have sold eight or ten million.

I still wanted Clive to buy LaFace, then cash myself out and go to work for him. The next time I talked to Clive about buying the company was during a late-night phone call to my home in Atlanta. This time he gave me an answer.

"I can't buy the company," he said, "because it will sink my bottom line and affect my company's bonuses, and these executives have worked far too hard. They can't have a year that they don't get bonuses because we bought LaFace."

Fresh out of Harvard Business School, I knew better. When you buy a going concern where you don't take a write-down, you amortize it over the years. If there is no write-off, it doesn't affect the bonus structure. It would basically be money borrowed over time. He clearly could have bought my company and not affected his bottom line. I knew this from an accounting standpoint, a legal standpoint, and a tax standpoint. I had asked him twice and I wasn't going to fight him over this, but I started to get a little attitude.

That was when Strauss Zelnick came calling again.

"Here's the deal," he said. "I know you've had conversations with Clive about buying the company, which he has no interest in doing. However, BMG is interested in buying the company, but only if you'll become the president of Arista, replacing Clive."

I couldn't believe he was serious.

"We're very serious," he said. "You can have your attorneys call and we can start the conversations."

The LaFace chapter of my life was going to close. I was going to sell the company and, for the first time since Duro Bag, take a job working for someone else. Given how long we'd worked together, part of me still didn't like the idea of replacing Clive, but because of his resistance to buying LaFace and the money issues we had with Arista, my options weren't great. Staying in place and treading water just didn't seem viable.

From the day Kenny and I started LaFace, this was the endgame in mind. Although I never worked for money, it was not that I didn't ever want to get paid. I'd watched the sale of Motown, the sale of Geffen Records, the sale of A&M, even though I was only starting out in the business, and, later, I saw Virgin and Island sold. I knew that I was creating something of value, so exiting LaFace while we were on top was something I'd been thinking about for a long time.

Kenny and I made the label out of nothing but our own creativity and hard work, and we meant something to music. We went from being a couple of kids producing R&B hits to finding talent that made some of the biggest-selling records of the day. In the process, I'd learned how to go beyond simply making hits; I'd learned how to make artists that would change the culture. We didn't just discover stars, we discovered a sound. We put Atlanta on the map. I might have arrived down South as a scrappy, hot songwriter, but I'd become a record man. While I'd taken some hard knocks along the way, I'd learned what I needed to know.

This new opportunity gave me the chance to start over—to formally end the partnership with Babyface as well as LaFace's dependency on Arista. But it also would let me leave behind the drama that had sprung up over the years. Proud as I was of what had been accomplished, all the struggles with Toni Braxton, TLC, Babyface, even Pebbles, had worn me down somewhere inside. I wanted to create a new, fresh life for myself, to begin again. I also sensed I was beginning to overstay my welcome in Atlanta—nobody said anything and there was nothing specific, but the music business had grown around us so much in those years, there was an element of competitiveness and residual resentment I could feel around the edges.

The move to Arista was a chance to expand my horizons, to push beyond simply R&B, and enter pop and rock. Sure I'd be working for someone else, but the scale of everything—the company, the artists, the city—would be bigger.

LaFace was a boutique label with only a handful of artists to work with at any given moment, and I found myself with too much time on my hands running the small company. I began to invest in restaurants and even started to build a hotel in Atlanta, but eventually decided not to and lost that money in escrow. I was losing my focus. I became a little too consumed with lifestyle as opposed to working hard. Now that I was no longer hungry, my edge was going soft and I could sense complacency settling into my scene. That was unacceptable. It was time to go. The only regret was that I sold too soon. My biggest successes turned out to be just up ahead.

My attorney Don Passman began negotiations and I went

back to running LaFace. Talks went on for some time, even grew quiet for a while. Clive Davis visited my house in Atlanta for dinner during the time I was holding talks with Strauss Zelnick about taking over Arista. Clive and I had already talked about buying LaFace and he had passed, so I didn't even bring it up when he came to my house. I already knew where things were going and I probably should have taken that moment for a heart-to-heart talk with Clive, but I didn't. One Thursday night that spring, the phone rang at my house in Atlanta. I remember the exact time: 11:36 p.m. It was Strauss Zelnick. "We've told Clive," he said. "He got up and he walked out of the restaurant. He's very upset. We need to conclude the buyout of LaFace and we need to conclude the negotiation of your executive contract. Pending approvals, you're now the president of Arista Records."

It wasn't a question. I hung up the phone and went to find Erica in the bedroom.

"We're moving to New York," I said.

12

ARISTACAT

Much like when Kenny and I had started LaFace, I never had any doubts that I'd be able to run Arista. The transition from hired producer to LaFace had been seamless; even though Kenny and I had known little about running a label or an office, we knew how to make hits and we figured that would be enough. And for LaFace it was. For Arista, however, I knew that making hits was just the start. Running a bigger label would mean that everything from my job to the music I heard would be on a larger scale, and to keep up, my vision for everything would have to be broader.

From the start, there was a lot to learn about running a big company. I had a very seasoned staff, some of whom joined me from LaFace, and they all knew a lot more about operational things than I did. I have always liked to surround myself with people who are arguably smarter than I am, and who allow my focus to stay on the music and the artists. I had learned enough about business to put great businesspeople around me, and I laid out some good money to hire the people I wanted.

As it turned out, I was going to need every one of them because, at the start, things were not easy at Arista. I had not anticipated the shock and awe that would greet the deposing of this beloved king of the record industry. Clive Davis can be very grand. He has an aristocratic way—dramatic, but very controlled. If Clive's in the room, it's Clive's room. He is a star. His pre-Grammys party is the single most prestigious invitation in the music industry.

He also has an impeccable ear. I've sat and witnessed his talent up close. He follows the journey of a song. As a song comes on and it goes to the first verse, then to the prechorus and the main chorus, I would keep my eyes on Clive's body. When it comes out of the bridge and goes into the vamp, I could read his body language and knew if the song paid off for him. If it didn't, I would know what he was going to say.

I had no idea why the Germans fired Clive, and I never asked. They fired him and then they funded his new label, so they weren't exactly getting rid of him. Clive had been hugely successful, and, at that moment, he was having yet another pinnacle of his career with, of all people, Carlos Santana. The *Supernatural* album was on its way to selling more than twenty million copies, behind the massive global success of a song called "Smooth"—an unprecedented comeback that nobody saw coming. But corporate executives, in my experience, generally don't like star executives, which may not have helped Clive's case.

Shortly after I started my new job, Clive invited me to breakfast at his Fifty-Seventh Street apartment. He greeted me warmly, ushered me into the breakfast room, and went straight to the point. He was very upset and he wanted to let me know that he felt like the victim.

"This is very hard for me because it's in the papers," he said. "My family's heard about it and I don't want them to read that I've been ousted and replaced by another executive. This is all very devastating to me."

He vented and then it was my turn. I told him it had always been my preference that he buy LaFace and we continue to work together. "Our failure to communicate is why we're here," I said.

I never even knew what a record executive was before I read Clive's first book. I didn't know there was a record executive behind Sly and the Family Stone, Blood, Sweat, and Tears, Janis Joplin, Bruce Springsteen, Miles Davis's *Bitches Brew*, until he pulled back the curtain. I was in awe of Clive and I never took him on. I wanted to talk with him. I needed to talk with the man who was, in many ways, the most fascinating man in the record business and the man who I shaped my career around, and the man whose heart I had broken.

Clive didn't see that I had grown to become this executive. He still thought of me as the kid he'd met at his Beverly Hills

Hotel cabana, a young songwriter with his partner Babyface eating tuna fish sandwiches. He couldn't see that I'd become what I'd become. I loved Clive. I would have never even talked with the Germans if he had accepted my offer.

"I can only apologize that we haven't treated each other better," I said, "because we could have had a very different outcome. Instead of people telling you and me what to do, we could be telling everybody else what to do. If we'd joined forces, we would have been more powerful."

Clive wanted me to know he was embarrassed. He was hurt—we were both hurt—but he was happy to be there to settle the score and so was I. That out of the way, we started to eat.

The breakfast took an interesting turn after we finished talking out our own issues, Clive started to tell me about the people I was inheriting. Some of them left with Clive to form J Records, some stayed with me whether they wanted to or not. Clive pointed out the people who couldn't be trusted. I wondered how much I could believe him, but, as it turned out, he was absolutely right about the people he said I couldn't trust. I had no idea how the politics of a corporation worked, but I was about to learn.

The public outcry that greeted the news caught me completely by surprise and hurt my feelings. In my mind I thought, okay, I put in the time with the artists and my career with music, I had success, I went to Harvard, I studied, I prepared, and then I reached this threshold and the press went crazy on me: "Rap guy takes over for Clive Davis." Rap guy? I heard it from all corners.

It was bittersweet for me. I liked that I'd moved to New York City and bought an apartment on Park Avenue. I was glad to become the president of Arista Records, a kind of crowning accomplishment in my music career. Within a few days in July 2000, I turned my world inside out. I signed the paperwork to

take over Arista, then Erica and I got married on the isle of Capri, took a four-day honeymoon, and moved to New York City
when we found out she was pregnant.

This was a complete life change—new city, new wife, new
family, new job. I liked that I'd sold the company. I liked that
I had a beautiful new young wife and we were starting a new
family. I was happy about my life, but I was unhappy with how
I was being received. I'm an artist. Yes, I'm a record executive,
but at the core of me, I'm still an artist, and artists perform for
their audience. I wanted to be able to celebrate this moment, to
take my bow before going on to new heights. But the backlash
made that impossible.

I knew that the remedy would be success. All I had to do was
have success and I wouldn't be news. The controversy would
be finished. Success isn't news. Unless you're an underdog and
become a success, you're not news, and I was long past my underdog days. In fact, in a way, I was seen as the victor and Clive
won all the sympathy votes.

Despite the controversy, I stayed focused on what I'd been
hired to do. Even though I never found out why the Germans
got rid of Clive, it was hard to ignore the timing of the decision. My move to Arista coincided with a larger shift going on
in the music industry. A new era in pop music had taken over.
Hip-hop and rap had not only moved into the mainstream, but
urban radio had taken over the dial. Top Forty radio was out of
date, and the market for black music had spread far beyond the
black community alone, a transition that the records we made
in Atlanta had no small part in making happen. When Babyface and I first started having hits with Whitney Houston and
Bobby Brown, we needed to slide in among all the rock and pop
records that crowded the Top Ten; now urban music ruled the
pop charts. The kinds of records that had made Arista successful
under Clive were no longer going to work. Every new big star

on the label had been discovered by me, and now my job was to take that track to bigger places.

At Arista, I was immediately dealing with a roster full of rock and pop acts that were far from the urban world where I had been operating. The funny thing is, though, I never focused on the fact that what I had been doing was with black artists and black music. I still looked for my records on the Billboard Hot 100, the top of the pop charts; I didn't have to look at the other charts to find my records. So when I went to Arista and started to work with other genres, other than the fact that I didn't have as much hands-on involvement with the creation of the music, it didn't feel that different to me. The biggest difference wasn't musical. The biggest difference wasn't genre. The biggest difference wasn't race. The biggest difference was that I was no longer an entrepreneur. I was no longer an owner. Arista belonged to the Germans.

At LaFace, you could complain to Kenny or you could complain to me or you could have a water cooler conversation or you could go tell your lawyer you weren't happy with your deal, but there was no higher person to talk to. That was the big adjustment.

The first record I signed was "Hit 'Em Up Style" by Blu Cantrell, written and produced by Dallas Austin. I was working in New York, but I still went to Atlanta on weekends when Dallas came over with the first recordable CD I ever saw (we were still using DATs, or Digital Audio Tape) and played me the song. Dallas sat there and as soon as I heard this thing come on the stereo, I knew it was a smash. It was a number two pop hit. The first copy I got, I sent to Clive. He made no comment. He countered with Alicia Keys. Gotcha.

From pop, I went straight to hard rock, signing a band from Bakersfield, California, called Adema and selling a half-million copies of the band's first album, the first rock record of my career, behind substantial airplay for the songs "Giving In" and "The Way You Like It." Of course, as soon as I expressed interest in the band, the managers began their wind-up—shopping the act to every other label in the world, trying to start a bidding war. This was completely new to me. I knew only about signing talent because of what the label represented. At LaFace, there was never a second label to consider. But now I worked for a corporate record company, and the process did not make me comfortable. By the time I did sign the band, I was a lot less interested.

Signing Adema, I got lucky, to be honest. That band didn't sign with Arista to work with me; they signed with the label because it was Arista Records. It was not something I was looking for, but I had A&R guys at Arista, and if they were excited about something, I wanted to hear it, I wanted to see it. If I liked it, I'd move on it.

Finding Avril Lavigne came entirely unexpectedly. I had agreed to go to a downtown studio for an audition in November 2000, but I was in a cranky mood and the closer to the time I was supposed to leave, the more I didn't want to go. Not wanting to stand up our A&R guy who had made the appointment, I went, but I was in a foul temper by the time I walked into the place. I was introduced to this shy, small sixteen-year-old girl who didn't have much to say, pretty, but not someone who had put a lot of thought into how she presented herself. She went into the other room behind the glass and she sat on a stool where I could see her. She started strumming her acoustic guitar, almost folky, and when that girl opened her mouth to sing, all the bad energy in my body washed away. And once again, God was in the room. I started smiling, loving what I was hearing. She had a voice that reminded me of Dolores O'Riordan, the girl in the Cranberries, a special tone, so pure and melodic. She never sounded like she was searching for the note.

With Avril at the Benefit for PENCIL cosponsored by Arista records.

She was a young girl from Napanee, Canada, right outside Toronto, and very different from any artist I'd ever signed. There was nothing even the slightest bit urban about Avril. She took me back to the campus of the University of Cincinnati with all the hippies hanging out with their guitars. I felt like I was at home listening to this girl. Sometimes that's all it takes to discover someone—being able to recognize how their voice has affected you, and that if it had that impact on you, maybe it will do the same for other people. It didn't matter that I hadn't worked in rock before. It didn't matter that she was working in guitar riffs instead of a drum machine. Looking at her, I saw little sign of the pop star she would become, but I could already see her for what she was.

It wasn't her songs that moved me; her voice was her superpower, and I didn't need to hear anything more than that. She sounded like strawberry lemonade, sweet and tart at the same time, ice-cold and bracing. I knew this as soon as she opened her mouth. The tingle that shot through me was more than a chill bump; it was practically orgasmic. I immediately offered to sign her.

"You just took a guy who was in the most rotten mood and put me in the greatest mood in the world, and for that, I thank you," I said. We gave her a recording deal worth $2 million.

As it became clearer that the blurring of the lines between rock, pop, and R&B would be the driving engine of my job at Arista, one of my LaFace development projects who embodied this trend started to pay off with a big hit record just as I was transitioning to Arista. Few artists captured the shifts going on in pop music in the early 2000s like Pink, but interestingly she was somebody I had been working with for several years already when I came to Arista and her first album was exploding.

I had first overheard a demo tape being played in someone's office while making my daily stroll through the LaFace
offices in Atlanta. I liked the lead singer, and when I asked if
there was a photo, I was surprised to see she was white. She
certainly didn't sound white. It was a female trio from Phil-
adelphia called Choice, and I asked the A&R person to fly
them to Atlanta before the end of the week. They did their
audition for me in the conference room and the lead vocalist, Alecia Moore, was sensational. Not only was she a great
singer, but she was this spunky, dreadlocked seventeen-year-
old girl with personality, character, and soulfulness.

Signing the group had been tricky. They were minors and
two of the girls came from strict Christian families, but we
worked out everything and whisked them to Atlanta to make
demos. Alecia Moore made it clear that she would not sign unless Babyface agreed to write and produce two songs with the
group. LaFace was always two people—me and Babyface—
and it was the musicality of my partner that lured Choice to
our label. Tricky Stewart did a few things with Choice that
I liked, and, since my custom was to showcase new talent, I
invited the girls to entertain at the annual LaFace Christmas
party. They weren't great, but my muse T-Boz heard them
and came up to me.

"I don't know who that group is, you need to get rid of
them," she said, "but not the lead singer. She's a star."

I had been fascinated by Alecia's singing because I always loved blue-eyed soul and never heard a young white girl
who could sing this black since Teena Marie, but I always
made note of T-Boz's opinions and began to see what she was
talking about.

A little while later, my son Aaron told me that he saw Alecia
working at a gas station. I am like a fucking drill sergeant about
my rules for my artists, like if you're an entertainer, I don't want

anyone to see you as anything other than an entertainer. I called her into my office and gave her the speech.

"Well, give me some money and I won't have to," she said.

Had me there. I gave her whatever cash I had in my pocket and went into heavy pursuit on getting her to quit the group. She started coming over to my house and hanging out when I had other artists there. She made herself a part of the LaFace community. I took her to dinner one night at Pricci, where they set the table with the salad fork, the dinner fork, the salad knife, the dinner knife, and the fish knife. She didn't know what was with all the silverware.

"You know what you need?" I said. "You need to go to etiquette school."

She never forgot this. Before long, she would play me a song called "Don't Let Me Get Me," with the line: "LA told me you'll be a pop star, all you have to change is everything you are." When I complained I never said that, she said, "You told me I needed etiquette class." Had me there, too.

Shortly after that, for her own reasons, she decided to take me up on recording as a solo artist. I was fresh back from Harvard and hadn't seen her in a few months when she walked into my office having sheared off her long dreadlocks. She was wearing a short, spiky haircut dyed hot pink and she had a rabbit's foot. She had completely transformed herself.

"My name is Mister Pink," she announced.

She had gotten the name from the movie *Reservoir Dogs*, in which the characters have names like Mr. White and Mr. Orange. She had created a character out of herself—it was what I'd been waiting for without even knowing it. I told her to lose the Mister and keep the Pink. We took tracks we recorded with Choice and turned them into solo recordings. I put her together with a new hot songwriting-producing team I had signed to my publishing company, Kandi Burruss and She'kspere, who had just recorded "Bills, Bills, Bills" with Destiny's Child and had done "No Scrubs" with TLC. The first single, a song they wrote called "There You Go," took off in early 2000. The video, directed by Dave Meyers, made Pink an instant sensation. By the time her second single, "Most Girls," released in September 2000, I was working at Arista. "Most Girls," which was written and produced by Babyface with a good friend of mine named Damon Thomas, was a Top Ten hit, leading the way for her first album, *Can't Take Me Home*, which sold about three million copies. She was the final new star to come out of the LaFace pipeline, but her success belonged to Arista. After Arista acquired LaFace, all the artists moved to Arista and the label ceased to exist.

Pink was outspoken, witty, and smart. It always struck me that this girl would find her own way quickly. When it came time to do her second album, it was Pink who came up with the idea of working with Linda Perry. She had been a fan of Linda Perry since 4 Non Blondes and "What's Up?" She made the whole thing happen; there was no label involvement. I put her together with Dallas Austin and they came up with some fantastic songs like "Don't Let Me Get Me," "Just Like a Pill," and, one of my favorites, "18 Wheeler." I went to Miami to meet Dallas and Pink. The album was taking on a direction I didn't feel all that comfortable with—in that delicate balance of pop, rock, and R&B, this had too much of pop-rockish edge, very different from the first album, which was sort of what I called white urban. The guitars were loud and there was a hard edge to the sound and the songs that was grittier and more abrasive than the records the pop stations were playing at the time.

I expressed some skepticism about the direction the music was taking. I loved the songs, but I worried aloud that she would be undermining the core support of her urban audience. We

With Pink at the twenty-eighth annual American Music Awards

had what I like to think was a healthy conversation, intended to show support, but I'm not sure that's how she took it. She went back and finished the album her way.

I didn't hear the record again until she brought the album to my office in New York around midnight one night and, man, did she finish it. I sat at my desk listening to the CD at full volume while she stood next to me singing every word, jumping on top of the table, acting it out, giving me the whole movie. From head to toe, she had completely crafted this character called Pink; she had come up with the concept and figured out how to use it to transform herself.

One thing I know about pop music is that when you can create a character that lives in your songs, you have it made. Michael Jackson took that to the highest level maybe of any artist to this day. He was the glove. He was the hat. He was the socks. He was the sequined jacket. He was the Moonwalk. When you can take ordinary items—clothing items like shoes, gloves, socks, hats—and make people see those things and think Michael Jackson, that's creating character. It is like Left Eye and her condoms or Jay Z and the Yankees cap. As he said himself, he made that cap more famous than the Yankees did. You can make your songs hits, you can make yourself famous, but until you've created a character, you haven't cracked the code of culture.

Watching this happen, watching her take over her career with her vision and painting her masterpiece, just the two of us in my office that night after midnight, it was something to see. I love nothing more than an artist who has a point of view and a vision for themselves. Whatever vision I had for her as a white urban soul singer vanished instantly as soon as I saw the vision she had for herself. I could tell she knew what she was going to be able to do with this character and that it would make her a star. She got it right on her own.

"My album is going to be called *Missundaztood*," she said.

"Get the Party Started," the first single she wrote with Linda Perry, shot straight up the charts in November 2001, and the album eventually sold more than ten million copies. Pink was officially a star.

"'Complicated' is a smash. Let's just put the damn thing out. How about that for a marketing plan?"

When I first got the first video for the second Pink album, I took it to a meeting with the chairman of BMG, Rolf Schmidt-Holtz, who had replaced Strauss Zelnick and Michael Dornemann. They'd been fired shortly after I started working at Arista, which was not good news for me. I felt uncomfortable without my support system, and, as far as I could tell, Schmidt-Holtz knew nothing about music. He stopped the video midway. "You need to take that shot out," he said. "It's not a flattering shot of her."

I didn't say anything. Of course, I never took the shot out of the video.

Having watched the miraculous transformation of Alecia Moore into Pink, I experienced a similar shock the next time I laid eyes on Avril Lavigne. Several months later, when she walked into my office for our first meeting since she was signed, she had long brunette hair, parted down the center, her face framed by rectangular blue glasses. She was in character now and she had become Avril Lavigne.

Avril hadn't yet turned in any music—it was a meeting to talk about what she wanted to do, our first full-on conversation—but much as when Pink had shown up to play me her second album, I saw everything in an instant that day. Avril didn't drop by simply to say hello—she was making a point. She came to my office with the intention of making sure that I understood that she had found her direction as a performer and as an artist with her own look and image.

I assigned her to A&R man Josh Sarubin and they went to work on her record. A couple of months later, he came to my regular A&R meeting, which could be a tough meeting. Nobody wants to go first; if you're going to go first, it better be great. Josh wanted to go first, and the song he played us was "Complicated." The instant it ended, I made him play it again. It was a fucking smash to my ears and to everybody else's in the room—rock and pop coming together in a way that none of us had heard before. I played it over and over. One of my old-time LaFace A&R guys, KP from Organized Noize, was there. He is a hip-hop guy who speaks in a deep, slow Southern dialect. "That shit jammin'," he said.

Josh went back to work on the record, and every time they'd bring in a song, it was better than the last. They brought me "Sk8er Boi." One night they sent me the song "I'm with You," a ballad that sounded so good that I didn't believe it was mine.

When the record was finished, we started to have marketing meetings at the company. Because this was a new kind of record for me, I waited for the experts at the label to make something happen inside the company. However, it quickly became clear that they were stuck in interoffice inaction. They wouldn't schedule a release and all I was hearing was a bunch of record company talk about what their plans were. I called Avril's manager, Terry McBride, and I told him I had thought about the marketing plan.

"Listen," I said, " 'Complicated' is a smash. Let's just put the damn thing out. How about that for the marketing plan?"

He agreed, and we went forward with scheduling a video shoot. Before we made the video, though, I took the album to a friend of mine at MTV named Tom Calderon. He liked what he heard, but he had one suggestion: she had to play guitar in the video if she was going to be taken seriously as a rocker. Since I hadn't done pop-rock before, this came as news to me, and I passed that information along. When they brought me the video, not only was she playing guitar, she was wearing this wife-beater shirt with a necktie around her neck. She came up with this whole thing—an instant home run. The album went on to sell more than ten million, but sales were just the start. That Halloween 2002, all the little girls in the suburbs were trick-or-treating as Avril Lavigne, which said a lot more than the sales figures ever could.

With Avril and Pink, I'd been able to make a clear statement about the kind of hits that my Arista was capable of creating. Two years after replacing Clive Davis, the label was bigger than ever, and given the difficult start that my tenure had, I found this particularly satisfying. Following the March 2003 Grammys, the *New York Times* ran an article about me with the headline that said it all: "And They Said He Couldn't Run a Major Record Label."

13

KAST OUT

t was after midnight in April 2002 in my office at Arista when I received a call from one of my longtime executives who went all the way back to LaFace with me, Dorsey James, with some disturbing news. He said Left Eye was dead. She had been killed in a car crash in Honduras, where she was filming a reality TV show, when she'd driven off the road after swerving to avoid another car while the cameras were rolling. At the time, TLC was no longer a fully functioning unit, and Left Eye had left Arista as a solo artist after her 2001 album, *Supernova*, a record I never felt really matched her stature. TLC never had anything but hits, and some of the songs may have been all right for someone else, but Lisa was a star who deserved better. I avoided discussions about the album with her, preferring to make my feelings known to the producer, but she insisted on releasing the album on a certain date. I don't know anything about numerology, but it had something to do with the date of her father's death. We couldn't get the album released in the United States in time, but we did manage to get it out in Europe. Lisa and I often had an uncomfortable relationship, but she was the original spark of genius at the heart of TLC, and her death was a pointless, tragic waste.

TLC had been the beginning of so much for me. They were my first real discovery and the first smash hit act on LaFace. They were also my first real challenge as a record executive, and navigating those waters cost me my marriage and years of my life. But I loved those girls through it all. The loss of Left Eye was devastating.

As I worked to move past her death, there were other challenges that I faced at Arista. Despite successfully meeting many of the changes that came with the move to Arista, the one area where I struggled was with the established Arista stars—whether it was dealing with the diamonds in Clive's crown like Aretha Franklin and Whitney Houston, or the fact that I kept mistaking Barry Manilow for Rod Stewart, apparently a common mistake made by many people. In 2002, we did an album with Whitney called *Just Whitney*, but from the start, it was clear that I didn't have the complete Whitney.

By the time I became involved with Whitney as a label head, her commitment to her career was very different than that of the young girl I'd met at the airport. Given my earlier experience, I was expecting her to bring the same level of professionalism to her work. But a lot had changed since I'd last recorded with her. Her work ethic, for one thing, wasn't the same, which came as a surprise—she wanted to spend more time with her family.

Any artist will tell you that comebacks are difficult to get right. I'm not sure you get more than one, and Whitney had already had hers. After having all those hits leading to *The Bodyguard* soundtrack, one of the biggest-selling albums of all time, she went through a quiet period until Clive was able to bring her back with a couple of 1999 chart hits, "It's Not Right But It's Okay" and "Heartbreak Hotel," and that turned out to be Whitney's comeback moment. When I was working with Whitney, we were trying to do that again, only this time it was harder. If an artist has the same commitment that I have, then we have a much better shot at making that comeback, but unfortunately it didn't go that way.

Of course, what I didn't know at the time was that much of this change in her commitment came from her substance abuse issues. I wasn't comfortable prying into her personal life, so I didn't learn how bad things were until I watched the 2002 Diane Sawyer interview—"Crack is wack"—and in an instant, I realized just how serious her problems were.

In more ways than one, that interview was a difficult moment for me, one of my biggest mistakes at Arista or anywhere else. I had gone to great pains to arrange that interview, introducing Whitney to Diane. Meetings with major media figures like Diane Sawyer were new for me, but my hope was to counter

The infamous Whitney Houston interview with Diane Sawyer

some bad publicity Whitney had created with her appearance at a recent Michael Jackson tribute concert. After all, we had an album to promote, and I figured that a high-profile interview would allow Whitney to take control of her story.

Instead, I watched in shock as Diane asked Whitney about drugs and she told her she made too much money to smoke crack. I called our ace publicist Laura Swanson in a panic.

"What have we done?" I asked.

There was no good answer to that question—to this day there still isn't. As a record man, sometimes the job is to help sell records and sometimes the job is to protect the talent. New as I was to Arista's bigger stage, I had to learn the hard way which of those is more important. That Diane Sawyer interview with Whitney was a terrible strategic mistake. I should have protected her; instead, I exposed her. No wonder we didn't have great success with the album.

I caught Whitney at the wrong time, just like I caught Aretha at the wrong time. They were the two great Arista heritage superstars. With Aretha Franklin, she welcomed me to the company when I became the president of Arista. I visited her in her suite at the Trump Hotel on Central Park West. Her bodyguard-assistant let me into the room. "Hello, Mr. President," she said. She walked up and pinned a flower on my lapel. She was the sweetest person in the whole world, so respectful. That was quite different from the first time I met her, when Clive Davis had introduced us at his pre-Grammy party many years before. She never looked at me. She put the cigarette she was smoking in an ashtray and handed it to me. Babyface and I had once flown to Detroit to work on a new track for her 1994 greatest hits collection. She cooked up a big batch of soul food for us. I asked her who were the singers she loved. She said, "Other than me?" She looked away and never answered. That's Aretha, the Queen of Soul.

The 2003 album I executive produced, *So Damn Happy*, never lived up to my hopes. With everybody from Burt Bacharach to Jimmy Jam and Terry Lewis cutting tracks with her, the album may have inevitably lacked focus and direction, but what it really needed was a damn hit single.

It wasn't always the inherited artists from Arista that were tough—sometimes there were difficulties with newer LaFace artists too. CeeLo Green was one of those. He was with Goodie Mob in Atlanta on LaFace. He did a fantastic rap on this song with Outkast called "Git Up, Git Out," and I didn't even know he could rap. He would stop by my office and expound like a philosopher king. He spoke with a golden tongue. I was always in awe of CeeLo and when he wanted to sign a deal for a solo record with Arista, I welcomed him. I always knew he was going to be huge, and while the 2002 album *CeeLo Green and His Perfect Imperfections* was a good record, it wasn't the big hit he needed. "Crazy" with Gnarls Barkley was still years away.

Outkast was a different story. With every new album, those guys grew and evolved as artists and musicians, and their audi-

With CeeLo, Babyface, and Jermaine Dupri

ence increased with every new release. By the time they put out their fourth album, *Stankonia*, in October 2000, I was running Arista, and I made sure the entire resources of the company were behind the release. The record debuted at number two on the Billboard 200 and eventually went quadruple platinum. They had grown so much musically. They had more depth, more edge, and they started to cross the threshold into rock. With me at Arista, Outkast was not going to be pigeonholed as hip-hop. We worked the record with alternative rock, Top Forty, and crossed them over to the mainstream without losing their edge or integrity with their core format at black radio. They had experienced musical growth that couldn't be denied. André had become André 3000. When you listen to "BOB," that is the same artist who would make "Hey Ya!" *Stankonia* opened the doors for Outkast.

Nobody A&Rs Outkast. They are as self-contained as any rock band. They write their own songs and they make their own records. Unlike every other hip-hop group I have worked with, they don't use samples (or only very rarely) and they don't shop for music outside their group or their Organized Noize compound. When they finished, they brought the record over to my house and we listened to their new album for the first time together, which became something of a tradition for us. In 2001, we put out a greatest hits collection with three new tracks, one of which won a Grammy.

Then in early 2003, I went to Atlanta to have a meeting with Outkast at their Stankonia Studios, named after their album. I went in assuming that we were going to talk about their new upcoming album, but right away it was clear they had a different conversation in mind. They told me at this meeting that they might not want to work together as a group any longer. In fact, I'm not sure Big Boi knew before this meeting that André had come to this conclusion—I couldn't tell. I was shocked and

Outkast at their CD release concert for Stankonia *in Atlanta, 2000*

stunned, but this was too sensitive to betray their confidence. Whether this was happening because of personal jealousies or divergent creative directions or whatever, they never let on.

Beyond that, I was uncomfortable being part of a conversation in which I didn't feel I belonged. I wasn't the third member. Whatever their verdict was, it was probably the manager's place to inform me. It sounded like a private conversation and I felt awkward, like I was hearing a family quarrel that I shouldn't have been privy to.

Outkast was my favorite act . . . ever. I had a commitment to them and I cared about them as people, but that decision about whether they wanted to work together or not was none of my business. I had seen acts break up. I was part of an act that broke up. I was part of a production duo that broke up. While it saddened me to think that their time together was ending, I didn't want to know any more. To this day, I've never asked, and I never will.

Sometime later, Big Boi told me he wanted to make a solo record. He went in the studio and he records, records, records, records. I started to hear the songs he sent me or his manager brought. I loved them. He played me one, "The Way You Move," that sounded like a real smash. Then he played me others that sounded so good I got confused. This album was full of songs that I really loved and I couldn't wait to put out. I went to Atlanta for his photo shoot. He had speakers everywhere, big speakers, small speakers. He was sitting on top of speakers. The name of the album was *Speakerboxxx*.

As it all came together, the company back in New York had been making plans to market and release the album by Big Boi, when I got a call from his former partner, André 3000.

"Reid," he said, "when are you putting out Big Boi's album?"

"The release date is five weeks away," I said.

"So if I want to make an album and turn this into a double album, how much time do I have?"

"Three weeks."

"Damn, three weeks," he said and paused, as if he was thinking it over.

"Okay. We're doing it."

About ten days later, I went to Atlanta to listen and he knocked me out with a jazzy hip-hop version of "My Favorite Things" from *The Sound of Music*. He played me a great song called "Prototype," which opens, "*I hope that you're the one / If not, you are the prototype.*" He was such a playboy with his words. I returned to New York, optimistic that this thing could happen.

Big Boi was fine with the idea of turning his single-CD solo album into a double-CD Outkast release, provided it did not delay the release date. He understood the power of the brand; he was still selling his solo album, only now to a larger market. His only concern was that his album was done, finished, accepted, and ready to go to market, and he didn't want to wait.

I felt like the luckiest guy in the world. I had committed myself to Big Boi's solo album, but I never turned my back on André. Although I knew Big Boi had a massive hit with his record "The Way You Move," when André decided to create *The Love Below*, I felt energized because, let's face it, Mick Jagger albums are never as big as Rolling Stones records.

André finished the album in three weeks. I don't know how he did it, but he brought it to play for me and I was blown away. I heard this song "Hey Ya!" and it was great, but I thought it sounded more like punk rock than a rap group from Atlanta. I was leaving the office and got on the elevator with a hip-hop kid in full Timberlands, sagging jeans, baseball cap, and jersey, who had overheard me playing the track in my office.

"Mr. Reid, that song you were just playing, that's a monster," he said.

He didn't look like a kid who I would have thought would like a song like "Hey Ya!" and I took note of that. When André called back to say he wanted "Hey Ya!" as his single, I told him that I had been thinking the exact same thing.

I decided to release both singles at the same time—serve the Big Boi record to urban stations and break André's single on alternative rock and pop radio. I thought that the dual single approach would work because the records were so different. "Hey Ya!" was kind of a pop-rock record and he was singing, not rapping; "The Way You Move" was a seventies-funk-hip-hop fusion record and he was rapping. Neither of the guys was featured on the other's record. These two records were so different, there would be no way they could cancel each other out. Both artists were fine with the idea. The only thing that was the same was the name Outkast, and I saw that as an advantage. I never thought for a second that it wouldn't work, and it will never happen again.

Now that it was an Outkast album, *Speakerboxxx/The Love Below*, André and Big Boi both shot their videos at the same time—André played every role in his green-tinted "Hey Ya!" video, including all three background singers—and the two of them filmed a piece that tied both videos together.

The band's manager liked the idea, my sounding board KP didn't give it a second thought, none of the people I trusted thought it was wrong, but the head of marketing at Arista simply didn't get it and resisted the idea. The marketplace couldn't take two Outkast records at once, he said. It was confusing—is it André's record, Big Boi's record, or an Outkast record? We delayed release for two weeks and it took me all that time talking my head off to get the company fully on board.

It worked like it had been choreographed that way since the beginning. Both records took off as soon as they were released in September 2003. They both went to number one in their format. We crossed the records over. They both went to number one in the other format. "Hey Ya!" was number one on the pop charts and "The Way You Move" was number two. *Speakerboxxx/The Love Below*, boom, entered the charts at number one and stayed for weeks.

The release cemented what the new Arista was coming to look like and what our approach to making hit records had become. We weren't tied to genres or formats—we were constantly looking for sounds that would cross over and blend. Whether it was the rock-pop charts, or urban radio, or R&B, all these different sounds were blending together into one incredibly addictive and popular brand of music.

In that spirit, we were working on the fourth album by Usher, *Confessions*, his first new album in more than three years. He had recorded more than forty songs when he first brought

With Outkast at "Arista Reloaded" at the 2003 BMG US Label Presentations reception

me the album, but I didn't think it was finished and sent him back in the studio to keep recording. I didn't hear the big hit I needed until my right-hand man Shakir Stewart found "Yeah!," a song by Lil Jon, who was breaking big with the new crunk sound out of the South.

With Dr. Luke and Ciara at the Record Plant, Los Angeles

Shakir had also brought me Jazze Pha, an Atlanta producer I had never worked with before, and he introduced me to Ciara, a seventeen-year-old beauty who turned out to be a very special artist. She sang to tracks at my Atlanta publishing company office for her audition. With a dancer's body and a dancer's way, she had hip-hop swagger, but beneath it was a sweet pop voice.

She was the last artist I signed to LaFace and I followed her demos closely. She and Jazze Pha were largely self-contained, but I paid the project serious attention, as I did Usher's record, which we were making at the same time. I thought she could be a star, and I knew Usher had another plateau to reach.

Unfortunately, those above me didn't have that same level of patience. One day in January 2004, I checked my appointment calendar before the weekend and saw an eight o'clock Monday-morning meeting.

"Rolf's office called and they asked to schedule the meeting," my secretary said. "They didn't say what it's about."

On Monday morning, I stuffed my briefcase with files. I really had no idea what the conversation would be about—release schedules, business issues, or my plans for the company. I got off the elevator at the Bertelsmann office at Times Square and walked past the receptionist. She didn't smile as she usually did. The office was quiet at eight in the morning—record companies don't start business until ten o'clock. It felt a little strange. Rolf Schmidt-Holtz greeted me at his office and we sat down.

"We've lost confidence and we'd like to make a change," he said. "We'd like for you to step down as the president of Arista Records, but we'd also like to offer you LaFace and all of its artists back and you can build your company from there."

As stunning as the news was, part of me was not surprised; part of me had expected to be fired the past two years, ever since Strauss Zelnick and Michael Dornemann had left the company. Beyond the team I'd built below me, I didn't have a single ally. Rolf Schmidt-Holz wasn't my ally. Clive wasn't my ally, and he retained considerable clout on the BMG corporate level. I was floating out there by myself and for some time had been thinking they were going to let me go.

But when it happened, it hurt. My heart sank; I felt that I had somehow failed. The blow was only softened because these weren't people who were friends or in any way vested in my career, who cared about my career or the artists who I was involved with. These were people with whom I felt no connection, emotionally, culturally, or musically. They were people somebody gave a job, they were in no way people who had anything to do with shaping the music industry or the culture. They knew nothing about how an artist worked or how to make the records that they sold, or even how the music business operated, so, in many ways, what they felt about me was irrelevant—but it still hurt.

I didn't like it and didn't entirely trust Rolf. On the surface, he was making me a great offer—I could have LaFace back—but somehow it felt like a step in the opposite direction. I'd gone from being the head of a small, taste-making label to running one of the most prominent companies in the industry; to simply return to where I'd come from felt wrong. It was hard to imagine life without LaFace—after all, Arista was still largely made up of LaFace artists. It was still Usher, it was still Outkast, it was Pink, it was all the people I brought to work there—it was still the LaFace culture. But it didn't take me long to see that, in spite of all the work I'd put into those artists and environment at both LaFace and Arista, it was time to make a change.

I opted out.

"I understand," I said. "I'm sure that this isn't easy. I'm sure that you've given this a lot of thought, but I'm going to take the first offer and step down and leave."

It had been fifteen years since I'd first arrived at Arista with the LaFace joint venture, and now the entire fifteen-year chapter came to a halt. Once again, it felt like I was leaving my family.

14

CULTURE CLASH

t didn't take long for me to land on my feet. I walked out of the Bertelsmann office, freshly fired, and called my lawyer Allen Grubman from the car. He told me he would call me right back. Two minutes later, he phoned.

"Doug Morris wants to see you right now," he said. "Whatever you're doing, go straight to Doug's office." It took only about fifteen minutes, but when I arrived, the security seemed to be expecting me and led me straight to his office.

Doug Morris was the chairman of Universal Music, the biggest music conglomerate of the moment. We had met privately once before, but I had never been to his office and barely knew him.

"I'm the luckiest guy in the world," he said when I walked into his office. "I can't believe they were foolish enough to let you go. I'd like to offer you the deputy chairmanship of the Universal Music Group. I want to do this immediately. You're an amazing talent. I've watched you for years. You make records that I love. You make big hit records and I really want you at this company." Doug and I shook hands and I left.

I hadn't been unemployed a half hour. I went home to tell Erica what was going on and headed to the gym to work out. At the gym, my cell phone rang and it was Edgar Bronfman, the chairman of Warner Music Group.

"What are you doing today?" he said. "I'd like to meet with you for lunch, if you can."

He had heard the news, obviously. Over lunch, he made me an offer to come to work for him at Warners. As with Doug Morris, Bronfman and I had met privately once before and he expressed interest in me coming to work for him. At lunch, I told him Doug and I had already shaken hands, but he suggested I still think his offer over. I was being respectful meeting with him, because really I only wanted to work with Doug.

I spent the rest of the week holed up in my apartment, frantically finishing my work on the new Usher album, *Confessions*,

At home with Doug Morris at Erica's book launch, New York

and the first album by Ciara. I didn't care about the label, but I am always committed to the artist. The albums needed to be sequenced, there were still final mixes to be approved, album art to be decided. Ciara had one last song. For my creative guys, it was just another day at the office, only at my apartment instead of the Arista office. They still needed me and didn't want to go on without me. The creative guys didn't fire me, the corporate guys did.

Even though I had left the label, I kept making hits for Arista. The same month I was fired, the company released *Confessions* by Usher, the masterpiece I always knew he had in him. *Confessions* sold more than a million copies the first week of release and went on to become the biggest-selling album of 2004, with more than eight million sold.

Ciara also needed some of my last-minute attention. Shakir,

who had found Usher's big hit "Yeah!," had also discovered a track for Ciara that would become her first hit, "Goodies." Lil Jon put the finishing touches on her album, which sold more than one hundred thousand copies the first week it was released in September 2004. The album debuted on the charts at number three and eventually was certified three times platinum, instantly establishing her as a new star. I was barely out the door when her record broke.

Between working on those two albums and dealing with the fallout from the Arista firing, there was too much happening. Plus, our daughter Arianna was two years old and the apartment was a madhouse. I needed a break.

I took Shakir Stewart and a few other staff people and blew out of town to Miami. Bertelsmann had already made their settlement, so I had a lot of money in the bank. My friends and I were eating, laughing, and having a good time. I wasn't really preoccupied with what my job was going to be. I had hot records on the charts and two excellent job offers. I felt fine, despite being fired, and wasn't down in the dumps or doing any soul-searching. In some ways I felt relieved to be leaving Arista behind. It was a big exhale, not necessarily a great exhale, but an exhale nonetheless. One stage had ended, and the next was about to begin, but, for that weekend in Miami anyway, I felt professional freedom for the first time since I'd moved out of Cincinnati. I had been locked into commitments, responsibilities, and strategies for so long, I had no idea what it felt like to be free. The concept was only beginning to settle into my brain.

I had been there for three days and was rolling down the highway on the way to Sunday brunch at the old Biltmore Hotel in Coral Gables with my man Shakir in the passenger seat, when the phone rang and it was Jimmy Iovine, Doug Morris's executive partner at Universal Music. They were the two kings of the music business. Iovine had also once talked about me going to work for him at Interscope Records. He couldn't hear me, because I was riding with the top down, and made me pull over to talk.

"Listen," he said, "Lyor Cohen just resigned from Island Def Jam. Doug and I have been talking. You are our number one, our number two, and our number three choice to take over Island Def Jam Music Group right now. So whatever you're doing, I need you to stop it, call Doug, and get back to New York, because this is urgent."

Island Def Jam were two labels combined in 1999 that brought together the pioneering rap and hip-hop label Def Jam and a British-based rock and reggae label, Island Records. Def Jam had been founded by producers Rick Rubin and Russell Simmons fifteen years before on the ground floor of the hip-hop movement and was a prime mover in advancing the cause. Island Records had been started in 1962 by a wealthy British expatriate who grew up in Jamaica, Chris Blackwell, who created an enormously influential and tasteful independent label with British rock such as Joe Cocker, Cat Stevens, and Traffic, and the worldwide success of Bob Marley and the Wailers. Blackwell was an iconic record executive whose discoveries ranged from Bob Marley to U2. Despite the disparate culture of the combined companies, Island Def Jam boasted the number one market share at the moment, and both labels had proud, distinct, and distinguished pedigrees.

We went ahead and had brunch, drinking wine and carrying on. After the meal, my son Antonio called. "Hey Dad," he said. "I just heard that you were taking over Island Def Jam. Is it true?"

Not only did the label have the number one market share, but Def Jam was the most cultural label of the day—even my kids were impressed. I'd gotten the call myself only maybe an hour and a half before. I hadn't told a soul. What the hell?

"Everybody's talking about it," Antonio said. "It's all over the streets."

I went back to New York on Monday and met with Doug

about this new post, something different from the vague position we had previously discussed. I would be taking over a bustling, sprawling label with a roster that ran from U2 to Ludacris. I would be the top dog at the top label. Our lawyers went to work and they were drawing up their papers right about Grammys time.

The morning of the Grammys in February 2004, a messenger brought the contracts over to the breakfast bar at the Beverly Hills Hotel, where I always ate. I signed them and sent them back. Now I was officially head of Island Def Jam and the word was out. I had made a brief, uneventful appearance the night before at Clive's annual pre-Grammys party, but when Erica and I arrived that night at the Grammys, we were swamped.

Jay Z and Beyoncé offered congratulations. John Legend shook my hand. I was feeling good from all these conversations in the aisles. Kanye West pulled me aside. He had yet to put out his first album, but I loved his first single, "Slow Jamz," which he did with Jamie Foxx and a rapper called Twista.

"Congratulations," he said. "I know you're coming to the company and I know you'll get me because you get Outkast."

Outkast asked me to sit with them. Ellen DeGeneres was seated on the other side of my wife. It turned out to be Outkast's night, and, at the end of the evening when they pulled down the big prize, Album of the Year, Big Boi surprised the hell out of me: first thing at the microphone, he asked me to join them onstage. The television audience may not have been aware of the drama behind that gesture, but the industry audience in the hall all knew I'd been fired by the label after delivering the year's biggest smash and picked up that day by the world's top hip-hop company.

"I want to thank Mr. LA Reid," Big Boi said. "This is the man who is responsible for our career, our big brother in the music business. When we wanted to change singles, he didn't really understand, but he gave us the creative freedom to do what we wanted. We love you. We still here and you already know what it is."

André echoed those sentiments as soon as he took the mic. "LA Reid," he said, "thank you for giving us the opportunity. We were seventeen years old, fresh out of high school, and you saw something in us."

Standing there with those two, my head somewhere in the clouds as I drank in this surreal moment of redemption, I could vaguely hear a warm, smoldering applause coming from the people in the audience who knew what had gone on. The thing about the Grammys is peer recognition. It isn't so much about the public. To the people who perform and participate in the

On stage at the Grammys with Outkast as they accept the Album of the Year award

Grammys, it is about the peer approval. That was the great feeling. That was the proudest moment of my career.

And yet, as I looked out at the faces of all those artists I respected in the front rows, I fixed my stare on Erica's eyes. Her happiness was even beyond mine. She knew what I had gone through. She had walked with me through all those dark days. I could tell from the joy in her eyes, Erica was the happiest person in the world, and I felt more warmth and appreciation from that than from anything.

But it wasn't just my wife. My mother was in the audience, too. For years I included my mom in my successes—taking her to the Grammys, sharing the good news about platinum albums—but I'd always tried to protect her from my failures. At the Grammys, all the glory Outkast heaped on me was on display, and she shared every minute of it with me, trying to figure out how that drum set in the garage had turned into all this.

Erica and I went to the party afterward that Arista threw for Outkast, but it felt weird. All the guys I worked with at the label were still there. The only one who wasn't was me. I definitely experienced mixed emotions being there, and, as soon as I said my thanks to Big Boi and André, Erica and I returned to our hotel room.

Two days later, I started work at Island Def Jam.

That Tuesday, after my driver dropped me off at Worldwide Plaza on Forty-Ninth Street between Ninth and Tenth Avenues in Hell's Kitchen, I walked into the Island Def Jam offices by myself. Nothing could have prepared me for the scene that greeted me.

From the moment I walked in, I felt the heat of the underground. If the movie had a soundtrack, this would be where you hear a long, low menacing note. I was taken to the office of Julie Greenwald, who was the president of Island Records, and she offered to show me around and introduce me to everyone. Def Jam was a world of its own. When I started at the company, the roster, while distinguished, had matured. In the hip-hop world,

With Erica at the Grammys after party

it had Redman, Method Man, and Ghostface Killah, Case, LL Cool J. There was the Roc-A-Fella label that Jay Z and his partner Damon Dash owned. Their big new signing was Kanye West, who was a brand-new artist and probably the brightest bulb on the label. Irv Gotti's label, Murder Inc., had Ashanti and Ja Rule. Ruff Ryders had DMX. Def Jam was hip-hop central, and a lot came with hip-hop central.

As I walked around the floors, the office felt dangerous, unruly. There were a lot of gang colors. There was definitely sort of a crime syndicate feel, far from my world. My music was always polished, not sugarcoated candy pop, but not street. There was an edge to the physical space that was unlike any other office I'd been in. On that first tour with Julie Greenwald, she opened one office door and someone had cut up someone's clothes and thrown the pieces all over. Chairs were turned upside down, like someone had had a fight. She closed it quickly.

"Ah, not this one," she said.

One of my favorite artists, Ghostface Killah, was down the hall throwing a little tantrum and he wasn't quiet about it. I walked down to see what was wrong and we had a good conversation that seemed to calm him down, but I wasn't used to having artists screaming in the hallways.

Right across the hall, a guy was getting a haircut at a secretary's cubicle. The barber was standing there, cutting away, and hair was flying everywhere. It wasn't a tidy, elegant environment, by any means. Where was I? This was different.

At the end of my tour, she ushered me to this tiny, narrow room. She pointed to this little fucking office.

"And that's your office right there," she said. "You should put your office right next to mine, so we cleaned this office up for you."

To me, this didn't look like the chairman's office. In Atlanta, I had a big, beautiful office. At Arista, even better. There were speakers built into the walls, mahogany shelves, and a giant mahogany desk overlooking Central Park. Julie Greenwald's large, spacious office was on the corner and I had been tucked in a cubicle by comparison. Down the corridor was another large office marked off with yellow tape like a crime scene, which was Lyor Cohen's former office. He'd left the company, but all of his belongings were there and his staff was there still working. Nobody showed me his office.

After this lukewarm welcome and a somewhat disturbing tour of the offices, it was quickly clear that I'd walked into a company that neither understood nor respected me or my legacy. They saw me as some pop music producer in a suit and tie, without any street credibility or tough guy swagger. Like what happened when I took over at Arista, I was not greeted as a conquering hero, but some kind of unnecessary interloper.

I went into my new office, closed the door, sat down, and cried.

I wondered what the hell had happened to my life. What happened to my career? How did I go from being the king of Atlanta to the head of Arista Records—winning album of the year two days before—to this little bitty cubbyhole?

Later that afternoon, my two most trusted A&R advisers, Shakir Stewart and Karen Kwak, came to visit. They watched in shock as Julie Greenwald came into my office and spouted out some off-the-wall nonsense they thought was inappropriate. They had seen my offices in Atlanta and Arista.

"What are you doing and why is she talking to you like this?" asked Shakir. "What the hell is happening here?"

The similarities with my start at Arista didn't end with office politics. Just as people had been worried about my ability to fill Clive's shoes, there was a lot of concern among the community that I wasn't qualified to run the most important hip-hop record label in the world. Def Jam was a company that the people felt belonged to them—the fans of hip-hop, the DJs, the artists, the culture. Everybody at Def Jam before me had been a part of the building of that culture, and I was the odd man out who had not made any contribution. I wasn't pop enough for Arista, and now I was too pop for Island Def Jam—how had I become a controversial figure? There was a lot of press, a lot of questions. Russell Simmons, one of the founders of Def Jam, went so far as to buy a full-page advertisement in *Billboard* magazine to post an open letter in August 2004. "My concerns, however, are about the future of Def Jam and the industry as a whole as to whether the legacy that Def Jam established will be maintained to the benefit of the artists and the culture," Simmons wrote.

He went on about how Def Jam stood up for the unjustly imprisoned rapper Slick Rick, and he questioned what would happen to Shyne, another Def Jam rapper currently facing jail time for a shooting incident in a nightclub that also involved Puff Daddy and his then-girlfriend, the actress Jennifer Lopez. "What will Shyne come home to?" his letter ended. I did go visit Shyne at Riker's Island, and we finished an album with him while he was incarcerated. He didn't come home for many years.

Six months later, we made a label deal with Russell Simmons. That was some strategy by Russell—point out a problem and offer yourself as the solution—but I was determined to quiet the controversy around me and assume command of the situation.

I started learning my way around the Island Def Jam Music Group, the artist roster, how things go, who does what. I took a series of meetings over two or three months to reorganize the company, which helped solve some of the office tensions. Julie Greenwald left the Island side and her counterpart at Def Jam similarly departed. I always thought Julie was a great executive, but I never for a moment thought we could work together, because she would always be loyal to Lyor Cohen. I moved into her corner office, but I decided I wouldn't remodel until the label got hot.

I brought in some people who'd been with me at Arista. I hired Shakir from Hitco and put the publishing company up for sale. I also had Karen Kwak from LaFace, who had been my head of A&R administration and my right hand for many years. I slowly put my players in place alongside the people who wanted to stay. Now all I needed was a big hit record to make my mark with the company.

15

EMANCIPATION
OF ME

One of the first calls I received my first day at Island Def Jam came from Mariah Carey. She and I were already friends—we'd first met many years before when Tony Rich had toured Europe as her opening act. She'd walked up to me backstage and asked, "How much did you have to pay TLC?" I tried to sign her when I was at Arista, but Rolf Schmidt-Holtz thought she was asking too much money for someone whose career was over. She ended up signing with Doug Morris and the Universal Music Group on the Island Def Jam label.

"Darling, I'm so happy that you're here," she said. "I've always wanted to work with you."

"You are one of my favorite artists and I think you're one of the most talented singers ever," I said. "I've always wanted to work with you, too."

She cut short any further chitchat and got right to business. She had been writing songs and she wanted me to listen to the demos. We quickly set a meeting at her apartment.

The fact that she'd called just as I was coming to grips with the challenge that awaited me at Def Jam could not have made for better timing. Cleaning house and bringing in new staff at Def Jam had been a good start, but I still needed to find a hit that would remind people why I'd been hired in the first place. I had no idea what was on the tapes she'd been working on, but I knew that I needed to prove myself in order to feel secure at Def Jam. Working with one of the most successful recording artists ever seemed like the best possible place to start.

Mariah lived in a huge penthouse in Tribeca, Old Hollywood glamour at its finest—art deco light fixtures, a beautiful piano that had belonged to Marilyn Monroe when she was a child. We retired to her Moroccan room, where Mariah likes to listen to music, and she played me a couple of the demos she was working on for her new record.

She was coming off of a tough spot in her career. A lot of

people thought she was through. She had made the movie and the album *Glitter* and neither was critically acclaimed or a commercial success. Her next album, *Charmbracelet*, was supposed to be a return to form, but it was not well received either. She was regrouping. She had divorced her husband, Tommy Mottola, the head man at Sony Records who was presumed to be the Svengali behind all her success. A cloud hovered over Mariah's career.

Many years before, Babyface and I had met with Tommy Mottola at his office when he was head of Sony Music. He pulled out these big, beautiful photos of this brand-new artist he'd discovered named Mariah Carey and asked us if we would produce her. I looked at the photos and saw that this girl was absolutely stunning. He played us a song that showed off her remarkable vocal range, and my initial impression was that she sounded something like Whitney Houston, except with this higher pitch she could get to that Whitney didn't use. I knew beyond a shadow of a doubt that this girl was going to become a big star—I knew it—but at that point, we were meeting with Tommy about finding a home for LaFace Records, and Babyface and I had resolved not to produce people outside our label.

The first time I really connected with Mariah was when I went to visit the studio in 1998 when Babyface was producing a duet between Mariah and Whitney Houston for the film *The Prince of Egypt*. We were no longer working together, but Babyface invited me to hang out. Clive was there, as was the head of the DreamWorks film studio, Jeffrey Katzenberg. When Mariah retired to her dressing room between takes, I went with her. She showed me potential album covers for a forthcoming greatest hits package and asked me which one I liked. "The one that shows your legs," I said. "Those are million-dollar legs."

She laughed and I guess I was flirting a little bit, but I knew in that instant that I was going to work with this lady someday.

ABOVE LEFT: With my siblings, Rosaland, Bryant, and Ivy

ABOVE RIGHT: Jamming in the bedroom with Bryant

BELOW: With my sticks, circa 1978

ABOVE: Pure Essence—with Tuck, Kayo, me, and Mouse

BELOW: The Deele—with keyboardist DeeGee Smith, Kayo, and that drummer

ABOVE: Give the drummer some!

BELOW: The Deele at our best

TOP LEFT: Antonio and Antonio, Cincinnati Jazz Festival—1983

TOP RIGHT: I'll always love my momma.

BOTTOM: Oooh . . . on the LaFace tip

TOP: With Toby Rivers, Bryant, Toni, and Mom

BOTTOM: Record Men: with Andre Harrell and Puff at my fortieth birthday bash, Atlanta, Georgia, 1996

TOP: Eddie F, Usher, Jermaine Dupri, Shakir, and KP at my wedding in Capri, Italy, 2000

BOTTOM: The South has something to say.

ABOVE LEFT: *Missundaztood* sold over 10 million copies

ABOVE RIGHT: Avril celebrates her success. *Let Go* went on to sell over 10 million copies worldwide.

BELOW: With Joey Arbagey and Whitney in Miami

RIGHT: Usher amid full-blown superstardom

TOP LEFT: Jimmy Iovine—one of the great record men

TOP RIGHT: Rihanna . . . enough said

BOTTOM: Partying with Usher, Mariah, and Erica

TOP: Having a blast with Hov at my fiftieth birthday

BOTTOM LEFT: Family is a beautiful thing—with Addison, Erica, and Arianna

BOTTOM RIGHT: In the studio with my boys, Antonio and Aaron

ABOVE LEFT: With my wife, Erica, and Rihanna. Barry Weiss is lurking in the background.

ABOVE RIGHT: With Ashley

BELOW: Def Jammin' with Kanye, Jeezy, Jay, and Fabolous

With Bieber-Usher—"Squad Up"

TOP: *X Factor* first season glory

BOTTOM: And THIS is . . . *The X Factor*, baby.

ABOVE LEFT: With JLO in Sag Harbor

ABOVE RIGHT: Motown on Broadway, with the record industry's boss of bosses, Doug Morris

BELOW: Travis Scott performing in Miami in 2014

ABOVE LEFT: With MTrain at her video shoot

ABOVE RIGHT: Backstage at a Sara Bareilles concert

BOTTOM: Outkast at Coachella

Once I did start to work with Mariah, I found her to be smart, committed, open-minded, and sweet. She was determined, not desperate, to have success. While I had no sense that her confidence had been shaken by her setbacks, I did know she needed reinforcement, validation from someone whose opinion she respected. The more I hung out with her, the more I understood what she needed from me and the role that I had to play. I had to see through the past surrounding her—to lend my ear and speak my mind—and focus on the music. Music made her a star, and it was going to bring her back.

Partying with Mimi

When she started to play me demos, the cloud lifted in front of me. I saw her future. And my hit record. God was in the room. The first thing she played for me was "Stay the Night," a song she had written with Kanye West, and I liked it. A lot. She played me two or three other songs that were works in progress. Mariah's music was similar to the music I'd been making—right down my alley. I listened to her demos with some considerable fascination.

"You're on to something," I said. "Just keep going."

I left it at that, although I asked if she would give me a copy of the demos to listen on my own. She trusted me enough to do that, and I took them with me and listened. She made more demos and sent those to me. The more I heard, the more I understood what this album needed to be. Mariah has many superpowers, but she is best known for her octave vocal, what I like to call that whistle note. Nobody else can do that with the strength and clarity that she can. For all her talent, I always thought Mariah in the past had been overproduced; I wanted to *under*produce her and let her be the incredible singer she is.

Mariah was managed by Benny Medina, whom I'd known since he was at Warner Brothers. He was the guy who took off his watch and told Babyface and me we had ten minutes to pitch him songs. Later he caused a stink when he threw Babyface, Pebbles, and me out of a Warner Brothers sales conference in 1988 after he invited us because we showed up with my girlfriend, who was an MCA Records artist at the time. Years later, though, we'd become good friends. Benny is a very popular, powerful manager known for being highly artistic and creative, but also a very shrewd business mind. Benny is quite the character; he grew up living with his schoolmate Kerry Gordy, son of Motown's Berry Gordy, at their family's Bel-Air mansion, which became the basis for the 1990 TV sitcom *The Fresh Prince of Bel-Air*, starring the young Will Smith. The process is always

Mariah and Benny Medina at Mr. Chow, New York

fun with Benny. The three of us began to spend a lot of time together, going back and forth over songs and the recordings, working on the album.

She did a song with Kanye West, two songs with Pharrell. She made songs with Jimmy Jam and Terry's piano player, James ("Big Jim") Wright, and had written songs by herself. Every song was solid. The gospel-influenced numbers had the peaks and valleys of gospel music and the soul-stirring, foot-stomping gospel piano. The album was really good, really soulful.

When we finished the album, Mariah called and told me she'd come up with a title for the album, *The Emancipation of Mimi.* "Mimi" was her private nickname among her inner circle, and the idea that she would go public with this identity was a clear message that she wanted to allow her fans closer into her life. I told her it was not only brilliant, but it sounded like the title of a hugely successful record. It was Benny who came up with the slogan for the campaign: "The Return of the Voice."

We rented a suite at the Mandarin Oriental for a playback party for the three of us, overlooking Central Park and the night lights of New York City. We laid out a generous supply of champagne and caviar. We listened to the record and raised our glasses to toast, but something was bothering me. I didn't want to say what I had to say, but I went ahead and said it with our glasses poised mid-toast.

"Guys, we're not finished," I said.

They put their glasses down and looked at me incredulously.

"Seriously, it's really close," I said, "but there's something missing. I need to think about it."

We didn't have the toast, but we drank the champagne and ate the caviar anyway. Mariah was disappointed, understandably. I had been encouraging about the album all along, and just when she thought she was finished, I decided something was missing.

I didn't hear the big single I needed, the monster. I heard hits, but I didn't hear the one big sure thing. I had to think carefully about objecting to the album being done. This was Mariah Carey. This girl had more hits than anybody I knew, fifteen number ones, almost all cowritten by her. How tough do you think it is to tell someone who wrote that many hits that you don't think she has another big hit at the moment? At its best, that's a very difficult conversation, and you have to take care how you communicate. What you say in that moment and how you say it is so important and so delicate to the relationship, because that's the moment when an artist can throw you out of the room and tell you to go fuck yourself. I thought about it a lot. It finally just rolled off my tongue.

"I don't think we have a smash. I don't think we have that

monster. I think we're close. I think we have the concept. I think we have the body of work, and I think it's a genius body of work. I think the performances are amazing, the vocal performances, but I don't think we have that big monster smash."

I felt so close to Mariah at that moment. I knew I was right, but she was an artist I respected—no, loved—who trusted me and my creative judgment, who allowed me to give my opinion and who listened to me. It was a risky thing to do. Making a song is not like producing a bottle of soda pop, where the product is already a proven success and the only issues are distribution, marketing, and sales. A song needs magic, but that magic is not a gift that keeps on giving. It is not guaranteed. Many times I have sent artists back to the studio and it didn't work—most of the time, in fact, it didn't work.

But I felt trusted by Mariah and I needed to feel trusted, because I was very sure. I had no doubts about what I was saying. She gave me the trust I needed, and, in that moment, we forged a lifelong bond.

The next day I called Jermaine Dupri. He had written my favorite Mariah song, "Always Be My Baby," for one of her previous albums.

"I need you on this album," I told him.

Jermaine was ready. He only wanted to know what kind of song I wanted. "I want a ballad," I said, "but a ballad with a beat."

I called Mariah and told her the same thing. She was willing, but not overly enthusiastic. This was testing her trust in me. I could understand her reluctance. She already thought she was finished, and I got the sense that she would do this extra work only because I'd asked. I chartered a private jet and sent her down to Atlanta and Jermaine the next day. This exercise nearly always fails if artists aren't committed to it, if they think I'm just making them jump through hoops, but Mariah knew that I had

Our Rat Pack: Usher, Mariah, Jermaine Dupri, and me, Las Vegas

a vision. Jermaine and I had a lot of success together with Usher, TLC, and other things, so there was an existing relationship between all of us. I was operating on a combination of instinct and faith.

Two days later, Mariah called. "We got it, darling," she said. "I'm going to come over to your house and play it for you."

She showed up and played me a rough version of a song called "We Belong Together." It started with a piano riff. As she got into the song, I was loving what I was hearing. She worked her way through the verse and I braced myself for the chorus, waiting to see if the song was really it. The chorus hit and it was magnificent. Pure gold. This was the fucking record I was looking for.

"Are you sure?" she said. "Because I'll go back to Atlanta again, if I have to . . ." She was playing with me now, but I vigorously assured her this was the smash I wanted and needed.

"Okay, I'll go ahead and finish it," she said. "But while I was there, we made another one."

The second one was a song called "Shake It Off," another brilliant track for the album. But she wasn't done. There was a third track, "It's Like That," an uptempo, fun record. All this was way more than I bargained for. They'd done the work and they'd knocked it out of the park. They could not have nailed it more perfectly.

All my career, since the early days with the Deele, I have always looked for the big hit single. I understand album tracks and I know certain sides work better in dance clubs than they do on the radio, but basically I like to swing for the grandstands and am not satisfied until I'm sure I hit one out of the park. I am a big hit single man.

But ever since I'd moved from producer to executive, I'd worked hard to forge relationships with each artist, to learn how to push for the big hit single while maintaining a clear sense of what the artist needed to get there. In a hit-driven business, learning to put the artist first isn't easy. My time with Mariah embodied that delicate balance perfectly. Throughout the process, Mariah, Benny, and I had collaborated in a truly unique way, and the end result brought all those pieces into place perfectly. I'd encouraged her and I was honest with her about everything, but she made the album. She willed that album into success. That was as much her determination as it was her talent. I was there to support Mariah's vision.

I went to Right Track Studios in New York to listen to mixes. As I walked into the studio, Mariah was putting some finishing touches on background vocals. I could hear what she was doing while I sat in the lounge. She was singing her ass off, and doing

Kanye, Jay, Erica, Patty Labelle, T.I., and Mariah at my "thirty-eighth" birthday party at Soho Grand, New York

it right. She was not simply doing vocal gymnastics, she was arranging the entire record to peak perfectly. I could barely believe what I was hearing. When she was done, I went into the studio and heard "We Belong Together" top to bottom, completely assembled, entirely mixed, for the first time. It was a transcendent event for me, almost an out-of-body experience. The record enraptured me as the rich, gorgeous sound washed over me. I knew at that moment it was one of the greatest records I had ever been involved with.

I rejected her first photo shoot for the album. "I need you to look expensive," I told her. We did a second shoot with a different photographer and we had the cover. Everything was coming together. We released "It's Like That" as a teaser single in January 2005. We did listening sessions for MTV and BET. We worked the press. Mariah shot a brilliant video for "We Belong Together" with director Brett Ratner. We released the single in March 2005 and it zoomed straight to number one and stayed there a remarkable fourteen weeks. It was the record that brought Mariah Carey back, but it was also the hit record I needed to establish myself at Island Def Jam. As it turned out, it was just the start.

After we began working together, Mariah became my best friend—my "musical wife," I called her. We talked on the phone constantly. I needed to find somebody to take over as president of Def Jam. With the attacks on my credibility when I took over the label, I was looking for somebody to run Def Jam who had standing in the hip-hop community. I explained to Mariah that I needed to find somebody who was smart, successful, and respected. She didn't hesitate: "What about Jay Z?" she asked.

At that very moment, with playwright's timing, Jay Z walked into my office.

"Mariah, you're not going to believe it," I said, "but Jay Z just walked in. I'll call you back."

I must have looked at him like I'd seen a ghost. He had visited the office only once before and was simply stopping by to say hello. Talk about God being in the room. He showed up like clockwork. The second she'd said his name, I realized the genius behind her thinking, and there he was. By making Jay Z the president, I would completely solve the culture conflict at the company, because he was respected by every artist, rapper, rap publication, DJ, and rap fan. With a brushstroke, I'd be able to stop watching my back and focus on making hit records instead.

Jay Z and I had met briefly only a couple of times. I'd once caught up with him in the hallways of Def Jam shortly after I first started at the label. He had recently announced his retirement from rapping and recording.

"You decide to retire just as I come into the company," I'd said. "What kind of luck am I having?"

He had then called me on the phone later when Usher's album *Confessions* sold a million copies in its first week to offer congratulations, but we never had much conversation beyond that.

Jay is a guy's guy. He has a jovial, fun way about him that puts you completely at ease, if he wants you at ease.

"Jay, what are you doing this evening?" I asked.

"I'm doing whatever you want to do," he said.

I asked him to meet me at eight o'clock at the Grand Havana Room for a cigar and a drink. "Let's get to know each other," I said.

Jay was waiting for me when I arrived. I am usually a few minutes late, but Jay is never late for anything, ever. He is a man who respects himself, others, and time. He is a man of integrity who thinks strategically—a king among kings. After an appropriate amount of small talk, I popped the question: "Would you be interested in coming to Def Jam as the president?"

He didn't jump up and down. Since he had just retired from rapping, his plan was to concentrate on his business empire, the Roc-A-Fella clothing line and his Roc-A-Fella record label. He did not need a job, and I knew I was going to have to work to get him to come to the company. Nevertheless, he did not dismiss the idea. "It's worth a conversation," he said.

At the time, Jay was the leading artist in hip-hop and the

most respected entrepreneur off the street. In three short years, he'd gone from selling CDs out of the trunk of his car to the career-making smash "Hard Knock Life (Ghetto Anthem)" in 1998. He cut a distribution deal for his Roc-A-Fella Records with Def Jam and he had recorded eight albums, each a trend-setting, barrier-breaking bestseller. He was the guy.

I called Doug Morris, the head of Universal Music, one of the most successful executives ever in the music business, and the only executive in history to have run all the major label groups. I was growing to love Doug. Some of my best days were sitting in his office talking over things. I told him my idea about Jay Z. "That's a great idea," he said.

As soon as I heard myself say it, I wondered if it was truly my original thought. Maybe Doug had already thought of this. Maybe he had talked to Jay about it. Maybe he had talked to Mariah. Maybe I was the last to know that this was a good idea, as opposed to being the originator of the thought.

We were not alone in our pursuit of Jay Z as executive talent. Trying to lure him to Warner Music Group was Lyor Cohen, the former head of Island Def Jam who had moved to Warner and had a long-standing relationship with Jay Z that I couldn't match.

Enter Jimmy Iovine, the master negotiator. "You've got to think about what you can offer that Warner can't offer," Jimmy said. "His masters. Offer him his masters. They're his. Give them back to him. Lyor can't offer that."

It was a brilliant move and we made Jay Z that offer. A few days went by without word. I told Doug I was tired of waiting and wanted to draw a line in the sand, give him a forty-eight-hour deadline to sign the deal.

"You've got a lot of balls," he said.

"I don't know if I have a lot of balls," I said. "I just don't want to be hung out here too long. I need to know where we stand, because if it's not Jay Z, I'm going to have to think about who it is. I've got to get somebody in there. It's not going to work otherwise. The confidence is not going to be there."

I told Jay Z's lawyer that I needed an answer in forty-eight hours or the offer would be withdrawn. I heard nothing the next day and all day the day after. Around midnight the second night, I was driving around Tribeca, thinking the deal was not going to happen. At about twelve twenty, my lawyer called. "He signed it," he said. "Jay Z signed the contract. We got the deal."

It had been total radio silence up to—and past—the deadline. I was impressed. This is somebody you absolutely want on your team. You do not want to negotiate from the other side of the table with this guy. You will lose. He is as good as it gets. I have never encountered another artist who's as much a businessman as any Wall Street broker. And he is the greatest rapper alive. I got him on the phone.

"Congratulations," I said. "You did it. You tried to drive me crazy, but you fucking signed it, man. I'm really happy. I'm proud of this moment, and we're going to do some great things together. I know it."

"Steel sharpens steel," he said. "Let's go."

I had forgotten he was a wordsmith too.

From the start, Jay Z was right: We made a formidable team. He was the rap and hip-hop man; I was the pop-R&B guy. Jay Z taught me all the subtle rules of hip-hop. Before Jay signed, I sat in Doug's office, voicing my doubts.

"Doug, if Jay Z becomes the president, you realize that no one will ever come to my office," I said.

"You think it will make you shrink," he said. "But you're completely wrong. It's going to turn you into a giant."

"It's like having Elvis down the hall," I said. "How do I become a giant when Elvis is down the hall?"

"You're going to learn," he said.

Learn I did. Jay Z became one of my great teachers. We quickly developed smooth moves working together. When Jay Z first brought Rihanna into the office for an audition in February 2005, we worked like a team.

I first laid eyes on her in the hallway. I didn't know she was a singer or anything, just a pretty girl standing outside somebody's office. Then Jay Z burst into my office.

"You have to see this girl," he said. "Come with me."

With Jay Brown and Jay Z at a listening event

We went back to his office and he introduced me. She was a startlingly beautiful seventeen-year-old from Barbados. She opened her audition with a Beyoncé song, singing, but the whole time piercing me with these laser eyes. I saw her determination, her commitment. I looked into those eyes and I saw someone who was going to be a big star someday. My head was spinning. She sang another song, "Pon de Replay," that would become her first hit single. After she was done, I looked at Jay Z.

"Don't let her leave the building," I said.

I left it to Jay Z's guys to close the deal, and she signed her contract that day before they let her leave.

That's the way it went between us. If he found something great, he'd bring me in. If I found something great, I'd take it to him. We would double up on our strengths, and with Jay Z and me together, we were pretty much unstoppable.

After signing Rihanna, Jay Z and his team did the A&R for her first album, and I had nothing to do with it. The funny thing about Rihanna's success was that we signed two girls at that time—Rihanna and a lovely young lady named Teairra Mari. We held an in-house company showcase and Beyoncé happened to be there with Jay Z. Teairra Mari, Rihanna, a four-girl group called Black Butterfly, and Ne-Yo performed. At the label, we thought Teairra Mari would be the big star. We spent more time on her, did more work on her, paid more attention to her. Rihanna already had a hit out of the gate with "Pon de Replay," but we still thought it was the other girl. A bell went off for me, however, when, after the showcase, Beyoncé came up to me, much as T-Boz had done after seeing Pink for the first time.

"That Rihanna girl," she said, "she's a beast."

Jay Z introduced me to Rihanna, who would become our pop star; I introduced him to Young Jeezy, who was our most cultural rap guy. I met Young Jeezy through Shakir Stewart. I heard his music at the same meeting where Jazze Pha first played me Ciara.

"Young Jeezy's from the streets," Shakir said. "I don't know if you really want to get mixed up with him or not."

I didn't meet Jeezy until a few weeks after I joined Island Def Jam and Shakir brought Jazze Pha and Young Jeezy to my office. He was draped in diamonds and gold chains, which he took off and laid on the table in front of him. Jazze Pha pressed Play on the CD player and Young Jeezy started rapping. His street stories were vivid and accurate, his delivery on point and strong. He looked like a star, much more accomplished and poised than the artists I usually audition.

With Teairra Mari, Jay Z, and Rihanna backstage at the World Music Awards, 2004

At a Kanye performance in London with Kanye, Gee Roberson, Jay, and Beyoncé

"First of all, I'd like to sign you to Island Def Jam," I said after he finished. "Whatever you're doing, stop. I got you from here."

He always remembered that I said that. Jeezy was a hustler, a hugely successful hustler associated with the gang BMF (Black Mafia Family). He also belonged to the rap group Boyz n da Hood and had put out popular mixtapes on independent labels. We won a bidding war to sign him. His advance was $1 million, and he didn't cash that check for more than a year, that's how well he had done in the rackets.

Jay Z was always careful about what rappers he would stand beside. In hip-hop, endorsement is everything. You can't just be a rapper from nowhere and become successful. You have to have an association. All the things Jeezy talked about on his record, he lived, and he had developed a serious fan base before ever putting out a commercial record on Def Jam. He was a real gangster with a serious gang affiliation. We didn't go to Jay Z for any endorsement—we knew he was our secret weapon—but he checked out Young Jeezy.

"He's real," Jay said. "This guy, I'll stamp." Jay Z stayed close to Young Jeezy, closer than I did, his entire time at Island Def Jam.

The first Young Jeezy single, "And Then What," got some attention, but when Shakir showed up in my office around midnight a couple of months later and played me the second single, "Soul Survivor," I knew we had a smash record, not just a street hit, but an across-the-board pop smash. When it was released in July 2005, the single hit the top of the charts and the album sold more than two million copies. Two years earlier, before widespread Internet piracy, that record would have sold more than five million. Now Jay Z was signing the pop acts and I was finding the rap guys.

From the start, our partnership highlighted the blurring of the lines between hip-hop and R&B, pop and rap, taking the work that I'd begun at Arista and pushing it a step further. In addition to rock, now rap was in the mix—all different kinds of sounds and influences competing to steal people's ears. What we were doing with Island Def Jam, without ever really trying, was creating a truly modern record label—one that could turn out pop hits just as easily as it could turn out artistic messages.

The vision for Def Jam had been created at the start by its founders, Rick Rubin and Russell Simmons, and it was one of the clearest mandates of perhaps any label in history. Jay and I had the responsibility of following the blueprint. We didn't have to supply the vision. It was there already. Chris Blackwell also had founded Island Records with a very specific identity, and my job was also to follow that plan.

The Island roster at the time included established acts like Melissa Etheridge, who needed only my support and encouragement. She had made many albums. I didn't pick her songs. I didn't pick her producers. I talked to her producers, but I talked to everybody's producers. I felt close to Melissa and would attend her performances to show support. Fall Out Boy and the Killers were both acts that had been signed to Island before I came to the label, but had not released any music yet.

A friend who knew the band from Chicago tipped me off to Fall Out Boy, knowing they were signed to the label, and when my A&R guy played me the demos, they sounded like hit after hit to me. "Mix" was my comment. The Killers I saw twice at South by Southwest shortly after I took the job at Island Def Jam, once at a little bar and once playing in a large open field, and both times they floored me. Brandon Flowers struck me as a young David Bowie, and they had a superstar drummer in Ronnie Vannucchi. The band had it going front and back. Julie Greenwald supervised the video for the first single, "Mr. Brightside," on her way out the door, but with the second and third albums, I would fly to Vegas and sit in the studio while they played me demos. Brandon would stare at me while I listened—it was a little uncomfortable—but it turned out that was how he got what he needed from me, just, as Joni Mitchell put it, "stoking the star-making machinery behind the popular song." That was my job.

Even if my expertise was more with Def Jam, I always stayed plugged in on the Island side. In particular I paid close attention to Jon Bon Jovi, who delivered his new album, *Have a Nice Day*, complete with frowny-face cover. Bon Jovi had actually been the first call I had received when I took over at Island Def Jam. I was surprised that an artist of his magnitude

With Bon Jovi at Kenneth Cole's "R.S.V.P. To Help" hosted by Kenneth Cole and Jon Bon Jovi

would think it was his place to pick up the phone to call me when I joined the company—more like the other way around. He had offered congratulations and asked for a meeting. A couple of days later, I met him at the heliport on the West Side Highway and we took a helicopter to his house in South Jersey. He lives in a French-style château right on the water. He wanted two things, he told me: to be on the cover of *Rolling Stone* and to be inducted in the Rock and Roll Hall of Fame. I told him *Rolling Stone* didn't seem too difficult—I already had Carlos Santana and Outkast on the cover, and I knew the publisher, Jann Wenner—but I didn't know much about the Hall of Fame process. I told him I would study up and help however I could.

We ate dinner with his wife, Dorthea, and he took me to his studio, a large barn filled with instruments—guitars, keyboards, drums. It was a candy store for a musician. He started to play me demos for his new album and ask me what I thought, but I was in no way ready to tell Jon Bon Jovi how to make anything better. I danced to the music and enjoyed myself, went back to the heliport and home, satisfied. It was a great introduction to the caliber of talent I would be working with on my new job. I had worked with stars before, but nobody like Jon Bon Jovi. He sells out stadiums, owns a football team. He is a very well-off rock star who isn't drunk or on drugs, hasn't aged one year, still the perfect twenty-eight-inch waist, rich as hell, and smart as they come. I saw what I'd signed up for.

When it came to his album, I wasn't intimately involved, as I was with Mariah, but I listened to the work in progress and made my comments. I had to teach myself how to relate to Bon Jovi's arena rock—at first I didn't know how those songs came to be or what the magic was. We put together a marketing plan and blasted that frowny-face all over London, Paris, and the rest of the world. The album sold more than two hundred thousand copies the week it was released in September 2005, the band's highest first-week sales ever.

Our hip-hop was killing it. Our pop music was on fire, our rock music going through the roof. Mariah Carey was back, bigger than ever. Jay Z reigned as president of Def Jam, and things were rolling. It was time to remodel my office.

16

KINGDOM
COME

With the doubters silenced thanks to Jay Z and the label turning out hits, I was able to refocus my attention and my passion where they belonged: with the artists. Over the years, the way I worked had changed dramatically. I no longer spent much time in the studio, and even when I did, I was often on the phone. I spent more time in meetings than in sessions. But working with the brilliant Jay Z alone quickly proved to be an education, a daily postgraduate seminar that redefined what it meant to develop talent and cultivate hits. You may have heard about how he went from dealing drugs on the street to being a superstar rapper, but when you meet Jay Z, you meet a gentleman, a complete artist, and a businessman. But as open as I was to new ideas, I had no idea how our partnership would challenge my notions of making hit records or how complicated my life would become.

As Jay Z and I both settled into a rhythm of looking for new talent and new producers, one of my first signings at Def Jam, Ne-Yo, began to emerge as a star. I'd actually signed Ne-Yo before I hired Jay Z, but at the time, Ne-Yo wasn't desperate to have a recording contract. He had already been signed to Columbia Records under the name Shaffer Smith, which is his birth name, and it hadn't worked out so well for him. He concentrated instead on songwriting. He wrote the 2004 number one hit "Let Me Love You" for the R&B singer Mario, and he was writing for a few different artists when he came to audition. He played me a couple of his songs, but when he stood up to perform one of them, I knew he was a natural. He was a very smooth R&B singer and had great dance moves. I told the A&R person who brought him in that I wanted him on Def Jam.

This all had gone down shortly after I first took over, when the label had been in a whirlwind. I didn't have my team in place and was scrambling to get the operation on its feet. I left Ne-Yo alone for a while, but kept his audition tape.

Later, after the team had been assembled and Jay Z was on board, I asked some of the artists we had signed to come into the office, not to audition again, but to refresh our recollections. Ne-Yo went to Jay Z's office, where the A&R staff had been assembled. He was every bit as good as he had been that first day. I asked which A&R person wanted to handle the account, thinking Shakir would stand up, but one of Jay Z's guys raised his hand. I always assign projects to the A&R executive who is enthusiastic. Once they started working together, Jay's guy started to bring me songs to hear. When he brought me "So Sick," I couldn't believe my ears. It sounded instantly like a number one record to me. I made him play it again immediately and danced around his office, singing the words I knew by heart after hearing it once. I listened to it all day.

With Ne-Yo, I had the right artist with the right presence, because whatever he did, it came from him. He had lived it and you could feel the sincerity. With pop music, the most important trick is to convince the audience that the singer is the song, that the song is about him, that he has lived the song, whether or not he actually wrote the song. Everything Ne-Yo did, he made real.

I realized I had not only a very good singer with a future hit record, but I also had a skillful A&R man—our team was working. We hooked up Ne-Yo with these Norwegian songwriters who called themselves Stargate, whom I had never worked with before, and it turned out they were guys who could be the anchoring producers for our label, like Dallas Austin was for LaFace. I closely supervised every cut, and, when they were done, we put together a four-song sampler with a cover message from Jay Z and me and distributed it to radio, deejays, press, and other tastemakers, hoping to build up a buzz before the release. We put out the first single, "Stay," to radio—we were saving "So Sick" for the surefire second single.

One night a couple of weeks before the album was due, I was having dinner with some of my staff and holding a debate about whether anybody knew the Ne-Yo album was coming. I stopped the waiter and asked him if he had heard of Ne-Yo. He not only knew Ne-Yo, but knew when the album was due and what it was called. When the album, *In My Own Words*, dropped in February 2006, it sold an astonishing three hundred thousand copies the first week, unbelievable coming from a brand-new artist. Ne-Yo struck a nerve. It was high-quality music, powerful songs, perfect production, and sincere, emotional vocal performances. The sampler had resonated. It was the first time Jay Z and I had put our names on something together, and people had paid attention.

Jay was critically aware of the power of association. As you define your brand as an artist or record executive, association matters. That was a point of view that I hadn't paid much attention to before, but Jay Z understood. And after a few months of working with him, I came to understand too. One time, Jay came to an audition for a little boy group I had already signed.

"LA," he said, "if this band has a hit and they're invited to the Grammys, will you sit next to them?"

"No," I said.

"Then they shouldn't have been signed," he said.

Jay was my protector, in a way, keeping me honest and making sure that I was focusing on the right thing: the quality of the music. He provided a balance; we both wanted to find success and discover new stars, but we came at this process from different angles. Because he always had a clear point of view and never hesitated to express himself to me, I quickly came to appreciate his perspective and combine that kind of thinking with my own.

While Jay Z and I worked well together, there was a lot that we did independently, especially my work with individual artists like Lionel Richie. I may not have had the Clive Davis touch at revitalizing once celebrated careers, but I had learned enough from my missteps with Whitney and Aretha at Arista to give Lionel his biggest hit since his popular peak with "Dancing on the Ceiling." I had met Lionel early in my career, shortly after we all moved to Atlanta, when I'd visited his home in Bel-Air. And even though it was still early days for me, he couldn't have been more gracious.

"The fact that you're here in my house says that you must be on your way," he said. "Congratulations in advance on your success." Charismatic and warmhearted, he meant that in only the nicest way.

We had been friends ever since, and when I landed at Island Def Jam, Lionel called to say that what I had done with my career reminded him of Berry Gordy and his time at Motown. With Lionel signed to the label, this would be our first chance to work together. He always made straightforward pop records and I suggested something different. I thought we should make a black album. He hadn't cut a decidedly black album since he had been with the Commodores.

With an established artist, the trick is to find the entry point. Lionel had been making pop records for so long—singing "Endless Love" with Diana Ross, writing "Lady" for Kenny Rogers—he had lost touch with his roots. One of the important parts of making a record is to know your target audience. You can't boil the entire ocean in a day. You need to focus on who you are actually making the record for. I wanted Lionel to let his core black audience know they were important to him.

Lionel told me that when he did the Essence Festival in New Orleans, one of his old fans came up to him. "When you're doing the pop stuff, you're Lionel," the man said, "but down here at the Essence Fest you're Lion-El."

I felt so strongly about reconnecting Lionel to the black audience I flew to Atlanta in July 2006 with his first single, "I Call It Love," and personally delivered the record to V–103 radio.

"This you have to play," I said. "I'm not some promotion guy pushing seven records. This is Lionel Richie, this is a very important record. I want to make a statement. I want the black audience to know that Lionel Richie has made a record for them."

We got the record on the black stations and it went all the way to number one on the black charts. We sold almost five hundred thousand albums, a substantial amount of records for Lionel to sell, and an outcome that everyone was quite satisfied with.

Despite successes like these, there were times that I struggled with the scope of the job in front of me. If Arista had expanded the scale of my operation, then Island Def Jam brought it to even greater heights. There were more artists, more genres, more styles, more hits, more covers, and figuring out what I needed to be involved with and what I could step away from was a challenge. Sometimes juggling everything proved too much, and unfortunately, there were consequences. I was moving at such supersonic speed that I became impatient with talent, something that had never happened to me in the past, which is how I lost Lady Gaga.

When I had signed Lady Gaga in April 2006, she was a complete unknown, all blond hair and thigh-high white go-go boots. She'd come into my office, pounded the piano, and sang her songs with such incredible passion, I was swept away. That energy and fire was there already, she just didn't have the sound yet. What she played me was along the lines of classic piano rock, Elton John, Billy Joel—powerful and emotional music, but not what we would think of today as her brand of pop. She looked outrageous, but she hadn't fully developed her famous character; her show business persona hadn't emerged. She didn't have the package tied together, but I could see that once she did, she was going to have it all. There was something about this girl that looked more than a bit like the star she would become. I told her that not only did I want to sign her, but that I believed she would change music.

Three months later, her A&R man brought me the demo tapes they had been making and I wondered what I had been thinking. When she played live in my office, I was taken by her voice—the tone and the emotion—and how she played the piano. On tape, though, she sounded static, ordinary, missing all those qualities that I had heard the first time. They were songs, but at that point, not great songs. Much like when she'd auditioned, her musical style remained undefined, only now she seemed to have lost that fire and passion that had drawn me to her in the first place.

The character I'd originally sensed in the room with me was nowhere to be found on the tape, her presence was missing. She was still building the vision. And if I weren't so impatient, all I had to do was nothing. But I wanted everything to be ready and served up for me—as it had been with artists like Avril and Pink, who'd brought such a clear point of view to their music and expression. Lady Gaga hadn't reached that point by the time I saw her, and I couldn't see past a tape that didn't have hits. Given a bit more time, she would have solidified that vision for herself much as Avril and Pink had, and everything would have fallen into place; instead, I dropped her from the label—the biggest mistake of my career. I had completely forgotten that I had I told her I thought she would change music, but when I spoke with her again—later, much later, too much later—long after she scored her hits and was officially Lady Gaga, she reminded me of what I'd said.

Why didn't I push her? I should have told her what I thought because she might have gone back and done what she ended up doing. I was spread thin at the time and perhaps looking too hard for instant success rather than putting in the work. I wanted the greatness to simply appear, and, when it didn't, I should have made the time and done the work. I'd spent years working with artists, learning how to guide them to the kind of vision they'd need for success, learning how to give talent the kind of support and incubation they needed to make hit records—it was something I'd come to pride myself on. But with as many as six other artists on my plate and the running of the label to look after, I didn't have much left of myself to give, and I quit on her when I should have doubled my efforts.

Jimmy Iovine eventually signed her and, of course, experienced tremendous success—she did change music—but she always credits being dropped by the label as the key event in focusing her drive in her career. It was nowhere but up for her from there, and she left me behind.

W hile there were numerous things competing for my attention that clouded my judgment about Lady Gaga, the biggest distraction at the time may have been that I was deeply involved with the upcoming Jay Z album—the first I had worked on with him—and I wanted to make sure that every aspect was handled in the right way.

The album had actually begun in the most unexpected of ways: with a movie soundtrack opportunity. Though I'd used movie soundtracks to launch artists like Toni Braxton and Usher, it had been years since I thought about using a soundtrack as a venue for an established artist. But when Kathy Nelson, the music supervisor for the Ridley Scott film *American Gangster* starring Denzel Washington, sent me a treatment, I read it with great care.

As I read through the description of the film, I recognized striking parallels to an artist I knew well. I walked into Jay Z's office and said, "I have an idea."

When we first met, Jay Z had retired from performing and recording. He did his next album, *Kingdom Come*, in 2006 entirely by himself. We held a few collaborative conversations, but *Kingdom Come* was all of his own doing. This marked the first time I'd gone to Jay Z with a creative idea for one of his albums.

Since we'd begun working together, our different approaches to making music had become a fascinating source of debate and discussion for both of us. More and more during our frequent and expansive talks about our philosophies of music, Jay Z made it clear he saw music as a social force, a means of expression and a vital avenue of communication, a far broader view than simply watching the chart numbers and sales figures. He respected my success with hit singles, but he didn't see hits as the be-all and end-all of his work. He understood that there was more than entertainment to music and often pushed me to think about the art behind it. Given how I'd gotten started in the music business, these were all things that I'd known once, but over the years, I had lost touch with them in my constant pursuit of hits.

For *American Gangster*, I started by telling him about this movie, the true story of Frank Lucas and his life as one of the biggest drug dealers. "It's a period piece," I said, "so the soundtrack has to be authentic. How about you make an album that's inspired by the movie and we'll call it the same title, *American Gangster*. We'll use the same key art. It's a platform for you to tell your story about your life before you became Jay Z, the rapper."

As an artist, Jay Z couldn't keep telling the same story over and over. This would give him a way to, once and for all, tell his story of his life as a gangster. In bringing him the idea for *American Gangster*, I was asking him to do something that I actually had learned from him: to make music that was important, to move people for a higher purpose—in this case, to tell a story that was incredibly personal to him. He loved the idea and agreed to it immediately, before he read the treatment or saw the art. All he knew was that the man's name was Frank Lucas.

It was a very short conversation and Jay Z went into production on the record. After a few weeks of work, he called me into the studio to listen. "I think I have something," he said.

I loved what I heard. I didn't hear a big hit, but I loved that, for the first time in my career, I wasn't working on an album with the idea of having a hit single. Jay Z reminded me of the value of music with meaning, and it was eye-opening.

He pulled together a genuine Rat Pack moment with the video for "Roc Boys," which he shot at his 40/40 club with P. Diddy, Rick Ross, Nas, all the hottest rappers. I don't usually attend video shoots, but this was not something I would have missed.

The album went platinum, but it wasn't designed to have a number one single—it was a concept album. In fact, we were so convinced of the unified nature of the work, we told iTunes we didn't want them to sell individual tracks, only the full piece. When they refused, we took the album off iTunes. Jay Z wouldn't stand for that—he wanted people to experience the body of work, and anything less was not acceptable. That's the beauty of Jay—no desperation. He wants to make money more than anybody, but he will not sacrifice the art in the process.

As sweet as the success was, on a personal level perhaps the best thing about this partnership went beyond the album's sales. After working together on this and seeing Jay Z put his ideas about art and music into practice, we understood each other in a way we hadn't previously. Until then, it had all been abstract conversations about art and creation. Now we had a better understanding of where each side was coming from.

With Jay Z, every day you feel proud to be working with him. Every day is a good day. Every day is a lesson learned. Jay and I would have three- or four-hour conversations in which we would shut the world out and dream out loud. The real payday was to be able to spend time with someone who is that brilliant, that artistic, that strategic, so in touch with himself and reality. Many stars live behind gates. They become delusional and out of touch. That will never happen to Jay Z. He stays surrounded by people who knew him before he was Jay Z. Too self-aware, too smart, too grounded.

Working with him solidified ideas about the relationship between art and commerce that would help me in the future as I continued to refine my approach with other artists. In *American Gangster*, I saw that priorities didn't always have to dictate the outcome—that music with a purpose could be successful specifically because it has that purpose. While this idea didn't remove the pressure or interest I had in finding hits, it did show me a new way to give an artist the flexibility he needed to create.

If *American Gangster* gave me a new perspective on making art, then Mariah Carey's next album reminded me of what got me to where I was in the first place—the hits. Jay Z can command an audience with *American Gangster* because he is a rapper. Mariah is a pop singer—she needs a single. And after the success of *The Emancipation of Mimi*, I felt pressure coming up with the next Mariah Carey album to find that single and more.

It's not that I hadn't followed up big hit albums before, but I worried that *The Emancipation of Mimi* had been such a phenomenon that it might be the comeback that couldn't be topped. I didn't question Mariah and I didn't have any sort of shaky confidence. I never vacillated in my belief in her as an artist, but I did wonder if the comeback thing had been a fluke, and I had very little experience with stars who had already been established and how to keep them growing and achieving. I'm not a renovator—I build from the ground up.

I stayed very close to Mariah during the recording of our second record together. I wasn't there for all the writing sessions, but I'd listen often to the songs, and while I did like the songs I was hearing, in my mind I worried if they were as good as the songs on *The Emancipation of Mimi*. She kept bringing me demos. We kept working. We'd have late-night sessions at her house, the studio, or my house. We spent hours listening. Benny Medina was still her manager and fully involved, but everything about this album felt different. With *The Emancipation of Mimi*, every song they brought me was better than the last. This time, every time they brought me a song, I wondered if it was as good as I thought it was. I never heard that big song I wanted.

I was on my annual Christmas trip to St. Barts in 2007 when Mariah called and said she wanted to bring some presents by for me and my family. She happened to be in Aspen, Colorado, at the moment, kind of a long way from the Caribbean, but she chartered two jets for her and her traveling party and flew in the next day. She kept calling along the way to say she was coming. She took a boat to St. Barts. By midnight, everybody had gone to bed except for me and Shakir, who waited up for her with me. Shakir was quite frustrated ("What are we waiting for? Why is she taking so long?"). She finally showed up around two thirty in the morning, trailing packages of expensive, generous gifts for everybody like Santa's sexy helper. We opened a bottle of champagne and toasted the holiday. "Do you want to hear the album?" she asked.

She slid a CD into the player and the first song to thunder through the speakers was "Touch My Body." In an instant, all my doubts and concerns vanished. I realized my problem had been that I couldn't let go of *The Emancipation of Mimi*. All I needed was to hear a hit. There it was, "Touch My Body." We spent the rest of the night listening to the whole album, but I was done worrying after I heard the single. We said goodnight at dawn and I went to bed buzzing.

Tinkering around on the piano with my main man, Shakir, in Vegas

She left the CD with me, and the next morning, first thing, instead of going to the gym, I went straight back to the stereo and played that record again. I watched my family all morning, as I played it over and over, like an instant focus group. My daughter, Arianna, is the biggest Mariah fan. She learned to play

"We Belong Together" on piano when she was three years old. When Arianna started singing along, I knew that we had what we needed.

Mariah writes prolifically and she has written or cowritten almost every one of her record number of number one hits. People don't think of Mariah as this extraordinary songwriter, but she is. She doesn't tour often, so she gives herself a lot of freedom and a lot of time to be creative. I realized that I had been holding on to *The Emancipation of Mimi*, but I finally got past it and I was able to sink into her new album, which she gave the genius title $E=MC^2$. And I did hear a hit. "Touch My Body" went straight to the top, and the album quickly followed to number one. So much for my sophomore jinx with Mariah.

As things grew busier and more complicated with the label, I tried to keep my personal life as straightforward as I could. These were emotional and rewarding times for me and my family, as we adjusted to life in the big city and felt New York City closing around us. We lived in a condo on Park Avenue, as opposed to the mansion in Atlanta, and, as we came together in New York, the experience brought our growing family much-needed structure and stability. In 2001, Erica had given birth to our daughter, Arianna, and two years later, in 2003, our son Addison was born. My stepdaughter, Ashley, came to New York at the same time to study photography at the School of Visual Arts. Aaron had stayed in Atlanta with his mother when I first moved to New York, but he eventually came to New York to live with us too.

When Aaron was a teenager, he was highly resourceful and a little star in his own mind. Living in New York, he was a social guy, got to know everybody. He pitched MTV about doing their show *My Super Sweet 16*, in which spoiled rich kids put on extravagant, indulgent celebrations for their sixteenth birthday. The MTV people loved the idea. When he came to me with the project, I didn't feel good about it.

"I really hate this idea," I told him. "It's like a reality show. You're going to put your family on television. It's a lot of exposure. I don't know, Aaron."

I quickly changed my mind when those big beautiful eyes turned sad and brokenhearted. He had put this deal together on his own. He wanted his rock star moment. I couldn't stand in his way.

A family affair, with Erica, Arianna, Addison, and Aaron at Hampton Classic, Bridgehampton, New York

Having fun with Arianna and Addison

They filmed him for a couple of months, at school, with his friends, planning the party. He put together a clever invitation, an audio greeting in an MP3 player. He came to me for help finding a venue and I asked Jay Z if we could rent his 40/40 Club. Jay gave me the club. I asked Kanye West to do me a favor and perform at my son's sixteenth birthday party for this MTV show. Rihanna was there. Aaron's godfather P. Diddy presented him with a gold Cartier watch and also did a number. Jermaine Dupri deejayed. Aaron arrived in a Rolls Royce Phantom wearing a white fur coat.

The show was a huge success; it ran through many repeat airings after the original broadcast in April 2006, and Aaron became quite the little star. He signed autographs. Kids came up and took photos of Aaron one Saturday afternoon in East Hampton, completely ignoring me and Usher, who was hanging out with us. At the Super Bowl that year, three young girls ran up to me, all excited. "Oh my god," said one. "You're Aaron Reid's father."

On one hand, it made me chuckle, but on the other, it kind of got to me. It might sound petty, but it touched a nerve because, in truth, I was struggling a bit with not getting recog-

At Aaron's graduation with family friend Ray Finley, Addison, and Antonio

nized for what I'd accomplished. A part of me had begun to worry that perhaps I was fated for a behind-the-scenes role in life. It had been like that for me all along. Babyface's partner, Pebbles's husband, Usher's producer, and now, Aaron's father. Even as chairman of Island Def Jam, I took a backseat to Jay Z. I was still itching to leave my mark in some definitive way on the music business and have my deeds acknowledged. I had to over-come criticism and doubt when I took over both Arista and Def Jam, and even after I turned out massive hits at both companies, I did not feel the respect I'd earned.

For basically my entire adult life, I had experienced nothing but success in the music business. My fingerprints were on some of the biggest records of the day, but I did not feel that my recog-nition matched my accomplishments. I rejected the notion that executives needed to be invisible. I was happy with my success, I loved making hits, but I wanted something more, which caused some vague dissatisfaction to stir in me.

For the most part, I was able to ignore this feeling, especially given everything that was going on around me. The hectic na-ture of work only grew in January 2008 after Jay Z didn't renew his contract. It had been an ongoing negotiation to get him to renew with Def Jam, and we'd hoped that he would stay, but ul-timately Jay decided to leave. He had a big deal on the table with Live Nation, so he had options, which he was always very forth-right about. He was transparent with me the entire time, and when we weren't able to make a deal to renew, I was clear why. There was no big moment. There was no dramatic confronta-tion. We talked all the time, and though I was disappointed, I understood.

None of this caught me off guard. We used to discuss his ambitions beyond the record business—to manage pro athletes, produce tours, sponsor festivals, explore other avenues of ex-tending the brand into the world of entertainment. Long before they were called that, Jay was dreaming up 360 deals. He and his partners decided to start a more wide-ranging talent management group, Roc Nation, and when it came to Def Jam, he felt he had done what he came to do and it was time to move on. There were no fights or animosity. He simply wanted to do something else.

After Jay left the company, I thought about a few different possible replacements, but, in truth, I didn't find anybody qualified to step into those shoes and I didn't replace him. I did the job myself. At that point, I had graduated from the Jay Z school of higher education. I promoted Shakir Stewart, who was already a senior vice president of A&R, bumping him up to executive vice president of A&R. While some people thought that he was Jay Z's replacement, he wasn't. Shakir was many things, but I didn't want to put that kind of pressure on him. I had come to rely on him in so many other important ways.

Since joining me at Def Jam, Shakir's skills as an A&R man only continued to grow. In 2006, while we were vacationing together with our families in St. Tropez, he played me a record called "Hustlin'" by a rapper named Rick Ross. It was such a definitive record, I didn't need to audition him or even meet with him. I just relied on another great record man and his recommendation and Shakir signed him. His first album, *Port of Miami*, sold an amazing 187,000 copies the first week and blasted its way to number one on the charts.

Still, not long after I promoted him, I began to notice that Shakir was changing. I first became aware of his problems on a trip to Las Vegas. In February 2008, he'd signed a girl group called Electrik Red and we went to listen to the album with producers Tricky and The-Dream at the studio where they were recording. We used to go to Vegas to gamble and Shakir would pop so much shit to the dealers and the waitresses, he would draw a crowd wherever he was gambling. On the plane to Vegas this time, he caught a text about something—I never knew what—and I saw him go dark. After the plane landed, he told me he couldn't stay.

"I've got something I've got to deal with," he said. "I've got to go."

He went back to Atlanta—he had never moved out of Atlanta, although he kept an apartment in New York—and I listened to the album without him, which was a downer, since he was the executive producer. But the next time I saw him, things weren't right with him. He seemed like he was trying to be the person that he had been, a strange kind of imitation of the guy I knew. Something was troubling him. I never knew what it was.

That year, Halloween fell on a Friday. We always held a costume contest at work and everybody—everybody except me, that is—would dress up in a silly costume and the employees would vote on who won the prize. Shakir came into my office and sat down. Nervous and fidgety—his hands were shaking—he kept trying to tell me something. He was moving his mouth, opening it like he wanted to say something, then he'd close it again, unable to get the words out. He looked like he was exhausting himself trying to say something that he couldn't get out.

I was concerned. Everything raced through my head. Is somebody bothering him? Does he have some pressure I don't know about? Are there financial issues? What the hell is this? He left my office without saying anything. Later I went to his office, where I found him staring off into space, and tried to hold a conversation.

"Whatever's bothering you, let it go," I said. "Take a break. Just let it go. You can take a break. We're fine. You're doing fine, I got your back, there's nothing to worry about. If you need some time, take some time."

He simply shook his head and I went back to work. A few hours later, I reached him on his cell phone and asked him if he wanted to go to Mariah Carey's masquerade party with me. He met me at the office, and as we drove downtown to the club, he seemed more at ease than he had been earlier. We listened to some music—he loved Morris Day and the Time; in fact, Shakir had conceived Electrik Red as a modern-day, all-girl version of the Time. At the party, he appeared relaxed, subdued, a little quiet, but at least he could talk. We drove back to my place together, listening to Prince, and shook hands as I left the car.

"That shit is jammin'," he said.

"I'll talk to you tomorrow," I said.

That was the last time I saw him.

The next day, Saturday, my son Antonio called me from Atlanta. "Dad, I have to tell you something," he said. "It's bad, Dad, it's bad. Shakir just shot himself in the head."

"What? Is he alive?" I said.

"No, Dad. He's not."

I broke down, started making calls, calls started coming in. I phoned his girlfriend Michelle and she couldn't speak. Neither could I. We both just sat there unsure of what to say.

I'd never looked to Shakir the way I'd looked to Babyface—they'd occupied different roles and had done different things for me—but it wasn't until that moment that I realized how much he'd come to fill that role as my partner in crime. More than that, though, he was my best friend.

I'm not fast to have friends. I don't open up to people. I don't tell people much about myself and I don't ask much about them. I'm not sure I know how to be a good friend. But I was a friend to Shakir and he was a friend to me. I never knew what happened, and how can you make sense of something like that anyway? Whatever his problems were, he kept them hidden from me. To this day, I miss him.

The loss was devastating—the darkest point of my life. I couldn't go to work and stayed home day after day. Every five minutes or so, I'd break down crying. I was fucked up, confused, angry. Then I started hearing word that people were pointing their fingers at me because they said I put too much pressure on him. That made me angry for an entirely different set of reasons. I had just lost my best friend, my company had lost a superstar executive, the industry had lost a leader, and his two children had lost their father.

I was still stuck in my house when Jay Z called. It was a warm, heartfelt conversation. He urged me to read a book called *The Seat of the Soul* by Gary Zukav. I must have read that book faster and with more focus than I've ever read any book, and I understood why Jay recommended it. The author explains that at the core of our bodies, we are simply carriers of souls, and though the body may die, that energy is never lost. Even though his loss left behind a gaping hole in my life, I felt better knowing that Shakir was still out there.

I had to find the strength to do what I love. I had to pick myself up and get back to work. Shakir and I used to think of ourselves as Shaolin monks. We used to talk about going into "monk mode"—it was something only between the two of us— and we always said that we would have our greatest success when we were in monk mode. I went into monk mode, which meant that I worked out harder in the gym, tried to eat better, tried to take better care of myself, to be more focused and able to work even harder because I knew that the road ahead would be much tougher and more complex than anything I'd encountered before. I needed to be strong—even stronger now that I'd learned the hardest lesson of all.

17

MY BEAUTIFUL DARK TWISTED REALITY

One afternoon in October 2008, Usher called me at Island Def Jam. Though we hadn't worked together since I'd left Arista, we remained close and spoke all the time. Over the years as he'd gotten older, ours had become much more of a friendship—especially since he was on a different label. He even still lived in my old home in Country Club of the South—a house that when he'd first entered at age fourteen, he'd looked around and announced, "Someday I'm going to own this." Damned if he didn't buy the place six years later.

As I'd tried to recover from Shakir's suicide, Usher and I talked quite a bit, and though those first weeks and months getting back on the job had been difficult, support from people like Usher had made the difference. By the time I got the call from Usher that day in the fall of 2008, I was finally beginning to feel like myself again—both at home and at work—using music to bring me back to how all this began. While I had learned a lot about making art from Jay Z, and I now thought much more about the transformative power of music, as I came back from these dark times what I needed most was something catchy and familiar, something that would make me look to the future instead of the past. What I really needed was a new star.

As Usher and I spoke on the phone, he asked if I was going to be in my office all afternoon because he had something he wanted to bring me. We often exchanged gifts, so I had no idea what to expect. Was he bringing me another painting or what? He told me to expect him at four o'clock.

At four on the dot, Usher walked into my office with this adorable fourteen-year-old boy. This kid was beautiful, like a woman can be beautiful and men rarely are, and he turned it on as soon as he stepped into the room. No one introduced him—he just sat down at the piano and started singing, then he took out his guitar and sang some more. He talked a little bit, almost like it was a nightclub act or something—punctuating his performance with pieces of conversation and storytelling before returning to pounding a rhythm on the desk and singing along. I looked over at Usher and gave him a silent "Whoa!"

"This is Justin Bieber," Usher said.

Fifteen years before, Usher had been the fourteen-year-old standing in front of my desk, and here he was now, an elder statesman of the tribe, the superstar I'd glimpsed all those years before in my office at LaFace, standing there with another kid almost the exact same age as Usher had been when he first met me. Usher didn't just bring me a kid with an amazing voice, he brought me a born entertainer, someone who would become the biggest of them all. When Usher said he had a gift, he wasn't kidding.

I always knew that if you left the door open and the lights on, something great will walk into your office. That's the day it became true. Justin had already started to become famous on YouTube. He built a fan base by putting up videos of himself doing all these classic R&B songs by artists like Ne-Yo and Boyz II Men. I knew what to do.

"I'd like to sign him right away," I said. "The sooner the better."

Since he was a minor, it took a couple of days to get his parents involved and signed off. Justin's manager was an Atlanta-based gentleman I had never met before, Scooter Braun, who discovered Justin from the YouTube videos Justin had posted. Within a week of bringing him to Atlanta, Scooter had Justin singing for Usher.

The next time Scooter and Justin turned up at my office, Justin had grown his hair down almost covering his eyes—a catchy look that was all his own. As with Avril Lavigne's under-shirt, and TLC and the condoms, I always looked for artists who could turn their style into a hook, but I was especially interested in hair. Hairstyles had done a lot for artists I had worked with as

A gift from Usher—the day we signed Justin Bieber, with Usher and manager Scooter Braun

diverse as Toni Braxton and Pink, and I could see immediately that Justin's hair would be every bit as important as his songs, his voice, his face, or his presence. It might not have been an intentional hairstyle, just that he hadn't had his hair cut in a while, but I knew right at that moment that when this guy hit the marketplace, kids were going to soon be wearing their hair like his. That boy had a hit haircut.

Justin was simply beautiful—his superpower was his face. But his hair and his appearance were only part of his charm. Justin had all this natural charisma that instantly transformed him into his own character. Whereas other artists had to work to develop the persona that they wanted to project, he was loveable and lively from the start, radiating personality.

As I listened to what he was working on in the studio, I was delighted to hear all those pieces I'd been impressed with in person coming through on the recording as well. I loved the demos, especially one song called "One Time" that we got from Tricky, which I knew would be our first single.

On the album, we took Justin more R&B than pop, taking off from the kind of songs he was singing on his YouTube videos. He was a natural-born blue-eyed soul singer, and I've always known they can have extraordinary impact, long before I recorded Pink. We didn't want him crooning and we did include pop songs on the album, but we cast him as an R&B singer. I heard this one song, "U Smile" and immediately wanted it for Justin. Unfortunately, the song belonged to another artist named Musiq Soulchild on Atlantic Records. The song had been written during an Atlantic writing camp, so Atlantic clearly outright owned this song. I didn't give a damn. I did everything I had to do to acquire the rights. I spoke to everyone I knew at Atlantic and basically bought the song for Justin.

In part because of Justin's age, but also because his YouTube videos had given him such a strong online fan base, we knew from the start that this record release was going to have a different look and feel to it—we had to figure out how to turn his age into an asset. When we put out the record in July 2009, we didn't get a ton of radio traction—even though it had been years since Usher first came onto the scene, the stigma against teenage artists was still there. Radio needed to be coaxed to put Justin's record on the air because his voice sounded so young that program directors thought he was more appropriate for Disney radio or Nickelodeon. Kids sound like kids, and radio doesn't like that, so we didn't get a lot of instant radio airplay. But Scooter took Justin on a promotional tour, visiting radio stations, and every time they went to a radio station, the crowd at the station would get bigger and bigger. Scooter and I developed a relationship. He would call and tell me there were thirty kids waiting at the station, and the next week he would call and say there were seventy-five.

In addition to the growing crowds, the video for "U Smile" became an instant hit online, encouraging us to keep using that medium to get Justin out there. On the album, Tricky and The-Dream had come up with a song they called "Baby Baby Baby," which we shortened to "Baby." As soon as I heard the song, I knew we would have a runaway smash. At the label, there was some controversy over the choice of the song as the next single. A couple of the executives didn't think it was the right song. I looked at them like they were crazy, but I was learning to defer to my staff, so I may have allowed the discussion to continue further along than I would have otherwise. One of the other executives settled the matter.

"I only want to know what *you* think the single is," she said, speaking to me. "I didn't come to work here for what anyone else thinks except you."

We made a video for "Baby" and the track blew straight to number one on iTunes when it was released in January 2010, where it ruled for weeks. The video turned into the biggest music video in YouTube history, with more than a billion plays. This kid, Justin Bieber, was simply an instant phenomenon at that point. Girls went wild. It was Biebermania. These kids went mad for this guy. Everywhere he went, mobs. No artist got more media scrutiny. Everything about him was amplified. Justin coughed, they said he's got pneumonia.

The more Justin built social media into his approach, the more his persona took on a new life. Justin and Scooter were a couple of the first artists to use Twitter, which he used to announce an in-store appearance at a kids clothing store on Long Island called Justice. The day of the event, Justin kept tweeting, "I'm on my way." The more he tweeted, the more people showed up at this mall. The place was packed with kids, thousands of them. The crowd grew impolite and police got nervous. They decided to close the mall and arrested the Def Jam sales representative Jim Roppo. Justin, by the way, never showed up.

Biebermania outside the premiere of Never Say Never *in Los Angeles*

It was Friday afternoon and the banks were closed. The cops were taking my mild-mannered sales rep to jail. I got a call telling me all this while I was on my way to a meeting at Mariah Carey's penthouse. I borrowed whatever cash she had and gave it to my lawyer, who whisked over to spring Roppo before the weekend, but he was too late. Roppo spent the weekend in jail, so we made "Free Roppo" T-shirts. That incident was when we first realized how powerful the Justin Bieber phenomenon had become. And how powerful social media could be.

Justin arrived at the beginning of a new era. Social media had already caught on with his audience faster than it had with the record company marketing geniuses. By the time the Web-driven groundswell had built up behind Justin, radio was late to the game and could only play catch-up. He rewrote the radio-dominant playbook that had ruled pop music until that point. We were finding new avenues for artists to connect with an audience.

While at the time we were still understanding the implications for all this, looking back it's easy to see what a transformative moment this release was. Justin wasn't just a new pop star, he broke new ground. In some ways the release was as it always had been—videos, singles, radio—but with Justin we were able to elaborate on that longstanding blueprint in a unique way. His age gave us the opportunity to reach younger kids who weren't listening to the radio but were just starting out online. That's not to say that there hadn't been hits that had begun online before, but a convergence of factors in this moment made Justin the ideal figure to become the first pop star created largely by social media.

For one thing, his age, which before social media would have been a detriment, was part of his success. But more than that, he was one of the first artists who did not hesitate to meet his audience in their own space and on their own terms. Though now it feels commonplace, in 2008 there was a lot of resistance among artists—and their managers, agents, and record companies—when it came to sharing themselves online. At the label, we were still learning about it ourselves, but just like when we were working with an artist who had a vision for the music, we knew when to take a step back. Because he was the same age as these kids, Justin had none of that hesitation, and it fueled every part of his rise, the first real star to emerge from the other side of the digital domain.

Through it all, Justin remained the sweetest kid. He would come to my office and hang, shoot pool, play checkers or backgammon. He was a prankster and he would run around the office like a little boy. Everybody liked Justin. This tidal wave of success was all the more reassuring to me because, after my awful

Scooter, Justin, Pete Wentz, Kristinia DeBarge, and Kenny at Island Def Jam's Spring Collection at Stephen Weiss Studio

mistake of releasing Lady Gaga, Justin simply walked into my office ready to go. I felt a little vindicated (although if I hadn't dropped Lady Gaga, I would have had the two most successful artists of the time). Justin may have gotten started by playing his guitar on sidewalks in Toronto, but within a few months of signing with me he'd become the biggest star in the world.

By the time we sold a few million copies of his debut album, *My World*, Scooter announced Justin's first tour, and one of the first dates they put up for sale, Madison Square Garden, went clean in minutes. The entire tour sold out. He was the king of thirteen- and fourteen-year-old girls (and a few of their cougar mothers, too). I came up with the crazy idea of filming the Madison Square Garden shows for a concert movie. I could tell this was going to be a peak moment, and if Justin was going to be the Beatles, he needed his *Hard Day's Night*. Scooter didn't mind filming the shows, but he didn't like the idea of making a movie, because he thought too much would be riding on whether the movie was a success or not and he didn't want to take the risk. I understood his point of view, but didn't necessarily agree.

"Maybe you don't know how big your artist is," I told him.

I'd been around record industry success long enough to understand just how unique a situation this was. Justin was a bona fide teen scream sensation the scale of which I had never before witnessed: packed houses of crying, yelling girls, heavy security details, massive press coverage. I could see this was bigger than simply hit records—that was why we should make the movie. He went off like an atom bomb and I watched from ground zero. I knew that he had what it took to launch a movie, even if Scooter wasn't convinced.

We found some interest at Paramount Pictures—in fact, they got excited about making a movie with Justin Bieber. Scooter remained apprehensive, but I went ahead and set up a meeting at Paramount. Scooter could be the next David Geffen—that is how brilliant I think he is—but he was very reluctant to make this movie and wasn't too keen on meeting anybody. Always prompt at our previous meetings, Scooter showed up an hour late. Eventually I dragged him into the room and made a deal for the movie.

We drove up to Hartford, Connecticut, for the first date of the tour. Backstage, Justin was goofing around with video games and playing basketball. A year before, he was this little kid who came to my office and now he was headlining an arena tour with buses and trucks parked outside. And here he was backstage shooting baskets like any other kid his age.

We did a 3-D movie with director Jon M. Chu, shot concert footage over a couple of nights in August 2010 at Madison Square Garden. The kids knew every song on the album and sang along with every lyric. Justin's vocal performance was excellent and his stage presence was killer, but more than that, he was comfortable. He looked like he'd been doing it his entire life. Justin's mother had been shooting footage of Justin since he was a baby, which Chu skillfully edited into the concert action. We called the movie *Never Say Never*, and when it was released the following year, it went on to become a $100 million smash at the box office, still the largest-grossing concert film.

While Justin became a pop artist who successfully blurred the lines with R&B for the Island side, Rihanna experienced similar success with a sound that moved her from R&B to pop for Def Jam. I'd been watching pop and R&B change over the years, but it wasn't until Rihanna emerged as one of the biggest stars on the label that I came to see just how close to pop it had become and how oversimplified those old categories were.

After we'd signed Rihanna, Jay's more than capable A&R staff scored a sizable hit on her first album, "Pon de Replay," one of the songs she'd sang at her audition. After they started work on her second album, Jay's man Jay Brown came to my office and played me a demo of a song, "SOS," and I went crazy. That was about all I had to do with her second album, but once that record hit, I paid close attention. I told the A&R people I wanted to hear every song. Before I would have listened to her records only after they were done, but I sensed that she was on the brink, maturing as an artist and also as a person. By the time she went in to record her third album, I saw the opportunity to lift Rihanna to a new level in her career, and with a massive breakthrough only around the corner, she and I started to develop a relationship based on mutual respect and trust.

For her third album, Tricky Stewart and his writing partner, The-Dream, brought us "Umbrella," a song they'd originally envisioned for Britney Spears until her label rejected the number. They'd also shown it to Mary J. Blige, but the minute Karen

With Rihanna at my Grammy dinner party at Cecconis, Los Angeles

Kwak brought the song to me, I knew it was perfect for Rihanna. I had to fight to get the song, but I made them an offer they couldn't refuse. Jay Z added a memorable rap to the recording and the song topped the charts for seven straight weeks after it was released in March 2007.

Our relationship really blossomed after "Umbrella." Rihanna started coming to my office and we would discuss her follow-up. Now that she was officially a superstar, she began to make decisions about her career, communicating more with me about music. From that point forward, I challenged her, and we gradually grew closer and closer, almost like a father-daughter relationship. She is an amazing talent with an extraordinary ear for songs and instinct for her music. One of the few international pop singers

since Bob Marley to sing in their native Caribbean dialect, she
has a powerful inflection that she doesn't hide. There's a freedom in her to live her life and express herself that is incredibly
rare, but the more I got to know her, the more I understood that
her excitement for life isn't limited to her art. She has the best
taste in everything—from wine to music—and always seems to
know what she wants.

I was sitting around my new house in the Hamptons with a
couple of my A&R people, smoking some weed and listening to
the new Rihanna album in the final stages. When we heard the
song "Good Girl Gone Bad," I knew I had found the title for her
album. I had no idea how ironic that would become.

Rihanna invited me to her concert at Staples Center and
played me a new song, "Disturbia," in her dressing room, which
I immediately knew would be a smash. We added the cut as a
bonus track to the repackaged *Good Girl Gone Bad* and rushed
it out as the next single. I was glad to see her take charge of her
own career and that she knew what a hit sounded like.

She was set to perform at the Grammys in February 2009.
The producer of the show reached me in my suite at the Beverly Hills Hotel the day before the Grammys. Rihanna had not
showed for the rehearsal, he told me. The next phone call came
from a publicist who worked for us. "Rihanna just had a car
accident," she said. "That's all I can tell you right now, but she's
in the hospital."

As it turned out it wasn't a car accident, it was her incident
with Chris Brown. I never knew much more about what happened than the public did. The details were kept from me. I saw
the photos of her battered face the same time everybody else did.
I managed to get through to Rihanna at the hospital, but it was
a brief conversation. I was able to voice some concern, which I
hoped was comforting, but I felt helpless. She was in bad shape
and embarrassed, and didn't want any visitors. All this was hap-

pening in her life at the point where she was moving beyond simply being a pop star with some hits into a lady the world cared about. It was tragic.

Several weeks later, her manager called to say Rihanna was coming to New York and wanted to see me, which somewhat surprised me. The fact that she was making my house her first stop in New York showed me that apparently our relationship was stronger than I had realized. It wasn't until then that I saw just how close we'd become.

Holding RiRi

She flew into town on a private jet, but the paparazzi still found her. She came straight to my apartment and they swarmed outside my building. I didn't ask her too much about what happened. We talked mostly about what her next career step would be. I ordered some Caribbean food and we listened to music. I played her a couple of demos, but there wasn't a lot of talk—most of our communication was telepathic. My only advice to her was to turn to music—it sounded cliché but that was what had gotten me through dark times. She stayed for hours. She already had her own A&R team—which I wasn't part of, although I was the head of the company. We decided to start working together more.

She had stayed at my house so long, I was late for a meeting with Bon Jovi at a private club up the street. I delicately extricated myself and told her to feel free to stay at my house after I left. Later, Erica told me she stayed another couple of hours.

Sometimes an artist needs help making art, sometimes an artist needs help making a hit, and sometimes an artist just needs help.

While Justin's and Rihanna's success reconfirmed everything about my pop music instincts, it was with Kanye West that I'd been able to continue to witness the artistry behind the music, culminating with the album that would become his masterpiece.

Not long after I took over as chairman of Island Def Jam, Kanye quickly became my favorite artist on the label. I had originally known him as a producer. We'd first met when I was the president of Arista Records and he was producing an artist we'd signed named Lupe Fiasco from Chicago. He came with Lupe for his audition, and after I agreed to sign the act, the A&R guy who brought them told me that Kanye was also looking for a record deal. Kanye ended up signing with the Roc-A-Fella label, where he served as house producer and was only reluctantly allowed to experiment with his own recordings. Throughout all of this, it was clear he had talent, but I wasn't sure that he was ready to step out in front of the mic.

That opinion changed quite a bit after our warm conversation at the Grammys the day I took over at Def Jam. Even though Kanye and I had held only a quick, simple discussion, this time, from those few words we exchanged, I could see he had the drive of somebody who was going to be a star. I had missed that completely at our first meeting. At first glance, Kanye wasn't someone you would expect to become one of the

With Doug Morris, Bieber, and Rihanna at the launch of Doug's brainchild VEVO, New York

most important artists of our time, mostly because he wasn't what you'd come to expect from hip-hop. He carried his beats in a Gucci backpack. He didn't wear the hip-hop uniform. He was a preppy fashionista. He wasn't ghetto. His mother raised him well and he went to college. His first album was called *The College Dropout*. He was a new breed of hip-hop.

With Kanye at the Soho Grand Hotel, New York

I got a copy of *The College Dropout* immediately upon joining Island Def Jam and listened to it constantly—in my car, my
hotel room, my apartment. It was an album that just stopped
me in my tracks—it was that good. He had a song called "Jesus
Walks" that took what was basically a straightforward declara-
tion of religious beliefs into the Top Twenty. It wasn't just some
crafty writing and production—it was the emergence of one of
the greats. Right from the start it was obvious that nobody was
better, nobody was on his level.

During the promotion and marketing of the first album, I got
to know Kanye more and I came to understand his vision for both
himself and his music with greater clarity. The first album was a hit
without me, but going forward, I got a chance to work closely with
him—his talent was obvious, and I wanted to do everything in
my power to support it. Kanye West was a brand-new artist at that
time, and with the company in transition, I didn't want his album
to get lost in the cracks. I spent time with Kanye and made sure
that the marketing team stayed involved, always preaching to them
that Kanye West was the greatest artist signed to the company—do
not fuck this up. Whatever he wants, give it to him. Those were my
instructions. If I did anything for Kanye West's career, it was more
when he wasn't in the room.

Honestly, much as I did with Jay Z, all I did was learn from
Kanye. I listened to him, I talked to him, I tried to give him
any information I could, but in truth, there wasn't much that he
needed from me when it came to the actual music. He always
had a clear sense of where he wanted to go and he looked for talent that would help him get there. Kanye used multiple producers throughout the time that I worked with him, and although
he was the primary producer, he used people like DJ Toomp,
Mike Dean, Jon Brion, No ID, and Jeff Bhasker—a guy who I
thought was one of the great producers, although his name isn't
particularly well known.

Riding with Kanye after his performance at Abbey Road, London

What made Kanye unique, though, was not the diverse list of producers that he worked with, but how willing he was to go beyond the limits of his own knowledge. When an artist is a producer and a performer and they're in the moment of their success, in the eye of the storm, so to speak, they don't usually look around for help. They don't look around for other producers, especially producers whose talents vary so widely from their own. Often they tend to get caught up in their own work instead of asking to hear what someone else thinks. Kanye West may have a public persona of being a very self-focused guy, but the truth about him is that Kanye is always searching for musical growth, always looking for new ideas.

When he makes records, for example, Kanye will have many

people come in and out of the room to contribute ideas. His sessions are always crowded, as he surrounds himself with creative people and pulls from these people, feeding off them. He wants to know their opinions and stays open-minded, collaborative. He edits or curates those ideas for his final records. The reason his music grows from record to record is because he allows the influence of other music people into the room. He doesn't live in a bubble, he doesn't write in a bubble, and he doesn't make his records in a bubble.

And then there's the actual energy he devotes—the man-hours that Kanye West puts into his music are probably unmatched. He is like Steely Dan that way, the pursuit of sonic perfection. He is always searching for a better beat, a better-sounding keyboard, a better lyric, a better chorus to the song. He makes three or four choruses to almost every song. He works at it. It's always a sound that determines when he's finished, because Kanye's sole interest lies in getting it right. I've heard different incarnations or iterations of his albums. They sound radically different from the time they start to the time they finish. The early demo tapes sound nothing like the finished product.

The first three albums represented his journey: *The College Dropout*, *Late Registration*, and *Graduation*. The next album in the progression was supposed to be *Good Ass Job*, but that never got made. Instead Kanye forged ahead into new directions and switched to *808s & Heartbreak*, drawing from his personal experience and the changes he was going through as a man. He started to sing and used autotune and other effects, he was making melodies—it wasn't traditional rap anymore. Sadly, his mom had passed away way too soon, and he put his heavy heart in his music. Our mothers had become friendly—I could understand his pain.

When I went to A&M Studios and sat in the control room and listened to some of the early tracks on *808s & Heartbreak*,

I couldn't believe he had come up with such an unpredictable album, and I was excited by his artistic growth and command. I gave him a speech.

"What you've done here is you've not only changed the course of Kanye, but you've also changed the course of music by doing this record," I said, "and you're going to see that you're no longer bound by the rules of hip-hop. You're now saying that you're going to take matters into your own hands and you're now going to do what you want to do creatively, and this album—I don't know if this is going to be thought of as your biggest album or your most important album, but I tell you what—for my taste, this is the album that defines you as a genius, because you're now doing what you do."

I paused for a moment, because I hadn't planned to launch into a monologue, but I knew that I wanted him to understand how special this was. I'd come to see myself as a protector and an advocate for Kanye, an incubator for his talent. "This isn't resembling what anyone else does. You've let go of all the rules, you've thrown away the crutches, and you're really walking on your own—and you're walking tall, my friend."

His response to all my compliments was a simple "Thank you." No proclamations about being the greatest or entitlement—he didn't act like my words were just stating the obvious. Despite how he's viewed by the public, there's a lot that people don't understand about him. I knew Kanye's mother, and he was raised well. The truth is, beneath the persona that Kanye projects, there is a sweet, insecure artist who is eager to prove that he works hard at being great. He's a student of design, and with that comes a meticulous, exacting nature that leads him to believe fully in the art he's creating, sometimes to a fault.

After his very public gaffe with Taylor Swift on the MTV Video Music Awards in 2009, Kanye went away, worked at a clothing design firm in Milan, and slipped out of the public eye.

He had been gone quite a while when his manager called and said Kanye wanted me to meet with him. I drove in from the Hamptons on a Saturday night to a Manhattan recording studio to see Kanye. He was there with his girlfriend and he was a little bit sad. I could tell he was still embarrassed by the Taylor Swift incident. I think it affected his confidence, because that night he was simply looking for approval. He played me some tracks he had been working on—"Lost in the World," "Runaway," and "Power."

I always find it great when you can hear in the music the change that an artist is going through, and this is something that can make an ordinary pop song into a lasting work of art. With true artists, you can hear when they're going through a life change. That album, *My Beautiful Dark Twisted Fantasy*, was a reflection of him going through a darker period—the Taylor Swift moment, the loss of his mother, probably some more personal things—but you could hear that he'd changed to a different person and he had a different message with a little less humor and a little more anger.

If you listen to "Stronger"—his big pop hit from *Graduation*, his third album—it was a sort of European underground thing that sampled Daft Punk. But "Power" sounded tribal with the drums and the chants, like he was getting more in touch with the black man that he is, as opposed to "Stronger," which was the pop star that he aspired to be.

Throughout all his records I could hear these changes, but that day in the studio, as I sat there listening to tracks that would become the cornerstone of *My Beautiful Dark Twisted Fantasy*, was a special moment for me. When I heard those tracks, I knew that this next album was going to be his masterpiece. That's not to say that he won't create more than one masterpiece, but that album went beyond everything he'd done until that point.

More than almost any artist I'd ever worked with, with

the possible exception of Outkast, I'd been able to watch him change as a person with every record, reinventing everything and yet somehow staying true to his vision and himself, that person who'd greeted me at the Grammys all those years earlier. Regardless of commercial success, seeing an artist I'd believed in achieve that level of personal growth through his music felt rewarding in a way that I'd experienced only a handful of times in my career. It wasn't about hit singles, or even just about art—though both of those were involved. Instead, it was about evolution, helping an artist come into his own while simultaneously achieving commercial success.

Working with Kanye allowed me to use the lessons of Jay Z—letting him go and simply lending my encouragement—but knowing when to step in and direct an artist's development was another important skill for me to learn: when to leave my guys alone and when to watch over their shoulders. I never wanted to undermine or criticize the best work of my staff, but I liked to think that my getting involved in the process could be helpful, even inspiring. I was named as executive producer on a couple of his albums—I took my name off *808s & Heartbreak* because I didn't feel I deserved the credit. I was the head of the label and it was a gratuitous credit. I picked singles, made suggestions for music videos. I gave guidance, I gave support, and I marketed him, but for the most part what I did with Kanye was enjoy him. He had his vision, and I recognized that my job was not to interfere but to sit back and help that vision become fully realized.

To me, there's Prince and Kanye. They are the most creative artists of all time. Kanye is the equivalent of Prince in a different time and space, in a different era of music where the values have changed. Kanye may not be the performer Prince is, but he is equally important. Rap success lives in other places than pop successes, certain cool kids who pride themselves on not being commercial, who want to be the first to discover the hip new thing. Kanye speaks to those people as much as he does to the pop charts. They are an important part of his audience. His success isn't defined by the charts.

That sense of contributing to a larger cultural conversation was something that I'd been chasing my whole career, and finally, as I hit my stride at Def Jam, I began to feel it. Throughout my career, I usually stayed focused on my own music. While I was generally aware of what was going on in the music world beyond my walls, I always tried not to get caught up in what other people were doing, so that it wouldn't taint my ears or my efforts with my artists.

Still, there had always been moments within culture that couldn't be held back. Whether it was the first time I heard Sugar Hill Gang and understood what rap music was, or when I heard the amazing influence that Prince's sound had on everyone around him, there were always these moments when it felt like the epicenter of culture was shifting a bit, and if you looked at things in just the right way, you could watch that transformation taking place.

That was the case for me in the early '90s when Dr. Dre released *The Chronic* and unleashed West Coast rap on the world. I spent days in the studio trying—and failing—to duplicate the drum sound he got on that record. As different as that was from what I was doing at LaFace, it was impossible for me not to take notice, to feel the gravitational pull suddenly coming from the west. A few years later, after my friendship with P. Diddy helped him get Bad Boy off the ground, I felt the pendulum swing once again, only this time it was back east, as every kid was dressing like him and his brand of hip-hop was emblazoned across every magazine, every music video. The shift was palpable and it was real.

But while I'd been watching these trends ebb and flow for years, I'd never actually felt at the center of them myself—never, that is, until Island Def Jam. With artists like Jay Z, Kanye, and Rihanna, I felt for the first time that what I was working on was truly cultural. We were changing the kinds of sounds that got made, the way people thought about the barriers between hip-hop, R&B, and pop. Once again, the epicenter of music had shifted, and I felt proud to watch it in rotation from my seat at the middle.

After all our long, philosophical discussions about music, Jay Z could tell what I was thinking often before I said anything. He had listened to me well, and, it turned out, had absorbed lessons from me, at the same time that I had been learning from him. And when it came to the success of his next record, I had more to do with it than I first realized. The problem was that the success went to another label.

Although he left Def Jam as president in January 2008, Jay Z still owed us another album on his contract. The album was called *Blueprint 3*, the sequel to *The Blueprint 2*, his widely acclaimed but not as popular follow-up to his landmark 2001 album *The Blueprint*. When he felt he was finished with *Blueprint 3*, he invited me to the studio to listen. I sat at the console and he played the record for me. I told him I loved it and asked him to play it again, sitting there grooving and jamming.

The next day Jay called me at the office. "You didn't like it," he said.

"Of course I liked it," I said. "What do you mean I didn't like it?"

"No," he said. "I know you and I know you didn't like it."

"Maybe I didn't hear the big single that I was looking for," I said.

Jay was right. Although I would never second-guess an artist of his stature and intelligence, we had already done the art piece with *American Gangster*, and I was looking for the big one. "I was listening in the studio," I said. "Sometimes I hear better outside of the studio."

I know my speakers in the office and my car. Sometimes I may hear music a little bit more objectively in my own space, but I was backpedaling and Jay knew it.

"I hear you," he said, "but I know what I know."

While he was disappointed by my response, I think he also saw an opportunity to own his future. He stopped recording and decided he wanted off the label. I understood, but on a personal level I was incredibly dismayed; after all we'd been able to accomplish together, to part ways like this wasn't what I wanted. He was the biggest artist on Def Jam, and I hated to lose him. He went to see Doug Morris and negotiated a deal to buy the album back from the label, something that rarely happens.

After he bought the album back, he went into the studio, reinvigorated now that he had more at stake, more to prove. We'd never spoken about whether he agreed about the need for a big hit single, but my words must have resonated because he came up with two monster hits from his new sessions. One was "Run This Town," with Rihanna and Kanye West. The other one was "Empire State of Mind," with Alicia Keys, which became his first number one and a song that went on to become the unofficial anthem of the city of New York. The album was a great big juicy home run.

After the record came out and was a big hit, I reached him on the phone. "You nailed it, didn't you?" I said.

He knew he did. "Oooh, yes, I nailed it," he said.

Happy as I was for him, I felt a bit let down—that album was the one that got away. In the end, it was my work as an executive, and honestly, my indifference to the early version of the album, that inspired him to come up with the biggest single of his career. I put a lot of man-hours into coaching, and, in my own way, I pushed him. In pushing him to be better, I also pushed him away. After being so in sync for years and coming to such a clear understanding of what drove us professionally and personally, I think he felt that, for the first time, I wasn't on the same page.

That Christmas, I went to St. Barts. Jay and Beyoncé ended up staying there at the same time, and one night, he called. "Hey man. I'm in your neck of the woods," he said. "What are you doing tonight?"

Erica and I joined Jay and Beyoncé at a restaurant for dessert. We adjourned to our house so Jay and I could smoke cigars. Jay knew Usher was on the island so we called him and Usher came over. We sat around a table in the warm evening breeze drinking, talking, smoking a little weed, laughing, and having a good time.

Beyoncé just had a smash with "Single Ladies." Both she and Jay-Z were on top of the world. They both had the biggest hits of their career. Jay turned to Usher.

"You know, I'm a little bit disappointed in you," he said.

"Why?" said Usher.

"Because you are one of our greats," Jay said. "You are supposed to be right now where Beyoncé and I are. Why isn't that happening?"

Usher shrugged. "I don't have my guy," he said.

"Who's that?" asked Jay.

"LA," said Usher.

"What do you mean you don't have him?" asked Jay Z. "He's sitting right here. He will do anything you want. LA is the reason why my album was so big. I don't know him nearly as well as you do, so if he can help me, he can help you."

We sat there until seven in the morning. By then I was so drunk and high, I crashed. I left Jay Z, Usher, Beyoncé, and

Erica at the table. The next day Jay called to say he was sorry for overstaying his welcome. I told him there was no such thing, and I was sorry for abandoning everyone. They left at eight thirty in the morning, but it had been a great night.

Jay Z is not the kind of guy to do all the political acknowledgments, thanking this guy and that guy at the label after he's won awards. The truth is that none of us deserve the credit. But in the dark of the Caribbean night, without even speaking to me, he gave me all the acknowledgment I needed. For all I learned from Jay, I guess I also taught him something, too.

18

X-IT

imon Cowell called me at Island Def Jam to clear a Ne-Yo record he wanted for a TV show. I had first met Simon at a BMG music conference at the Beverly Wilshire Hotel in Los Angeles when I was about to become president of Arista Records. We bumped into each other in a corridor and were introduced. I remember thinking that he looked more like a star than a record executive. He was wearing a V-neck sweater with his pecs sticking out like tits, and a signature hairstyle. We attended the music presentation the next day, where each label head would present his upcoming releases and discuss them. These presentations usually lasted about forty-five minutes, although I've seen Clive Davis take twelve hours. I listened to Simon present his music and I knew mine was better. I had not spoken to him since, but I was glad to help him clear his record.

At the time, though, it struck me that he'd never personally called to clear a record before. They use a lot of my records on his shows and they usually go through legal, but, for whatever reason, this time Simon called me. It planted a seed in my mind, because, at that point, Island Def Jam and I were both going through changes.

Doug Morris, my longtime friend and mentor, was being kicked upstairs as the chairman, and taking his place as CEO was Lucian Grainge, coming in from the British end of the operation in June 2010. Lucian and I had tangled over *The Emancipation of Mimi*, which failed to experience the same kind of success in the British Isles that it did in the United States. On a trans-Atlantic call between Lucian, Doug, and me, I asked him point-blank: How could the album of the year in this country have done so poorly in his country?

"The album is too urban and we invested six million dollars and got nothing back," he said.

I didn't mince words. "I think that's bullshit," I said. "I don't think you pushed the record and I don't think you've invested that kind of money and I'm not happy with the results we've gotten. If we can have these kind of results in America, you have to explain to me how a superstar like Mariah Carey can't have that success in the UK."

That conversation probably wasn't taken that well, but I fight for my artists.

When news of Lucian's promotion spread, I wasn't surprised to find that he didn't especially care for me, and I knew that was a problem. I remembered well how vulnerable I had been at Arista after I lost my corporate support upstairs. It was beginning to occur to me that I might need to transition out of Island Def Jam. I could see that my days were numbered. When the shift occurred, I tried what I could to win Lucian's acceptance, to win his trust, but once it became apparent I couldn't, I knew I had to get the hell out of there.

Island Def Jam was a massive success—even without Jay Z, we were still making gigantic hits with Justin Bieber and Rihanna—but I knew corporate politics. I had watched it for years and I had seen power struggles. I'd seen the winners, I'd seen the losers. I had watched the civilians come in, gain control, and make decisions that had nothing to do with the creative empires that they were supposed to be running, but more to do with what is best for shareholders. You have to respect and understand it—it doesn't work for me, but at least I understand it. I've studied the various kinds of leadership, and I know the difference between the creator and the executor, the facilitator. I know I'm not all of them—I'm going to create something. I knew what I was and I also knew that I wasn't Lucian's style and type.

I don't know whose style and type I am. Doug Morris and Jimmy Iovine respect me, but they are the only two of the other remaining record executives who have actually made records in the studio. I long ago grew accustomed to being the single black face around a meeting table. I've never been what I'll call Mr. Black Power or Mr. Promote That I'm Black. What I do like to promote is that, in my industry, I am the only one who does what I do. I happen to be black. I'm the only chairman of a major label who happens to be black, so it can be a little strange. Every room I go in, I stand out. If I have a cold, it's pneumonia when I walk in. I never feel like I'm one of the boys or a member of the club. I've always felt like the odd man out. I know that some of that is insecurity. I always know that I can't slip up, because I won't get the brother pass.

One of my fellow executives asked me one day why everybody calls me Mr. Reid. I told him I had never asked anybody to call me that and that I always introduced myself as LA. "Then why does everybody do it?" he said. "Everybody says that you make them say it."

I told him it might have something to do with the fact that I'm older, that I have been doing this for some time now, and that it might be respect, but it was so insulting. I wondered, damn, does Clive have to deal with this?

While the tensions with Lucian had nothing to do with race, they did highlight something personal to me that had been lingering beneath the surface for a while. Because I knew my strengths and I knew how much creativity and awareness I brought to my work, I recognized how unique they were in the music business whether Lucian saw it or not. I'd been at Island Def Jam for six years, and I'd presided over a series of hits that had rivaled anything I'd done in my career. I'd been able to discover talent, to incubate, and to work with artists—all my passions were on display and they'd all been on my own terms.

And yet, in my quieter moments, there remained a part of me that thought I hadn't gotten all the credit I'd deserved. Even though I'd helped create some of the biggest hits and stars of the last twenty years, I still had the feeling that I was in other people's shadows. The longer I stayed at Island Def Jam, the louder this feeling of wanting recognition became. My deeds spoke for themselves, but there was something in my ego, something in my pride, that needed additional validation. I didn't totally understand where it came from or what was behind it, but eventually it grew to a volume that was difficult to ignore.

When Simon called, I didn't know about his plans to bring his British TV show *The X Factor* to the United States. I only knew that Simon was a big television producer, that he had many shows in many countries, and that we liked each other. But it triggered the thought in my mind that maybe, just maybe, I should consider something like this. Apparently my instincts were right, because shortly after the call, I learned that Simon was not only bringing *The X Factor* to this country, but that he wanted to have lunch with me to discuss my being on it.

Even before we'd spoken about the show, I was intrigued. The more I thought about it, the more I began to see it as an opportunity for the public to connect the dots of my career. If I did the show, people would see the work I had done, tie everything together, and recognize the common thread from Babyface to Boyz II Men, Usher to Justin Bieber, Mariah Carey to Whitney Houston, Pink to Rihanna, Outkast to Kanye. I wanted the acknowledgment, if not necessarily the fame.

"I think you have what it takes to do this show," Simon said when we finally sat down together. "You like show biz. You like the starry kind of thing. And I remember your presentation at the Beverly Wilshire Hotel. You kicked all of our asses."

"I'd love to do the show," I told him. "There's only one problem. I work for the Universal Music Group. Your show is part-owned by Sony. It's going to be pretty difficult to do your show while working for the Universal Music Group."

Simon agreed that could be a problem, but we both decided it was a good idea to keep the conversation open. I don't know where I got the idea I could run Island Def Jam and join a television show cast at the same time, probably because I have a bloated idea of who I am and what I'm capable of doing. I actually thought that my TV notoriety would give me a competitive advantage that could attract more talent and one-up my competitors.

A couple of months passed while we thought about it. He looked at several candidates and eventually came back around to me being the most suited person. He called a second time.

"Do you really want to do this?" he asked.

"I very much want to join the cast," I said.

"I'd like to offer you the position officially, but Lucian's going to be a problem," Simon said. "How are you going to handle that?"

"I'm going to have a meeting with him soon. If you're serious, Simon, I'll bring it up with him and see how he takes it."

I met with Lucian at a restaurant called Toscana in Brentwood. I sat down with him and tried to pretend that he and I loved each other. He didn't try so hard. When I told him about the TV show, he was skeptical.

"Are you sure you're ready for something like that?" he said. "You'll be famous. You won't even be able to walk in a restaurant without people bothering you."

At that moment, the waiter came to our table. "Mr. Reid," he said. "How are you, sir?"

I thought, *Maybe Lucian doesn't realize that people already know me when I walk in restaurants. I don't really need a TV show for that.* He said he would think it over. A couple of people we knew wandered over to the table to say hello. We broke up the meal and went outside. "I have some ideas," he said. "Let's talk tomorrow."

The next day, our conversation was brief. "If you're really serious about doing the show," Lucian said, "I don't know how you think you can run the label and do the show. It's a time commitment that's more than you might think it is. It's not just showing up for two hours a week. This thing will take over your life. You'll have to have a really strong number two in your company and I don't think you have a strong number two, so I'm not sure how you're going to do both."

That was pretty much the end of the conversation. With one exception: Lucian also floated an intriguing thought during our short talk. He suggested that, instead of running Island Def Jam, perhaps I should create a joint venture that I could run with Universal Music Group and take a handful of artists with me, which could be more manageable than the entire company—not a bad idea. I thought about that for a couple of months while I went back to work running the label.

After a few more weeks, Simon and I started negotiations for me to be on the show, but immediately the talks hit a snag, with the Sony board insisting that I couldn't work for Universal Music. The only way I could join the show was to leave my job. In all my thinking about being on TV, I had never considered quitting my job for the show. I knew it would be difficult to negotiate, but I didn't think it would be impossible. Now that it was, I really had to think about the stakes. There were tons of moving parts. The label was keeping me more than busy. At the time, we were in the process of finishing Justin Bieber's movie and Rihanna was doing her next album, a raunchy new direction she was going to call *Loud*. And I had started working on a comeback album with Jennifer Lopez. My mind was so consumed with day-to-day work, it was hard for me to focus on what I'd actually be giving up if I left for the show.

The Jennifer Lopez project had come about quite by accident and had its beginnings on my Christmas trip to St. Barts the previous year, in 2009. Benny Medina, who managed Jennifer as well as Mariah Carey, was staying with me, and I picked up a fax intended for him. It was a video treatment for the new Jennifer single, "Louboutins."

I went to iTunes and pulled up the song. "Benny," I said, "did you notice that the song is number one hundred and seventy-eight and dropping? Why are you making a video on the song? This song's a stiff."

I was talking friend-to-friend—I had no stake in Jennifer Lopez—but I couldn't help giving Benny a hard time. Benny asked me if I would mind telling Jennifer what I thought. She wasn't my responsibility—I didn't want to tell her, but Benny asked me to do it as a favor, so I found myself talking on the phone with this lady I had met once, but hardly knew.

"Baby, what are you doing?" I said. "This song, 'Louboutins,' you're talking to the point-one percent of the society who can buy it. It's way too aspirational. The brand isn't famous enough and the song isn't that good. And you are trying to make a comeback here. What are you doing? This is a mistake, Jennifer."

She expressed her appreciation for my candor and she and Benny decided shortly thereafter not to make the video. Sometime later, Benny confided in me that Jennifer wanted off Epic Records. I was reluctant to meet with her—although who doesn't want to meet with Jennifer Lopez?—and I wasn't sure what I could do. She came to my bungalow at the Beverly Hills Hotel and won me over with what she said.

"Thank you, because you were right about the song," she said. "My years at Epic were with Tommy Mottola, and Tommy helped me and guided me and we had massive success. Then my life changed. I got married and had children.

Celebrating J. Lo's Icon award at the Billboard Music Awards at Hakkasan Las Vegas, with Benny Medina, Casper Smart, and Erica

Now I want to make a comeback. I'm very serious about that, but I need someone who can guide me."

She let all that sink in before continuing.

"The advice you gave me the other day was really valuable advice and I felt a connection. I really would love to have you work with me and help me craft my comeback album with Benny. I think I can get out from my label and if you'll have me, I'll do it for no money. If we have success, we share the profits. If we don't have success, we both walk away."

I liked that deal, so Jennifer and I started to work together. She had most of the album already in the can, but she needed the singles. I went to work finding songs and she would come over and listen. We discussed who she was as an artist. Because Def Jam had been having a good run with Rihanna singing pop songs, we both agreed those songs were not much different than the kind of songs Jennifer wanted to do. She tried a few things in the studio, but some of the tracks were leaked and that didn't help. I didn't want them out, because I didn't believe we had nailed it yet. I felt certain we could get there with Jennifer, but I needed some trial and error time. I needed to try some songwriters, some producers, until we found the magic.

I had a Skype conversation with a producer named RedOne, and after connecting the two of them, he and Jennifer came up with this song called "On the Floor." She called me over to the studio in Long Island where they were working near her house and played me the track. I told her that it was the one I was looking for. She brought the finished mix to my office and I listened again, outside the studio, comfortable in my own environment, and confirmed my initial reading—smash hit. I suggested we add a rap by Pitbull, the sensational Latino artist who was breaking big in the rap and dance worlds. This whole process took almost six months.

As all this was going on with Jennifer, Simon and I continued to talk about the show. Many nights he called me around one o'clock in the morning and he would try out his ideas for the show on me. We discussed other judges who potentially could join us. We talked about what we would do with the talent from the show, whether we would produce records with them and sign them to our labels, whatever those labels might end up being. Simon was helping me develop a television mind-set.

At my next meeting with Lucian, he again pushed the idea of my setting up a new label with Universal. He told me he would back the operation and that I could take Rihanna, Kanye West, Justin Bieber, whoever I wanted. The idea that I would partly own this label was attractive, so I decided to explore it and see what it would look like. If I didn't end up doing the TV show, perhaps this smaller label would be a better option.

But as the deal for the smaller label was being negotiated, I began to grow sour about Universal Music Group and more excited about leaving the company to join *The X Factor*. The prospect of taking my pick of artists to my own smaller label was appealing, but it also felt like a step back. I'd be going from being the head of the biggest label with the biggest market share to something much more boutique and intimate. Though I liked the prospect of being able to focus on a few artists, I struggled with the notion that the scale was smaller. I had been at a small label that I'd owned half of once before, and I'd moved on from that part of my life.

I didn't know what waited for me on the other side of the record business if I went to *The X Factor*, but that uncertainty felt a bit exciting. I knew what came with running a small label; I didn't know the TV business, but the prospects were appealing. There was risk and I knew it, but my situation at Universal was no more stable.

"If I leave Universal Music Group and I join *The X Factor* and whatever else comes with it," I said to one of my friends, "it's risky and there's a chance my career might end. But if I stay at Universal Music Group with Lucian, my career will absolutely end."

I couldn't deal with the doubts and indecision. I drew an arbitrary deadline in my mind that if Universal didn't have the deal finished by the time I left for vacation in St. Barts on December 16, I wasn't going to take it. I didn't tell anyone, except Erica, who totally supported me. She issued me a wake-up call.

"I don't like the idea of anybody trying to make you afraid," she said, "with all that you've done in your career and all you're capable of doing. I don't like the idea of someone trying to strike fear in you about what your future might be. When have you ever been afraid? Frankly, I don't even like seeing that in you. I don't know who that person is."

When we got to St. Barts and the deal still wasn't done, I phoned my attorney and told him I wanted out. He was furious, but my mind was made up

"I don't want to work for the guy. I don't like him. He doesn't like me. The deal didn't get done in the time that I thought it should have gotten done and I'm simply not taking the deal."

And with that, I began to negotiate an exit agreement from Island Def Jam, while making a deal with Simon to go to work for *The X Factor*. My attorney was worried that I was giving up a lot of money at Universal for an uncertain future with a television producer. "You'll just have to dive in and see," I told him.

I called Doug Morris to tell him my decision. He had advised me to take Lucian's offer of setting up a label because he thought I could make a lot of money in a few years. He was surprised when I told him I was not taking the deal.

"Are you serious?" he said. "You're not taking it? You

have a lot of balls and I love it. What are you going to do?"

I told him I wanted to make the deal with Simon to do *The X Factor* and beyond that I didn't know. "By the way, Doug, I heard that the head of Sony Music was leaving," I said. "Why wouldn't you take that job?"

"How do you know I'm not?" he said.

"Get the fuck out of here—you're going to Sony?" I said.

"If we can work it out."

"Can I go with you?"

"Absolutely, you just showed me what you're made of. You've had nothing but success and you're a friend. Let's go. Enjoy your vacation."

I did just that.

I came back to the company at the top of the year. No one expected me to return to Universal, but I did because I hadn't resigned or been fired. I was still negotiating my exit deal and there was a lot of work to be done. We were about to give the new Jennifer Lopez single the biggest launch I had ever witnessed.

In an odd convergence of worlds, as we were working on her album, Jennifer had been offered a role as a judge on *American Idol*. Ironically, she had also come under consideration as a judge on *The X Factor*, but they couldn't come to terms. She and Steven Tyler of Aerosmith joined returning judge Randy Jackson that season as the new panel on television's most popular show. At the peak of its cultural currency, *American Idol* was attracting twenty-five million viewers a week and had been minting stars such as Kelly Clarkson, Clay Aiken, Ruben Studdard, and Carrie Underwood. Benny Medina arranged to debut the video to "On the Floor" on *American Idol*. You couldn't have dreamed of a better platform to launch the Jennifer Lopez comeback. The next day, the song exploded on the iTunes charts, where it shot to the top and stayed. The single sold six million. Jennifer's back.

I had left the company a couple of weeks before that happened in February 2011. Doug Morris was not taking over Sony until July, so, for now, I could concentrate on becoming a television star.

19

HERE COMES THE JUDGE

The morning I woke up for my first day at *The X Factor* in March 2011, I went to the gym, got a facial, put on my Tom Ford suit, and rode down to CBS Television City. I pulled up to a huge crowd of cheering kids, waving signs for Simon and *The X Factor*. They didn't know who I was, but they were cheering for Simon's show. I knew he was a big deal, but I hadn't seen this firsthand. My first impression of him in the hotel hallway years earlier turned out to be completely accurate. He's a star.

Simon Cowell and the British impresario Simon Fuller had reinvented the TV talent show, and *American Idol* had changed the music scene landscape dramatically in the twenty-first century. What they started in England, they took to a global scale, and they broke radio's stranglehold on the record business. As record executives, we were often at the mercy of radio. If I made a record and the radio programmers decided it was not a hit, that artist never saw the light of day. The two Simons understood that not all music fit on the radio, and that television could make stars, too. They built a platform that could keep artists on television in front of an audience for long enough to catch on, regardless of radio. Simon had started *The X Factor* in England in 2004. The immensely successful boy band One Direction came off the show. People in the United States watched the British program online. Simon had imported one of his judges from the UK edition, a pretty dance artist named Cheryl Cole, to be a third judge on the US show.

Going in, I assumed that everything about this world would be different from being a record exec with one exception: how I discovered talent. Because I'd been finding stars for twenty years, I'd built a lot of confidence in my instincts, and I didn't doubt that I'd be able to re-create that skill on camera. What I didn't realize at the start, but learned very quickly, was that the kind of talent that would audition for a TV talent show was much different from the kind of talent that I was used to seeing—there was a reason these voices were walking into a soundstage and not my office. Further complicating things was that the actual art of discovering someone on a show also proved to be entirely different; as I came to see, the skills that had made me good at making hit records were not the same as those that would make me a good judge on a TV competition show.

I got out of my car, did a couple of red-carpet interviews, and went inside to the large dressing room shared by all three judges. Benny Medina came with me to keep me company. It would have been a very lonely experience without Benny, going to work by myself, not being the boss for the first time in twenty years. To produce a TV show takes a cast of hundreds. I was a little overwhelmed by the size of the enterprise and the massive investment it represented.

I was the first to arrive, and as I sat in the large green room, I had the strange realization that, for the first time, I was the talent. I was not in control of the schedule—my only job was to sit and wait until they were ready for me. When Cheryl Cole arrived, I introduced myself and we chatted briefly, but she was a bit reserved. She went off into her corner. A few minutes later, in walked Paula Abdul. I had heard they were trying to make a deal with her, and they had closed it only the night before the taping. That was an instant relief—somebody I knew. Other than Benny, I didn't know a soul. I didn't know the camera people, I didn't know the makeup artists, I didn't know the hair-stylists, I didn't know the guy who went to get coffee, I didn't know anybody. I hadn't seen Paula in years—our Pebbles-era drama had been forgotten long ago—but we gave each other a big hug, both happy to see each other. She went to her makeup mirror to prep.

About an hour later, Simon walked in. Everybody in the room stood up. Caesar had arrived. This wasn't the Simon I knew. This was a new Simon. This was Simon the king, the media star, the mogul, the multimillionaire. He seemed twenty-five feet tall with an aura of power and authority surrounding every step.

"Okay, kids, are you ready?" he said. "It's time for the show to start. Let's go."

Ready? We had been given no instructions, no script, no idea of even how the show ran. No conversations, no "you do this, you do that"—we were simply going to start and figure it out as we went.

"This is what we'll do," Simon said. "We'll go out and we'll introduce ourselves. I'll go first, then I will introduce Cheryl and pass the mic to her, she'll talk for a second, then, Cheryl, you'll introduce Paula. Paula will talk and hand the mic to you, LA, and then you talk for a second. That's it."

That was all the stage direction we would receive. We walked out to a jam-packed, loud, screaming audience. I wasn't sure what to think. I hadn't experienced the adrenaline rush of being onstage since my days in the Deele. We did exactly what Simon told us to do. Simon introduced himself. They went absolutely wild. Paula introduced herself, and they went wild again. Cheryl introduced herself and they made a little noise. I introduced myself and they politely clapped.

Looking out at the audience, I found it hard to imagine how the next several months were going to go. We would spend the next two months on the road filming the first show and auditioning the nation. We collected candidates from two cattle call free-for-alls in Los Angeles before heading out on a six-city tour and selecting performers for a boot camp. At the *X Factor* boot camp, each judge would be assigned eight performers to coach, cutting them down to a final four before the end of the first show of the season. Each judge supervised one of the four categories of teams; the Young Boys, the Young Girls, the Overs (older than young), and Groups. The ultimate winner would receive $5 million.

We adjourned to the judges' table, the cameras started rolling, and they brought on the first talent. Simon bantered with the guy, he sang, and Simon turned to our table.

"Okay, let's see what the judges say," he said. "LA, what do you think?"

It was my first time. I sputtered—"Well, I thought you were good" or something—and another judge jumped in. Soon they were talking over each other. It was all very clumsy. For the first time, the thought occurred to me that, wait a minute, Simon did *American Idol* and *X Factor* in England, Paula Abdul was an *American Idol* judge for years, and Cheryl Cole came from *X Factor* in the UK. I was the only one who didn't know what he was doing.

We auditioned talent for two hours before taking a break. Backstage, Simon was noticeably upset, but I had no idea what was wrong and figured it must be me. I'd taken on this job, changed my life, and now I was a complete failure. Nobody came up and talked to me, and that made me even more uncomfortable. Simon and his production team were holding a meeting in the corner of the room, and, damn, I was not used to being on the outside. I was used to sitting at that table.

Simon broke up his meeting and came over to talk with us. This time he had more specific instructions, a little form, a little choreography. We went back out, and in a much more orderly manner, we auditioned talent for another six hours. After that, we were steered into the press tent and sat for interviews for another two hours. It was eleven o'clock at night before we were done. It all started again the next day.

I soon learned that the biggest difference between auditions as a record executive and auditions on television is that, as a record executive, I never had to tell people what I thought or why I thought it. Working for a label, I would watch the audition and I would rock my head, but it would throw you off. You never knew whether I was loving it or not. Often I was a little ambiguous on purpose. On television, there could be none of that ambiguity—I had to explain myself in a way that I never had to before. I had to learn how to talk and I had to tell everybody my thought process every step of the way. Every audition, all the way down to the final episode of the final show, it all came down to my opinion. You couldn't say the same thing over and over. I had to develop a vocabulary, a style, a speech pattern. I had to put hooks in how I spoke and I had to build tension and not give it away too quickly, a yes or a no, stay or go home.

All the time I was judging talent, my mind was buzzing. Instead of focusing intently and developing a vision for the artist in front of me as I always had during auditions, I was concerned with my personal stagecraft and listening to myself, so that I knew exactly what I was going to say. At the same time, questions were scattering around my brain about my role on the show. What did I need to do? Should I try to be funny? Should I try to be smart? I needed to figure out my mojo. Who was the character I was creating? What was the personality? Who was I supposed to be? Was I LA the record executive? Was I supposed to be a comedian? Was I supposed to be the talent expert? Who was *my* character?

I had thought about all this, particularly my character, quite a bit before I went back for the second day. I'd spent years helping others create their own stage personas and now I was trying to understand my own. I picked up a lot listening to Paula and Simon. I started to figure out what I was supposed to do, even though I wasn't getting much guidance.

After a couple of takes, Simon looked over at me and he winked. "That was really good, LA," he said. A couple of producers gave me tips. "Don't be so quick to say yes and no," one producer said. "We need you to give it a little pause. We need to create some jeopardy here. We don't want you to give away your answer quickly. This is television."

Much as I'd always been eager to learn in my old job, I found every suggestion helpful now. Before we started our six-city tour for auditions, the producers caught up with me while I was with my family—finally giving me some feedback about my character.

"LA, we just wanted to have a word with you about wardrobe," said one producer, "because the first day you wore your suit and you looked like an executive. The second day, you wore sweaters and were a little bit more casual. We want you to keep your executive profile. We don't want you to be casual. We want you to be the talent expert, the seasoned executive. That's the character we want you to play. Otherwise, you're doing really good and we'll see you in Chicago."

This was nothing I didn't know already, except for the part about the necktie, and I never mind dressing up.

After the second day in Chicago, one of the producers took Simon, Paula, and me aside to shoot some YouTube promos. I wondered about Cheryl, but didn't say anything. After we finished, Simon asked me what I thought about Cheryl. I told him I thought she was good. Then he asked me about one of the cohosts, Nicole Scherzinger, a singer I knew who recorded for Interscope Records. "Do you think you'd like Nicole better next to you or would you like Cheryl next to you?" he said.

"I like Nicole," I said.

"Okay, then it's done," he said. "We're sending Cheryl home. Nicole's going to be the judge."

What? Did I just get somebody fired? Doubtful. They clearly had already made their decision, but he wanted to run it by me. At the next city, sitting next to me was Nicole. While we were on the tour, all of us became friends. At night we would hang out after the show and maybe have a drink at the hotel bar.

The last day on the road shooting the show, I was woken early in the morning by a phone call from Erica telling me that

With Mom at my fiftieth birthday celebration, New York

my mom had died from a heart attack. She had had previous episodes, surgeries, so it was not altogether unexpected, but damn, it hit me hard. I didn't say a word to anyone. I struggled through the taping, went home to Erica, and flew to Cincinnati to take care of my mother. I told Simon only after I left.

My mother was where I got my people sense. She had unerring insights into people and she was always proud of my accomplishments—my gold records covered the walls in her home—but she was also always straightforward with me if she didn't like something, which was often the case. She had gotten to know all my children; traveled the world to Japan, China, South Africa; she could shop for what she wanted to shop for. I didn't visit her in Cincinnati as often as I would have liked, although she was a regular presence at our family functions in Atlanta and New York, and when I did go to see her, I always took a private plane so I could leave when I wanted, worried in the back of my mind that somehow I would get stuck in Cincinnati. I managed to pull myself together and get back with my work, but she never leaves my thoughts. To this day, I can't bring myself to sell her house.

On the show, I tried to regain my focus. My character began to emerge from my banter with Simon. We became bookends. Simon was on one end, me on the other. Simon was the famous TV executive who had done this for many years and been hugely successful. I was the record executive who had actually discovered famous stars, so I played the professional expert. We would pick on each other. He liked to team up on the girls. Nothing was scripted. I wore cool glasses and expensive suits. When I started *The X Factor*, Justin Bieber was one of the world's biggest stars, and we definitely used his name and his association with me to promote *The X Factor*. The same was true for Rihanna, whose appearance with me as a celebrity mentor with my team was one of the highlights of the first season.

Simon and I developed a genuine chemistry between all the judges. Sometimes there would be backstage wheeling and dealing, such as when you needed to lobby the other judges if you wanted one of your acts to win.

"LA, you're going to have to help me," Simon might say. "I really want to keep the girls."

And we'd bullshit each other. "Okay. No problem, Simon," I'd say. "I'll keep the girls." Get out in front of the cameras and turn on him. "Girls, I'm going to have to send you home." It was fun.

When I was on break with my family, Simon called from London. "LA, I've been sitting in the edit for the past two weeks," he said, "and I have to tell you, you are fantastic. You are a complete star on this show. You're going to be the surprise. As I look at the whole thing, you're the breakout."

This made me happy. I went through the entire process never knowing, never looking at tape or photographs. I just did the work. I didn't know how I looked or sounded. Now I was ready for the season.

For the season opener, Simon threw a red-carpet premiere at the Chinese Theater in Hollywood. I was used to music business press, but TV press was a whole different animal. There was a mob, from networks to bloggers. Simon made us sign up for social media (which is why I still have 1.3 million Twitter followers). They did a great job at building up anticipation for the show. I still hadn't seen anything, and when the lights went down, I saw it for the first time.

The edits were beautiful. I had gone through those auditions in kind of a daze, but the way they cut it together turned out really well. The crowd in the theater was laughing and exploding into applause. "I'll be damned—I can change my life," I thought. "I'm a television personality."

When the show aired the next night, fourteen million people tuned in. The only problem with that was that Simon had crowed to the press that he would have twenty million people watching *The X Factor*. The press jumped all over him and trumpeted the show as a failure because it didn't live up to Simon's exalted expectations. Anytime you can get fourteen million people to do something, it is not a failure, but the press didn't see it that way. "*X Factor* doesn't have the X factor" was the way they saw it.

In spite of the response, I was having a ball, hanging out with Paula, Nicole, and Simon. Some of the crew were becoming buddies and I looked forward to seeing them every day. I loved the whole ritual of getting ready for the show, going to the gym in the morning, working out really hard, deciding what to wear, listening to music to get pumped up and to go on the stage and do the show. A couple of times, I rented out restaurants and threw big dinner parties while we watched the broadcast on large-screen televisions. After the slickly produced season premiere, the show went live every week and each judge guided his or her final four through the season, gave them songs, and coached them.

When I went out in public after *The X Factor* started running, my life changed completely. All of a sudden, everybody knew who I was. The first time I noticed was when I went to an art exhibit at my children's school in Brooklyn, and every kid in the place came running over to me. The whole school crowded around, all the grades: "Hey LA, can I have an autograph? How's Simon? How's Paula?" My kids loved it. Everybody wanted to take a photograph and my kids jumped into the pictures with me. The little ones were the best. Our audience demographics skewed either very old or very young. The people in between didn't pay us any attention. At the Starbucks or Footlocker, it was always the young kids that got the most excited.

This was my new life. Finally, after all these years, I was receiving recognition for myself, not for something I did for someone else. For five minutes, I really loved it.

During the summer leading up to the show's premiere, I'd closed my deal with Sony to start my new post as the chairman-CEO of Epic Records. I was still on the road and doing these long days with *The X Factor*, but as of July, I was also running a record label. In August, I had the month off the TV show to work at the label, but in September I had to go back to the West Coast and start shooting weekly episodes. It quickly became clear that I had no idea how I was going to do both jobs.

For starters, I needed to build a staff. Only one person came over with me from Island Def Jam because Lucian had been so angry over my departure that he threw large bonuses at my executives to stay, so I was forced to work with executives I didn't know. But even more dire than the staffing situation was the fact that I'd been hired to breathe new life into Epic. Epic was the ugly stepchild of the company's prestigious main label, Columbia Records, and had long been in decline since the glory days of Sly and the Family Stone and Michael Jackson's *Thriller*. The label had no roster to speak of and it was at an all-time low in the label's long history. This would require a complete rebuilding effort, a tough task under normal circumstances, but with the show going on, it was much more complicated than I'd ever envisioned.

The show was taped on the West Coast and I worked out of the Epic Records office during the day, but I was going through the motions running the record company while my mind was completely absorbed by *The X Factor*. Being a record executive is one of the most labor-intensive jobs in entertainment. It's the staff, the roster, auditions, mixes, marketing meetings, hiring. I could barely take phone calls during the day. Although I had become something of a record industry brand, so to speak, I wasn't attracting the executive talent I needed, largely because I was now running a label that wasn't having much success.

Making both of my jobs harder was the fact that finding talent for Epic and finding talent for the show were two very different things. The deeper in we got, the more I understood the difference between talent on a show and at a record company audition. On a TV show audition, something is wrong already because you're there—it's pretty much a foregone conclusion that you're not going to make it in music. Why else would you be trying out for a TV show?

In our shop talk backstage, the judges always said that Prince would have never auditioned for a show like this. Or Bono. You don't get Jimi Hendrix. You don't get Led Zeppelin on a show like this. You don't get Diana Ross, Drake, Lady Gaga, or Kanye

West. You get talent who are okay with people telling them what to sing, what to wear, how to dance, when to dance. Nobody could have ever told Madonna what to wear or made Bob Marley sing "Tie a Yellow Ribbon Round the Ole Oak Tree." I'd always thrived around artists like Pink or Avril or Mariah, who, even though they wanted to make pop music, all had their own visions for the kind of artist they wanted to be. They were creatively open-minded but with their own strong point of view. On *The X-Factor* there was little of that vision from the contestants themselves.

Still, working with the contestants on my team had plenty of fun moments. On the show, I sat on my back deck of my Hamptons place next to Rihanna to pick my final four. They auditioned for us and then came back, one at a time, to learn their fate. You would have to build up to it—*You were really talented, you were much better in the auditions the first time I saw you, this time you weren't quite as good, you weren't as convincing; I'm not certain that you're a star, but I love your dedication, I love your voice tone, and this is a very tough decision to make. . . .* Big pause. "You're in my final four."

Of course, they always went crazy. But if you were sending someone home, they would occasionally get a little angry and security would have to escort them away.

One of my favorites was Astro, a fourteen-year-old rapper with an attitude. He stood out right away at boot camp when he refused to sing, dance, or do any ensemble pieces. "I'm a rapper," he said.

A rebel like that might be the last thing you'd think you would find on a TV show. I loved the kid. Finding material for Marcus Canty, an R&B singer who could really sing, was easy, but getting songs for Astro was always difficult. Sometimes clearing a song with music publishers could be an issue. You might want to sing "When Doves Cry," but Prince would never allow it. I called Eminem's manager to see if I could land "Lose Yourself" for Astro from him. It turned out Eminem watched the show and liked the kid, so we could clear the song. I was able to get Michael Jackson's "Black and White" for him on an all-Michael Jackson show. We had to rewrite the chorus for him, but we nailed it.

Chris Rene was a trash collector and a drug addict in early recovery from Santa Cruz, California. He turned the place out with an original song that the world had never heard, "Young Homie," and rocked that crowd.

Out of the first season, I signed Chris Rene, and we did an album with him, but "Young Homie" didn't turn out to be a hit. We also signed Marcus Canty, the soul singer who could sing his ass off, and he didn't work for us either. I signed the winner of the first season, the girl who took home the $5 million, Melanie Amaro. She came to the office exactly one time and she had about as much drive as a broke-down car. She called me once around eleven o'clock at night to ask if she could get a discount at the Sony store.

Despite enjoying my artists on the show, by the time we were halfway through the first season, I couldn't ignore the reality that Epic Records had become an increasingly serious project for me. As I built the label, I was hiring executives, and they had to come to the set to hold our meetings. By the end of the first season, my dressing room was filled with Epic executives. I grew impatient to spend time with my label.

As I struggled to balance both the show and the job, the two became entangled in a way that undermined my efforts at Epic. For one thing, how I listened and evaluated talent changed. For my entire career, when I'd discovered talent, there were always aspects about the performers that I liked that I couldn't articulate. Seeing potential in an artist isn't always something that you can easily put into clear words. However, as I was forced to do that on the show, I found myself gravitating toward the artists and suggestions that were safer, easier to explain, that had the kind of potential that can be communicated in a fifteen-second sound bite. My feedback became more superficial because it's what the medium demanded.

But more than that, I didn't focus on the same things that I once did, because what made for good TV wasn't necessarily what made for good music. Sure, part of that was because the caliber of artists we had on *The X Factor* was not what I was used to, but the other, and arguably bigger, part came from the fact that the goals of the show were not consistent with my own standards. Good TV is fueled by conflict—between the judges, between the artists, between the judges and the artists. Almost by definition, the process of competitive auditions lends itself toward this kind of drama, but it doesn't necessarily produce the artists most capable of making a hit record. It's a very specific kind of talent and mind-set, one that often rewards a shallower approach.

Initially, I thought I could manage to make a distinction between TV talent and hit record talent, but over time, it started to cloud my judgment. By the end of the first season, it became apparent to me that working on *The X Factor* had taken me further away from the music rather than closer to it. By joining the show, I'd taken a step away from my passion—the first time that had happened in my career.

As that reality hit home, I had some dark private moments, wondering what I was doing, where my friends were. I found myself fixating on what my artists were thinking and whether or not people like Jay Z or Kanye approved of what I'd done. I worried that Rihanna thought I'd lost my mind, and Mariah assumed I'd abandoned her. Perhaps Jennifer Lopez was wondering why I was trying to be a star, and Justin Bieber figured I didn't like him anymore. I tend to overthink things, but I couldn't shake these feelings of being judged by people whose opinions I respected.

And then there was the stardom itself. Of course that had been part of the excitement at the beginning, but the more time I spent in the spotlight, the more I realized that all the clichés about the trappings of fame were clichés for a reason. It didn't take long for the appeal of the notoriety to wear off. When it did wear off, all that was left was a painful irony: while I was finally getting the credit I'd long sought for my accomplishments, I'd been forced to move away from my passion for music to make that happen.

In spite of all these frustrations, I really did enjoy that first season of *The X Factor*. In many ways it was an experience that I needed to orient me toward the future. The camaraderie among Simon, Nicole, Paula, and myself was real, and taking on a new life doing television for a year turned out to be the break I needed between Island Def Jam and Epic Records. I'd been on the same grind for so many years and had gone through a lot emotionally. I needed to regain my energy, remember why I'd gotten started in this business to begin with.

With that out of my system following the first season, I was ready to sit down and focus full-time on Epic. I had no desire to stop, no anticipation to stop. I didn't want to stop. The show had given me focus by reminding me what my true passion was, and going back to TV would be an unwelcome interruption. The only problem was, I'd already committed to doing a second season.

I had no desire whatsoever to do the second season. Zero. In fact, I almost didn't do it. I waited until the very last day, the final day that the auditions were supposed to start. I spoke to Doug Morris, who told me it was too late to back out.

"But now that I've gotten Epic started," I said, "this is what I want to do. I'm a record man."

At the Fox upfronts with the X Factor *season 2 cast: Demi Lovato,*
Britney Spears, and Simon Cowell, Central Park, New York

"I told you that before the first season and you went ahead and did it," he said. "Now you've got to finish it."

I went through the second season, but with a bit of an attitude. The thrill was gone. While I tried to do a good job, I knew the second season would be my last. The second season was a different panel. Simon and I were back, but with us were Demi Lovato and Britney Spears. I became fond of Demi, but I could never get particularly close to Britney, even though she was seated right next to me. I was used to having fun, silly Nicole Scherzinger beside me. Britney was an introvert and not as communicative and, frankly, not a lot of fun. I worried about my stress showing on TV; they say a television camera is like an X-ray. I was already tired of the show. I was ready to get back to my real job.

When the producers phoned—I took the call on camera—to tell me I had been given the Overs to coach, I slammed down the phone and walked out of the room. I wanted to quit right there. The old guys? What am I going to do with the Overs? That's not my thing. I signed Usher at fourteen, Avril at sixteen, Rihanna at seventeen, Justin Bieber at fourteen, TLC at seventeen. I don't do adults. I simply didn't have any interest in it. Once I got into it, I did end up having fun with the talent and even won the second season. My contestant, Tate Stevens, was a country artist, and it turned out that I love country music and didn't even know it. He introduced me to Garth Brooks songs like "The Dance" and "Friends in Low Places" and taught me the difference between country and bluegrass. That was something brand new.

By the end of the second season, all the realizations I'd had after the first season were still staring me in the face—only this time they were amplified. I was embarrassed about my record label and where it stood. I was embarrassed that I'd paraded myself across the television network like a clown. I was embarrassed that I had this desire to be famous or to connect the dots. I was embarrassed by my decisions. I had reduced myself to being unimportant talent, and that made me upset with myself.

The second season had also complicated things for me at home. Being away from home so much, living in Los Angeles while my family lived in New York, had grown stressful on my wife and kids. I didn't see them enough. I was trying to do my job on television and working hard on the record company, struggling to stay focused. Meanwhile my wife and family were not impressed or happy that I had become a TV star and was living in Hollywood, which added to my stress.

I will say that I was a decent actor. I wouldn't win an Academy Award, but, looking back, I covered up my tension and unease. But as soon as the camera went off and my adrenaline came down to earth, there was this unhappy soul. Doing live television in front of a live audience will send your heart racing, and I had tough times at night coming down. I found myself trying vigorously to be normal when the truth was that my adrenaline had me floating. I made the mistake of putting a Google Alert on my name and read everything that was written about me. Some things were good and some, they took you to the cleaners. Either way, it was all having a negative effect on me. For the first time, I could feel my lights dimming, like I had lost my grounding, my all-important sense of self. I needed to get my mojo back.

I pulled something of a fast one on my way out. I gave an interview to Shaun Robinson of *Access Hollywood* and gave her the exclusive on my leaving the show, provided she held the interview until after we taped the last episode. I never told anybody I was leaving. They aired the interview an hour early and the whole time I was taping the last show, Simon was glaring at me. At the first commercial break, Simon wanted to talk.

"What have you done?" he said.

"Simon, I've just had enough," I said. "I did the best I could do for you and I'll do anything for you, you know I will, but I really just can't continue."

"But why the interview? Why didn't you tell me?"

"Honestly, you want me to tell you why? Because if I had told you, you would have spun it to the press that you fired me. You can't give a record man control of the media. We're cut from the same cloth. I beat you to the punch."

20

EPIC LIFE

Quitting the show gave me room to focus on the label, but just because I had more time, it didn't mean that everything suddenly ran smoothly or that the hits started rolling in. In fact, at first, things only got worse.

When I came back at the top of the year after my Christmas break and the end of *The X Factor*, I had to deal with the reality that, for the first time in my life, I was no longer that guy. Epic Records was the smallest of the company's three labels. Columbia had Beyoncé and Adele, the top artists in the world, and RCA had the biggest roster of stars—people like Justin Timberlake and Alicia Keys, not to mention all my former LaFace performers. At Sony Music's corporate meetings, I was sitting there with no hits, no roster. I'd never known how that felt and I didn't like it. I didn't know how to walk the halls and not be the hottest guy. I didn't feel the same when I walked into a room. I didn't know what to say, how to talk, what to wear. I felt empty. It was a psychological adjustment, and a painful one at that.

I'd never been cold in my career, not from LaFace to Arista to Island Def Jam. That ten years of Island Def Jam and Arista meant going to the Grammys every year with nominations in many categories. Now I didn't have a reason to go to the Grammys, because none of my acts were nominated. I didn't have a reason to go to the American Music Awards. I didn't have a reason to go to the Billboard Awards. None of my acts were on the show. I was out of the game.

It didn't help that I was still struggling to assemble a staff. With the craziness of the show behind me, I looked over the team I'd put together and realized that when I was working on *The X Factor* I'd made a lot of bad staffing decisions I now had to live with. I'd spent years putting together and fine-tuning a team at Island Def Jam, and I hadn't invested the same energy in team-building at Epic. I was in a company with people I didn't know well, with artists that for the most part hadn't done well. I felt that I was punching beneath my weight class.

The worst part, though, was not the corporate dynamic, it was the fact that I remained under the influence of the shallow when it came to finding hits. Despite being aware of how the show had altered my ear for talent, I found it hard to counter that change. Not only did I sign five acts from *The X Factor*, I signed other acts that resembled *The X Factor* acts and had failure after failure after failure with them. The one bright spot was that I signed the girl group Fifth Harmony from the show's second season and they went on to become the most successful act off of the show, developing into a girl band that I quite like. But beyond them, I signed acts because I thought they had a platform and thought maybe it would work for me. It didn't. I couldn't get it right.

My bar had lowered too far. When I'd had success in pop music, it had come from being able to fuse and cross genres— R&B and rock, traditional pop and R&B. I'd never worked with cotton-candy, sugarcoated pop music. Coming from the show, I was trying to duplicate that bubblegum pop, only I couldn't figure it out. I took it as a challenge, remote as it was from my R&B roots: *Okay, I can do sugarcoated cotton candy, too, let me show you.*

It took that string of failures to show me that I couldn't do it. I began to question everything—my taste, my sense for talent. Perhaps those two seasons had taken such a toll on me that the music and the world had passed me by. The pace of the music world is unrelenting, and I considered whether I no longer understood what was hot and what was not. I lost interest in most of the talent, and then I lost confidence in myself.

It took Babyface to set me straight.

Kenny and I never stopped talking and always stayed in touch. When I was at Arista, I had negotiated a deal to get

Kenny off Epic Records and executive produced an album with him. That was the beginning of our working together again, and when I left for Island Def Jam, I took him with me. But the truth is I never felt that Kenny and I had completely broken up. I think it's safe to say Kenny is the guy who knows me better than anyone. He is more like a brother than a best friend, and he has been since the day that he walked out in that studio from singing "Slow Jam" with Midnight Star. We became brothers that day and we've been brothers ever since. When we fight, we're fighting like brothers fight. We might fight one day about something or another, but we will always be brothers.

Not only does Kenny know me as a person, he knows me musically, and what he told me was that I was just going through the motions.

"I know you are living this great life," he said, "the big apartment on the Upper East Side, the big house in the Hamptons, your kids in private school, drivers, cooks, and nannies. You and your family have this wonderful life and you're just a guy going through the motions, paying the bills keeping up this life, but it has nothing to do with who you are and your soul.

"That's not who you are," Kenny told me.

"You've painted yourself into a box," he said. "It's not who you are. You like to feel it. You like to feel love. As much as nobody likes to feel pain, you get inspired from feeling pain. You wrote certain songs off the pain you felt. You wrote certain songs off the love you felt. You made certain career decisions and signed certain artists because it spoke to where you were in your life at that moment."

What I heard Kenny telling me was that as long as I wanted to be safe, my music was going to be safe. He was trying to push me out the door. Babyface was saying there was no point to making soulless music. It doesn't stand for anything but a number on the pop charts.

"We used to write songs in your living room," he said. "Now when I come in your living room, it's so quiet I'm afraid to touch the piano because it's going to disturb the house, because it's no longer a music environment. It doesn't feel friendly. I come in and I can look at your piano, but I can't play it."

I knew Kenny was telling me the truth as soon as I heard it. As I'd been trying to diagnose my problems, I'd been focusing on the wrong things. I'd paid attention to whether the problem was me and my ear—whether I'd missed the moment and couldn't get it back. Instead the reality was I'd gotten caught up in a vision of myself that wasn't me—like one of my artists trying to force a sound that didn't come naturally. I was trying to make music that I couldn't relate to, that I had nothing in common with. When I looked at what those artists and signings had in common, I realized that if something wasn't coming from my heart, I quickly lost interest in it.

Hearing Kenny's words drove all that home. I thought back about everything we'd been through and how far it had all come. From my mother's garage in Cincinnati, to my old house in Atlanta, to my office across the halls at Def Jam. The one thing that all those places had in common was that, in my mind, each one conjured my passion—got me excited about my music. That was the feeling that I needed to re-create. It wasn't enough to identify that my ear had gone saccharine—knowing that was important, but alone it couldn't do anything. I had to find the sound, the artist who would give me that spark back.

If you're a record man, musical taste and direction are the determining factors of your career. This isn't true if you are a business executive, working in finance or in legal or some operational function at a record company; then taste doesn't matter. But if you're a record man, it's all about your taste. I found out that I was not a TV star. I learned that I was a record man.

I sat there, trading glances between Kenny and the piano

sitting in my living room, and still hearing his words beating around my head. I was now clear about what my career was, about who I was as a professional. I didn't start out to be an executive. I started out as someone who loved and cared for music and artists and tried, sometimes desperately, to make music that I could be proud of. I had to do a lot of deep digging and soul searching to figure out how I got lost—and more important, how to get back on track.

To reconnect with my spiritual and musical roots in both the most broad-reaching and deeply personal ways—as well as reignite the Epic brand—nothing could have been better than a Michael Jackson album, and that was exactly the project I launched.

As with most people in the world, Michael's death in 2009 had hit me hard. So much of the work he'd done had influenced my own tastes. His album *Thriller* was the pinnacle of Epic Records' history—and perhaps all of pop music history—and his absence was still felt years after his death.

I had dinner with executor John Branca in Los Angeles to talk over the possibilities of working with the Jackson estate. I convinced him to let me put together an album of the existing unreleased recordings. They delivered all the music and I sat in my office, unpacking the boxes and listening to every demo that Michael Jackson ever made. It was like being left alone with the crown jewels, and I slowly started to sort through what Michael had left behind. I sat alone late into the night in my office overlooking the Upper East Side skyline and listened, feeling the magic of Michael Jackson engulf me.

Because Michael recorded specifically for albums, there were surprisingly few complete pieces sitting around unreleased. Not only were there not as many as I thought there would be, but my

With Michael Jackson at the Dorchester Hotel, London, 2007

first time listening through them, I could see why they hadn't been released. Still, I kept listening and listening.

A lightbulb went off when I heard a piano demo of songwriter Paul Anka playing and Michael Jackson singing a song called "Love Never Felt So Good." That one was different, really good, and it had never been finished. It was only a piano and vocal. Now we had something to work with, and that one song sealed the deal for me and made me commit to making an album. I searched through the tapes for all the songs that Michael had sung from top to bottom. A lot of takes were partly finished or only had stacks of background vocals. I found about eighteen and whittled those down to ten, nine by the time I released the album.

Yes, I was, at that point, working with remnants, but remnants from one of the greatest artists who ever lived, and if that doesn't take your bar up higher, nothing will. Hearing his naked vocals in the studio with all the tracks turned off, hearing just his voice, you could feel his energy and the perfection of his delivery. He was a flawless singer, flawless. He later became known for his dance moves and even some of the craziness that surrounded his life, but at the core of it—back to the very beginning with the Jackson 5—we're talking about one of the most brilliant singers who ever opened his mouth. That talent never left him. When I got these tapes and I listened to those naked vocals, I realized that this guy was really the greatest and I was back working with the best.

I gave the tapes to Timbaland, who is one of the most incredible producers ever. Timbaland took the tapes, stripped away all of the original music tracks, and built the records around Michael's vocals. He created the music tracks. It was Timbaland who convinced Justin Timberlake to sing on "Love Never Felt So Good," which gave the record a boost with contemporary radio, where Michael Jackson is no longer a fixture but Justin Timberlake is.

The whole time, I paid close attention to Timbaland's work. I spent more time in the studio working on the Michael album than I had in twenty years. I immersed myself for six months. I was in the studio for every mix, day and night, listening intently in the dim light late into the night. I basically kind of took over and I probably even got a little heavy-handed about it, but it was hard to help it—my passion had come back.

When I was searching for a title to the album, I spoke to Babyface.

"This is a Michael album," he said. "No one titles Michael's albums. Michael has to title it."

I wondered what Kenny meant by that, but as I started listening to outtakes of Michael from the *This Is It* concert movie, I heard Michael talking between songs. "It's about escapism," he said. "People want an escape."

I already had a song called "Xscape" that he wrote and produced with Rodney Jerkins, and now it was my title track and Michael had named the album.

With everything coming together, I had one more, very personal, piece to add. Deep in my own tape vault, where nobody knew it was there, I had "Slave to the Rhythm," the one song Babyface and I finished with Michael in 1989. We did that music under a private arrangement with Michael and the record company never knew about it. As I pulled that out, dusted it off, and handed it to Timbaland so he could work his magic, I couldn't ignore the symmetry: I was working to complete a track that Babyface and I had put together almost twenty-five years earlier. Babyface and Michael, working together to bring me back to myself. Kenny and I had always wondered whether this session that we'd worked on all those years ago would see the light of day. Now, sitting there in the studio, with the mixing board in front of me, the song we'd begun more than twenty years before finally finished and jumped from the speakers, I knew it was worth the wait. Satisfied, I stretched my legs out in the engineer's chair, catching a glimpse of my reflection as it bounced off the darkened studio glass. I knew we had something special, but I wasn't thinking about any of that—I was too busy having fun.

For the release of the album, we made a groundbreaking holographic Michael Jackson performance of "Slave to the Rhythm" for the Billboard Music Awards, and when it finally dropped, the album sold three million almost as soon as it came out in May 2014.

I was on my way to Japan earlier in the year to preview the album for Sony executives when another act I had signed to Epic blew up. I was sitting on the plane checking iTunes when "Say Something" by A Great Big World hit number one. Ian Axel and Chad Vaccarino were two Brooklyn kids who had studied music business at NYU and released a record on their own that had picked up some steam.

I first heard the band while I was on an equestrian weekend with my family in Miami. My daughter Arianna loves to ride horses. Richard Palmese, a long-standing friend who used to run MCA Records, emailed me a demo and I downloaded the track to my iPod and played it all weekend, debating with Arianna about how good the group was. All my kids, whether they like it or not, work for the label, and I have often relied on Arianna's opinion, but this weekend I couldn't help but feel I liked this group a lot better than she did.

Like all my favorite artists, Ian has a distinctive hairdo, his very famous Jewfro, as he calls it. Their voices reminded me of Simon and Garfunkel, not that they had a kind of retro sound, but, without being a copy of that era, they felt as special to me as everything I'd heard back then. They had already tapped into a unique sound all of their own. For me, that was enough. When they came to my office, I didn't even have them audition for me. For whatever reason, I simply had them play me demos and I listened to their songs. I convinced the band that I would kill for them. I even told them I believed they would be the first act from the new generation of Epic Records to win a Grammy, a boast I later repeated to my staff when I played the group's music at a meeting. I loved their sound, I loved the way they looked. They had everything I needed. Whatever they would become as performers was yet to be seen, but I was fine with that. We had everything we needed to launch. I had my first something at Epic Records.

We put out their song "This Is a New Year," and although it was not an out-of-the-park smash, it was a great song to display the band's talent and enough to set up promotional tours and make them familiar. They did a music video that became a You-Tube sensation and was great ground-laying. The next batch of songs they sent me included a number called "Say Something," a beautiful piano ballad, just their voices and a piano: "*Say some-*

thing, or I'm giving up on you / Say something." It was just the most beautiful, heartfelt lyric, so sincere, so soulful that it would bring tears to your eyes. It was at that moment that I knew we had something great. I played it for everybody, but I did not release the song as a single right yet.

Then I got lucky. Doug Morris liked to say it is better to be lucky than good, and what happened next had nothing to do with anything I did. The TV show *So You Think You Can Dance* used a forty-five-second slice of the song in its dance competition. The next day, we sold fifteen thousand units at iTunes. The next day, we sold another fifteen thousand. And the next day. There was no radio play, no music video. The song plays forty-five seconds on a TV show and starts to sell.

But, wait. Christina Aguilera heard the song and asked if she could sing on the record with the guys. She quickly went into the studio with A Great Big World and did the most tamed, beautiful vocal performance that perhaps she'd ever done in her career. She sang on the song with the guys, but she never took over the record. She provided a simple, tasteful complement to the guys. Christina Aguilera is one of the great singers of her generation, and perhaps even underrated in how great she is. You'd be hard-pressed to find someone who's better than her. Her manager, Irving Azoff, who had always been something of a godfather to me, was kind enough to allow this to happen. A month after the TV show in November 2013, we released the version of the song with Christina Aguilera and A Great Big World, and it starts selling a hundred thousand copies a week. By the time I was on the plane to Japan, the song was on top of iTunes.

I said to myself, *Wait a minute, this is actually working. Babyface was right.* That was the first moment that I started to find myself again, because this was a song that had a soul. It was a song that had a pulse. It was a song that had real meaning, a song that meant something to my life, to other people's lives. It wasn't just an empty, saccharin-filled pop song, but a meaningful ballad so great that Christina Aguilera, who clearly isn't desperate, who is a big star on *The Voice* and who has a wonderful career, felt compelled to sing on it. That was the turning point for Epic Records right there.

I started to feel some internal momentum, even if it wasn't obvious to the industry or the public yet. We began to attract some talented executives. I was listening to all the music that came in, taking every audition that came through the door, still digging for that needle in the haystack, still trying to thread the needle from across the street, still looking for the impossible. That was when I signed the Kongos, an alternative rock band of four brothers who grew up in South Africa and London, but lived in Phoenix. Their father, singer-songwriter John Kongos, had made records in the seventies with Elton John's producer, and the group was already having great success in South Africa.

Dennis Lavinthal and Lenny Beer of the influential industry tip sheet *Hits* came to my office, opened up a laptop, and dialed up this song, "Come With Me Now" by the Kongos. It sounded like a smash to me. Things were definitely starting to change.

"I love this band," I said. "Can I see them?"

"The guys are actually not here," Dennis said. "They're in Phoenix. They have another offer from another label that they're about to take. There's no chance of you seeing them right now because they're on their way back to South Africa in the morning, so you can't physically see them, but you can get on the phone with them."

Now I faced the challenge of talking on the phone with some guys I'd never met. I wasn't sure whether they knew me or not, so I had no cachet to play. Why would some alternative rock band out of South Africa know me? I was going to take a shot

At the Nickelodeon Kids Choice Awards with Meghan Trainor

in the dark. I conferenced up with the guys and told them how great I thought they were and how great I thought their song was. I promised them that I would get their song to number one alternative. I told them they would be the first alternative rock success at our label. We started talking about music and

I asked them some questions and discovered they were actually jazz musicians and very familiar with jazz fusion, which I grew up loving, so we shared our enthusiasm for Jaco Pastorius, the Mahavishnu Orchestra with John McLaughlin, *Bitches Brew*, all that. Instantly we found common ground and ended up having the greatest phone conversation in the world and the guys agreed, without them meeting me or me meeting them, based on the song I heard and my response, to sign with Epic Records.

We put the record out not more than a week later. Boom. It goes on the radio. This was an alternative rock record, but everybody in the company had their radio on, because KROQ was going to premiere the song. Everybody in the company was excited—the hip-hop department, the pop department, the alternative rock department, every department—and everybody had their radios tuned to KROQ. When "Come With Me Now" came on the air, the entire office exploded. The company started to rejoice. You could feel the energy in the halls. It felt like Epic Records had been reborn.

At Grammy week 2014, the guys came to my hotel room to meet me. I'd finally seen them perform the night before, opening for an act called Imagine Dragons at the Wiltern Theater. I loved them and was so happy we'd signed them. We had a great meeting, sitting in my hotel room, talking about music, listening to songs, looking at videos of their live shows. After they left, their A&R man, Paul Pontius, who I had only recently brought on board the company, stayed behind. He had been with me for many years before at Island Def Jam and was responsible for signing bands like Incubus and Hoobastank. "I got something I want to play you," he said.

He sent me an MP3. I opened it on my laptop and out came this charming voice: *"Because you know I'm all about that bass, that bass . . . no treble."*

I was like, holy shit, play it again. This is a smash. "Paul, who is this?" I asked.

"I don't know," he said. "It's a songwriter out of Nashville and this producer, Kevin Kadish, sent it to me. They're looking to shop the song for an artist. I just wanted you to hear it."

"Okay, who's that singing?" I said.

"That's the girl that wrote it. That's Meghan Trainor."

Meghan Trainor was a nineteen-year-old girl who grew up in Nantucket, but had been living and working as a songwriter for a number of years in Nashville. I couldn't stop playing it. I knew this was a fucking home run. I couldn't believe my ears. "Paul, I need to meet this girl," I said, "so make arrangements to bring her into the office while I'm here in LA. I've just got to meet her and she's got to sing for me."

"She's not so much a performer," he said. "She's a songwriter."

Paul went about making arrangements for me to meet her and I kept playing everyone the song, "All About That Bass." I was hooked on the song, the thing was so catchy and carried this powerful message of empowerment for the plus-size gals. I knew she had something special.

A few days went by, and, meanwhile, I agreed to audition a beautiful female vocalist from Madagascar. She was a gorgeous, young biracial woman with curly hair, skin that glowed. She played piano and sang, then sang along to her demo tapes. Part of me, the old LA, thought this might work, but I was still on the fence. I told her manager that I thought I would like to sign her, but would she bring her back the next day for a second audition. She said they couldn't come back during the day, but they would return the following night for another audition.

The next day Meghan Trainor showed up at the Epic Records offices in Los Angeles. As usual, I gathered the girls, a couple of the A&R people, put everybody into an office, and Paul brought in Meghan. "How y'all doing?" she said.

She held a ukulele in her hand and exuded warmth and character. The moment she walked into the room, I started smiling. I couldn't stop smiling and I wondered why. I loved this girl. She talked a little, made everybody laugh, and then started strumming her ukulele and singing "All About That Bass." I looked around the room and everybody was smiling. The girl from Madagascar disappeared from my thoughts.

Meghan was nothing like any of the artists that I'd ever signed before. She didn't have Rihanna's looks. She wasn't a crooner like Whitney Houston, Toni Braxton, or Mariah Carey. She was something different. And whatever it was, I couldn't stop smiling. She did two songs and I asked her to step out of the room. She went down the hall to wait in a little room and I asked the people in the room what they thought. Everybody in the room said they loved her, unanimously. Paul went down the hall and told her she had landed a record deal.

When Meghan and her producer came to meet at my office after the deal was done, they told me that now that I loved the song so much, they wanted to keep it and not give it to another artist. I didn't have to convince Meghan to become a performer, because the truth is, behind every great songwriter there's an aspiring performer. Because when they're born, they're all the same. They're people who love music and they're people who have the gift. Maybe somewhere later in life they come to the conclusion that perhaps they shouldn't be performers, but they're all performers at first. She wasn't even twenty years old. She was ready. "All right, baby," she said. "Let's go, boo."

She talks like that. Speaking with Meghan is like eating comfort food. There is something so soulful about her, like there is an old black woman in there somewhere. When she calls you "baby," it makes you feel good. Meghan didn't have any doubts; she rose to the occasion immediately.

I was feeling good. I had signed the Kongos and A Great Big World and now I had Meghan Trainor and "All About That Bass."

Meghan and Paul told me they wanted to make a couple of changes to the song, give it another mix. "I will hear of no such thing," I said. "You're not making any changes. By the way, you can't even mix this. We're going to put this out just like it is. I don't want you to breathe on it. Don't touch a thing. This record is perfection. This record is flawless."

"But we didn't mix it yet."

"I don't want to hear it. We're mixing nothing."

And we put the record out exactly as it was. The demo that Paul played me in my hotel room after the meeting with the Kongos is the very record that knocked Taylor Swift off the top of the charts and became a global smash that sold more than seven million copies. I had my first Epic Records number one. But the statistic that truly blew my mind was when "All About That Bass" became the longest-running number one in the label's history, eclipsing a record set by "Billie Jean" by Michael Jackson.

At last, everything was happening at the same time and the company started to hit a stride, and in many genres: the alternative field with the Kongos, the pop charts with A Great Big World, a brilliant execution of Michael Jackson's *Xscape* album, and, if that wasn't enough, we signed a kid out of Brooklyn named Bobby Shmurda and his song "Hot Nigga" became the hip-hop phenomenon of the year.

But it wasn't just that the hits had started coming, it was something bigger than that. As things at Epic took off, I began drawing together the different corners of my career, creating hits but also connecting my past to my present in new and unexpected ways. Such was the case when I signed the rapper Future.

Future was one of the first acts I signed when I got to Epic, but more than just a talent, he's also steeped in my history. A cousin of Rico Wade of Organized Noize, Future was part of the next generation to emerge from the Dungeon Family in Atlanta. With this background, I knew he would be a different breed of rapper, and I couldn't have been more right. He sings in a rap style or raps in a singing style—it's magnetic, hooking you in a totally unique way. After a series of successful mixtapes, he finally released his debut album, *Pluto*, in April 2012, which included the big hits "Tony Montana," featuring Drake, and "Magic," with rapper T.I. He rolled out hit after hit. The true revelation, though, came with his third album, *DS2*, which *exploded* to the top of the charts when it was released in July 2015. That launch was a smash, but two months later, he was back with a joint mixtape with Drake, *What a Time to Be Alive*, that proved just how insatiable his drive is.

Future's talents also lie beyond his own music. He is equally capable of writing and producing hits with other artists, such as Rihanna and Ciara, and that has quickly cemented him as one of the most important artists on the label. Future is turning out to be the crown jewel of Epic, but to me, my bond with his music extends far beyond these last three years, all the way back to Atlanta.

I had a similar run-in with my past when I signed Travis Scott. T.I., another alumnus of LaFace University, brought him to Epic. Travis is a visionary rock star cut from the Kanye West cloth: graphic designer, director, songwriter, producer, and one the most electrifying performers I have ever worked with. One of the things I saw in him soon after he signed was the sweep and depth of his talent. His creative energy is a force of nature, and even before he'd put out a thing, it was clear he was destined for greatness. We had him on the label for three years before we released his first studio album, *Rodeo*, in September 2015, but once he was out there, the word of mouth started to take hold pretty rapidly, as his hit single "Antedote" landed him a slot on his first arena tour, with the Weekend. The album made number one on the rap and hip-hop charts, but we had to settle for number two on the pop charts. Like

Future he is able to make records for himself as effortlessly as he does for many other artists, including Jay Z, Kanye, and Rihanna, whose single "Bitch Better Have My Money" he co-wrote and produced.

Both Future and Travis are prolific young musicians who constitute the future of Epic Records, but my satisfaction in their success runs deeper than just record sales. Each of them in their own way speaks to my past and where I'd come from. I'd started my time at Epic by chasing the sugar-coated pop that was so unnatural to me, but as I rediscovered my ear for talent, it opened up new possibilities from the entire breadth of my career, reminding me of how I'd gotten to where I am. I was drawing on my history in order to discover new voices and make an impact. With Kenny's words still echoing in my head, I knew that my instincts and my taste—and above all my drive to make good music—were at the root of this resurgence. I'd brought the music back into my living room and it sounded better than I ever could have imagined.

So my little label was starting to kick in and attract an even higher caliber of both creative and executive talent. Suddenly Epic Records was the place to be.

The real success of a label is measured by its ability to attract talent, and we started to attract real competitive talent. When I first took office at Epic, the label was on the brink of closing the doors and turning out the lights, and we successfully brought it back.

We accomplished this turnaround in difficult times, when the record industry was still adjusting to the realities of selling fewer records, struggling to find its way. This is a much more challenging proposition than when Kenny and I were the songwriters or working with all the different producers. We did this with no help, no mergers, no acquisitions, no big superstars handed to us, no nothing. But I'm like James Brown. I don't

Still together after all these years

want anybody to give me anything. Open up the door, I'll get it myself.

Today I am trying to dig the roots even deeper into the earth, into the soul. I am surrounding myself with friends and family who represent my musical legacy. When you come to my home, you should feel me, the history of me, who I have been and who I am always going to be. I brought back Mariah Carey and Jennifer Lopez, who both have history not only with me, but with Epic Records as well. I signed Outkast again and brought Puffy and Bad Boy Entertainment to Epic. We are aggressively seeking and finding new talent—that is the lifeblood of the industry and my specialty—but I want to mix and merge that with my life and my work. These artists are

Standing between a legend, Ozzy Osbourne, and a "Future" legend

more than mere metaphors; they are the giants who helped make me who I am.

That way I will have a much greater chance to see into the future and to attract the future talent, and that was exactly what happened. At the 2015 Grammy Awards, I was back in the audience with acts in the running. Meghan Trainor was nominated for Song of the Year and Record of the Year, the two big ones, and A Great Big World was nominated for Best Group or Duo in Pop. Meghan didn't win, but damned if A Great Big World didn't walk away with the trophy, just as I had predicted, the first new generation on Epic to win a Grammy. All that made me happy, and made me feel that we'd gotten our company on track. What we will become is yet to be seen, but from where we have come, it's clear that we've improved. We're no longer a work in progress. We have progressed.

SHOWDOWN AT COACHELLA

oth Big Boi and André from Outkast called me separately to say they had accepted a booking at the gigantic Coachella Valley Music and Arts Festival in the spring of 2014. They had decided to celebrate the twentieth anniversary of the group with a headline reunion performance at the annual music festival in the California desert, followed by a round of performances at European music festivals that summer. They had not been onstage together since winning the Album of the Year award at the Grammys in 2004 and had turned down numerous offers for large, large sums of money to perform over the years.

All the time, they had vacillated back and forth about whether they were going to be a band again or not, whether they were going to make a new record or not, whether they would tour or not. Now with the contract signed and the appearance officially announced, I reserved my excitement. I didn't want to be disappointed, because for me—as, first, an Outkast fan and, second, as sort of the father of Outkast—this was one of the most important events ever in our musical family. I started having regular conversations with Big Boi and André to see if there was anything I could do to help, but I really couldn't help but look forward to this momentous occasion.

I had never been to a music festival, but let me tell you, I was excited and ready to dive in and figure it out. I was told traffic getting into the site was horrendous, so I chartered a private plane and booked a hotel room. In the car on the way to the festival grounds, we were surrounded by kids everywhere. I'd never seen anything like it. There were massive parking lots filled with cars, police officers directing traffic, valet parkers, and people selling paraphernalia and T-shirts on the streets. We made our way through the crowd in a golf cart, every so often hearing someone shout out "Hey LA." Whenever I'm near my artists, people know who I am. Once the artists aren't around, nobody knows or gives a fuck.

As I approached the Outkast dressing rooms, my heart was pounding, I was so excited. Familiar faces from Atlanta popped out of the crowd—Rico, Pat, and Ray from Organized Noize, Big Gipp from the Goodie Mob, everybody with a red cup in their hand. I walked into the dressing room with the sign ANDRÉ 3000 on the door, nervous as a little kid, no idea what to expect. André was jumping up and down, doing some stretches, which he broke off to give me a big hug. I looked at him in awe. I think André 3000 is one of the most fascinating people in the world, not only a massive star, but such a recluse. You never see him at parties or out in public. This guy is always off the scene, but just a gorgeous man and such a creative, complex guy, always kind, always nice, but painfully honest, too. I asked him how he was feeling and he told me he felt great.

Then I went to Big Boi's room and what a difference. He had a party going on, stuffed the place with uncles and aunts, kids, family, and friends. Big Boi went on and on about how excited he was to have Outkast back together. He was pumped and ready to go. I slipped away with my people just before show-time and found a spot where I could watch from the side of the stage. I looked beside me and there was Paul McCartney. What a moment. I was dying to ask to take a selfie, but I restrained myself. I was filled with anticipation, my mind frantically wondering what the opening number would be when the piano riff dropped that introduces "BOB." The place went crazy and all I could think was *Oh my God*.

My problem was I couldn't see all that well from the side of the stage. I was surrounded by people from the label, but, oddly enough, they weren't from LaFace, they were with Epic, and they hadn't been involved in the act. I could tell from the looks on their faces that it didn't mean the same thing to them that it did to me. I couldn't see the video screens. I couldn't see what they saw out front. I left them and went out front, by myself, no staff, no nothing, just one big security guy, and watched the rest of that show, and I did not move. I sang every lyric, I jumped up and down.

The show was a little odd. André, who is usually a fashion extravaganza, sometimes wearing a blond wig, was dressed in a plain pair of overalls. If this was such a big moment, why didn't he dress for the occasion? He usually knows how to show up. He didn't seem to care, didn't seem to be giving it his all. It wasn't perfect, but they got through the show and it was fun, exciting, had some great moments, and I had a great, great time, but I left just a little concerned. I made arrangements to meet with André and Big Boi before their next show the following weekend in the desert.

The next weekend, Irving Azoff gave me a beautiful, big sprawling estate with a pool and a staff. André came over the night before their performance. I was sitting out back by a fire pit and in walked André. The desert night was warm, but there was enough of a chill in the starry sky to sit by the fire. "This is surreal," he said. "This feels like a movie set."

That was the beginning of a three-hour conversation. We talked about everything under the sun, we shared music, we talked about books, we talked about values, we talked about the past twenty years and how his life and my life had changed, what Outkast means to him and what he's thinking about going forward, both in movies and in music. He talked to me about the Jimi Hendrix movie that he had recently finished. And we talked a lot about focusing on inspiration and answering the bell when it's time. I gave him all the coaching I could.

We talked about what had happened the previous week. He told me he'd spoken with Prince, who gave him some ideas. I think he let himself down a little bit, if I'm honest. He knew he had been reluctant and didn't completely show up. For the second performance, he intended to show up. When he left, I felt so inspired, just sitting on top of the world, because here was the guy who I felt was the biggest star that I'd ever discovered, the most important star I'd ever discovered, coming to talk with me about his life, his career. I learned so much about how he thought. People change in twenty years, they grow, evolve, become wise and experienced. That night, I realized that I didn't know him and I became acquainted all over again. I grew to love and respect him even more. But more than anything, I was proud.

The next morning, I went to see Big Boi at the house where he was staying. Again, the place was filled with people, hectic and happy. His mother was cooking in the kitchen and the smells wafted through the whole house. It was a very comfortable, homey feeling. Big Boi, who fully showed up the previous weekend, was chomping at the bit to go again. "Hey man, we're gonna go kill it this time," he said.

There wasn't much we needed to discuss, so it was a short meeting. I gave everybody hugs, we took pictures, and I asked him if there was anything I could do to help.

This time I brought someone from LaFace with me to the show. Bille Woodruff, who had been our music video director, had gone on to become an amazing film director with movies such as *Honey* and *Beauty Shop*. He discovered Jessica Alba, but he started with us at LaFace and knew what Outkast meant to me.

Before Outkast's show, Bille and I decided to check out the dance music stage in one of the other areas of Coachella. We had never seen an EDM event before and it was eye-opening. We watched Ellie Goulding and Zedd both whip the crowd into frenzies with wicked and wild combinations of thumping beats, great songs, and lavish lights. My only regret was that I wasn't on the same drugs that everybody else was. All the time, the people were dancing and moving. They sprayed the crowd with water to cool them down. I was blown away—but the whole time I was thinking, *How does Outkast follow this?*

When it came time for the Outkast set, this time I didn't go backstage. I went straight out front and planted myself where I could see everything up close with nobody in front of me. Again there were a lot of familiar faces from Atlanta and elsewhere in the crowd—I saw Q-Tip from A Tribe Called Quest. The instant the band took the stage, it was night and day from the previous weekend. This time, André showed up. He was wearing his blond wig and an all-black jumpsuit with a big red tag hanging from it that said FOR SALE on one side and SOLD OUT on the other.

It was such a great message because André was conflicted about having to go out and imitate himself. He felt like he was selling out, so he hung that retail sign on himself and came out ready for action. It was brilliant.

The show went perfectly—lights, sound, the band, everything worked beautifully. Bille and I jammed all night. I rediscovered Outkast songs that I'd forgotten I loved like "Gasoline Dreams." They went back to their first album for "Player's Ball" ("This is for the real Outkast fans," they said). They did "Southernplayalisticadillacmuzik." They played "Crumblin' Erb." They played "Elevators" and did songs from *ATLiens* and *Stankonia*, as well as all their big hits from the *Speakerboxxx/ The Love Below*—"Hey Ya!," "The Way You Move"—a flawless performance.

And when it was over I went backstage and simply smiled and gave them both a hug, then I got in my car and left. That was it. I had no worries for them. I didn't have to say a word. I just gave them that look, and they knew. It was the most important music experience of my life.

Coachella was a celebration in front of a new generation. These young people knew all the words—they didn't come to be at Coachella; they came to see Outkast. That's when I realized that this thing had outgrown my perception of it. It was bigger than even I knew and much more important than I thought. Outkast had stood the test of time. At the root of it, they were always originals. They copied no one. They didn't even sample. All original music. They always spoke the truth. It wasn't always easy for them. They didn't call themselves Outkast by accident; they have always been outcasts.

For starters, they came from the South. The first hip-hop came from the Bronx; the music then became wildly successful on the West Coast with NWA. But hip-hop in the South hadn't emerged in a significant cultural way until Outkast, so they weren't readily accepted by hip-hop culture at the start. I was there when André and Big Boi won an award at the Source Awards and the audience booed. André stood up, accepting the award. "The South got something to say," he told them.

It turned out that in the years since Outkast had stopped performing, they had become even more important in their absence. Their unavailability only increased their mystique. I watched the looks over all those fans' faces, and I realized that I'd been dreaming of something, I'd been prayerful about something that had actually taken place, and I hadn't realized it. I had always said I wanted my own U2. Where's my U2? I'd been a record man for a long time. Where's my Coldplay? Where's my Rolling Stones? They were right there all the time.

Coachella made me realize, *Wait a minute, Outkast is an authentic cultural phenomenon, a rap group that became a rock band and reached the masses.* This wasn't traditional hip-hop. This wasn't a rap concert. This was a rock concert. Although the crowd contained every kind of face you can imagine, Coachella was mostly white kids, not at all like the crowd when Outkast started out, when they were a hip-hop band from Atlanta. Now this was a world-class band, a world-class act, world famous. My prayer was answered.

It was always Outkast. It's a hard question to ask: What is your favorite act of all the ones you've worked with in your career? That's a dangerous, loaded question. What do you say to that? Usher? I love Usher. If I say Usher, then somebody else will get upset. I could say Pink, but then what's Avril going to say? I could say Toni Braxton, but what's Mariah going to say? I could say Mariah Carey, but what's Ciara going to say? I could say Jennifer Lopez. I could say all kinds of names. But the one name I can say and no one can say anything about is Outkast. And I've said that from the very beginning: Outkast is my favorite act that I've ever signed—and no one's ever complained about it. I think that for every act in our history, in our musical family of LaFace, Arista, Island Def Jam, and now Epic, we can all agree it's Outkast by a mile.

All the greatest acts and artists I have worked with, like Outkast, Usher, TLC, Kanye West, Jay Z, Mariah, Rihanna, Babyface, and the others, all have one thing in common. Those acts have high quality in common. They never worked to appease the most common fan. They always worked in an aspirational way.

When people first listened to the early Babyface albums, his songwriting voice was so distinctive, he influenced many other songwriters at the time. When Kanye West came on the scene, a middle-class, educated backpack rapper, he broke the mold of the gangster rapper, and created a different style of hip-hop that many artists would emulate, some more successfully than others. His contribution improved music. Jay Z's contribution improved music. Rihanna, Beyoncé, Usher, Outkast, a lot of these artists came along and they more than improved music; they became almost the gold standard of what greatness was.

I always wanted to be surrounded by the people who were cutting-edge, people who were making what I call aspirational music, people who really didn't care to be regular. They didn't want to be normal. They didn't want to fit in. They always wanted to stand out.

As I look back at all those artists that I have worked with over my career, the one thing that comes through to me is that I am really proud of the music that they made beyond what it sold. Beyond numbers, I was proud of it. That's what matters. When I listen back to Babyface's second album, *Tender Lover*, I hear the quality of the music, the quality of the writing, the quality of the production, the quality of his singing. Or, fast-forward, if I listen to Kanye West's *My Beautiful Dark Twisted Fantasy*, I hear quality that was superior to almost anything in the marketplace. And beyond his Grammys and all of his accolades, I was proud of the music he was making.

When I go back to the very beginning, listening to jazz fusion bands and loving Miles Davis, or digging what James Brown represented, or even in my rock days worshipping at the shrine of Led Zeppelin, I always loved the things that were a cut above the rest. And while I always liked having hits, my hits were never based on making music that I thought fit urban radio or alternative rock radio or Top Forty radio. I always aspired to simply do what I thought was superior music—superior to me. Not every person would necessarily agree with the assessment, but to my ears, Outkast was superior. To me, Babyface was superior. To me, the Tony Rich Project was superior to music that was happening at the time. To me, Jay Z was superior to almost every rapper, and what he and I put together under one roof at the Island Def Jam label went about actually making what I call a cultural contribution to music, not just hits.

Many years, I had the biggest album of the year—Usher's *Confessions*, *The Emancipation of Mimi* by Mariah Carey, or

Speakerboxxx/The Love Below by Outkast. They were not only the biggest-selling albums of the year, but, in many cases, also the most critically acclaimed. That can be debated, because some critics like rock more than they may like hip-hop, or soul more than they like pop. It can be debated a thousand ways, but I know that in those moments, those records were not only hit records, they were also critically acclaimed and influential records, records that helped shape the culture.

When I use the term "cultural," I mean that someone has cracked the code of culture. Whether it is pop culture or urban culture, it means that what they've created can last forever. Jean-Michel Basquiat the painter was cultural. What he created will last forever. So is Jay Z. His work will last. Outkast is cultural—not just their hits, but with what they've created; they carved out a piece of history. As a record man, if I can't do something that becomes cultural, then having a hit record doesn't mean that much to me. I don't want only hit records—I did that. I always wanted more.

I want to be involved with the artists who make the music that will shape the culture, whatever it might be, and I can tell if that's happened—like seeing little kids going trick-or-treating dressed up as Avril Lavigne. I want to work with a John Lennon or a Bob Marley.

I think that music is only more powerful and more popular than it's ever been. It's the most widely pervasive element of the entertainment business, a thread running through all of society. People in music today can sell any brand. I don't care what it is. If you want social media to be successful, if it doesn't include superstar music artists, it won't be successful. Or if you're launching a fashion line and you don't have some superstar associated with it, it won't have the success. We're seeing the power of music in a different way today. Where we don't necessarily see it in record sales, we see it in influence. Ticket sales haven't suffered while record sales have declined, so people still spend money on music. It is how they are listening to recordings that is changing.

With CD sales stalled and downloads slowing, streaming music over computers looks like the future of the music business. Rather than focus on the negatives, I see the current landscape as possessing more opportunity, not less. If only the consumers of music today decided that it's better to spend, say, ten dollars a month for music to consume all the music that they can, our industry at that point will become more successful than ever before. Imagine if we could convince only the people who buy music right now—not the people we don't have, just our existing customers—that instead of buying six CDs a year with a handful of songs, they should pay a modest subscription and get all the music they could want. When we get the world to that place, artists will make more money than they've ever made. The prediction is that in fifteen years, it will be a $72 billion industry.

I always wanted to be known as that guy who was pure music, because that's what I am, pure music. Many other guys I admire have gone beyond music, like Jay Z with his Roc Nation, or Sean Combs with his Revolt TV and clothing line, or Jimmy Iovine and his Beats headphones. I admire their success and their wealth, which I can't match, because I've been a little bit one-dimensional. I don't know whether it's a blessing or a curse, but I have always been about the music. I could make movies, I tried television, but I'm music. At the beginning of the day, when I wake up, I always remember to be music. I never forget. It's second nature. I wake up, I listen to a song, and then I brush my teeth. Music enriches my day. I always notice that my mood changes if there's no music. When there's music, I come alive. All my friends know that about me. The other night, Jay Z came up to me at a party and threw his arm around my shoulder. "Want to drink some champagne, Record Man?" he said. That's me—I'm a Record Man.

Passion is my superpower. I still don't think I've done my greatest work and I understand that I've had to clean up my act, straighten my mind, and get back into the head space to be prepared for the great one to walk in. I'm ready for company now, and I do believe that the greatest acts that I will work with have yet to walk into my door. I firmly believe that. Auditions are a fundamental part of my professional routine—three or four times a week, I see people. I'm always looking. The only reason I get up and go to work every day is that I'm getting up with great hopes that today will be that day that they walk in.

The door is open and the lights are on.

ACKNOWLEDGMENTS

would like to give a special THANK-YOU to this long list of extraordinary people who are everything to me:

My dear wife Erica- you are my rock!! I love you.

My wonderful children; Antonio, Ashley, Aaron, Arianna, and Addison. The greatest kids in the world! I love you all more than life itself.

My siblings, Rosaland, Bryant, and Ivy—even while I was largely absent, you weren't.

My aunt Katrina—you have always been my shining light.

Kenny—my brother, my friend, my partner, my truth!

Kayo—the pure essence of brotherhood

The Deele—Dee, Carlos, Stick, and Daryl—you all taught me more than you may know.

Ali Hasan—my brother from another mother . . . the true definition of an unconditional bond.

Doug Morris—you are the very best ever! Your friendship, wisdom, guidance, and support have been invaluable.

Clive Davis—an ever inspiring example.

Clarence Avant—my godfather.

Richard Johnson—decades my friend, decades.

Joel Katz—your intelligence and wisdom have guided me well my friend.

My dear friend and media guru, Laura Swanson.

The countless executives, managers and attorneys whose presence in my life made everything work.

This book would not have been possible without the tireless efforts of Jan Miller (elegance and talent together equals YOU), Nena Madonia Oshman (you made this process fun!), Jonathan Burnham, Matt Harper (you are a star), Courtney Walter (your passion is contagious), David Dalton, and my genius collaborative co-author Joel Selvin.

And a very heartfelt *THANK-YOU* to all the amazingly talented artists, songwriters, producers, and performers whose music is the soundtrack to my existence.

Joel Selvin needs to acknowledge: Everybody associated with LA Reid, who made this a pleasure, starting with Hope Rippere, who made everything happen. Jan Miller and especially Nena Madonia Oshman of the Dupree-Miller Agency both went above and beyond. Frank Weimann of the Literary Group, always. Carol Mastick did the excellent transcriptions. Author David Dalton did the preliminary archeology. This book would not have been what it is without the extraordinary care and attention to detail paid by editor Matt Harper at HarperCollins. Most of all, the greatest thanks go to LA Reid himself and Erica Reid, who welcomed me into their home and made me feel like family. Special thanks to Pamela Turley for everything and, as always, my darling daughter, Carla.

ABOUT THE AUTHOR

ANTONIO "LA" REID has been a key
figure in shaping the sound and experience of popular music for over twenty-five
years—as a record producer, songwriter, and
label executive. Reid first broke into the music world in
the 1980s as the drummer for the R&B band the Deele.
Along with bandmate Kenny "Babyface" Edmonds,
Reid made his move behind the scenes of the industry in
1989 when he founded LaFace Records. Prior to becoming chairman and CEO of Epic Records in July 2011,
Reid also served as chairman of the former Island Def
Jam Music Group from 2004 to 2011 and as president
and CEO of Arista Records from 2000 to 2004.

Reid's excellence in the music world is not limited
to his work as an executive. Winner of eighteen BMI
Awards, he's also a talent in his own right. Reid has
produced and/or co-written dozens of number one sin-
gles and has won three Grammy Awards. He has been
presented with numerous acknowledgements, including
UNICEF's Spirit of Compassion Award, the Recording
Academy's President's Merit Award, and the prestigious
Harvard University Alumni Award for Excellence in
Media and Entertainment. Reid lives in Manhattan

with his wife, Erica, and his two children Arianna and Addison. He has three grown children, Antonio, Ashley, and Aaron.

J OEL SELVIN is an award-winning journalist who has covered pop music for the *San Francisco Chronicle* since 1970. Selvin is the author of the bestselling *Summer of Love* and coauthor, with Sammy Hagar, of the number-one *New York Times* bestseller, *Red*. He has written twelve other books about pop music.